GLOBAL ECONOMIC STUDIES SERIES

# CROSS-CULTURAL
# ECONOMIC MANAGEMENT

# GLOBAL ECONOMIC STUDIES SERIES

**The U.K.'s Rocky Road to Stability**
*Nicoletta Batini and Edward Nelson (Editor)*
2009. ISBN: 978-1-60692-869-1

**The Financial Crisis and the European Union**
*Klaus G. Efenhoff (Editor)*
2009. ISBN: 978-1-60741-987-7

**Cross-Cultural Economic Management**
*Rongxing Guo*
2009. ISBN: 978-1-60741-343-1

GLOBAL ECONOMIC STUDIES SERIES

# CROSS-CULTURAL ECONOMIC MANAGEMENT

## RONGXING GUO

Nova Science Publishers, Inc.
*New York*

For permission to use material from this book please contact us:
Telephone 631-231-7269; Fax 631-231-8175
Web Site: http://www.novapublishers.com

### NOTICE TO THE READER

The Publisher has taken reasonable care in the preparation of this book, but makes no expressed or implied warranty of any kind and assumes no responsibility for any errors or omissions. No liability is assumed for incidental or consequential damages in connection with or arising out of information contained in this book. The Publisher shall not be liable for any special, consequential, or exemplary damages resulting, in whole or in part, from the readers' use of, or reliance upon, this material. Any parts of this book based on government reports are so indicated and copyright is claimed for those parts to the extent applicable to compilations of such works.

Independent verification should be sought for any data, advice or recommendations contained in this book. In addition, no responsibility is assumed by the publisher for any injury and/or damage to persons or property arising from any methods, products, instructions, ideas or otherwise contained in this publication.

This publication is designed to provide accurate and authoritative information with regard to the subject matter covered herein. It is sold with the clear understanding that the Publisher is not engaged in rendering legal or any other professional services. If legal or any other expert assistance is required, the services of a competent person should be sought. FROM A DECLARATION OF PARTICIPANTS JOINTLY ADOPTED BY A COMMITTEE OF THE AMERICAN BAR ASSOCIATION AND A COMMITTEE OF PUBLISHERS.

LIBRARY OF CONGRESS CATALOGING-IN-PUBLICATION DATA
Guo, Rongxing.
 Cross-cultural economic management / Rongxing Guo.
    p. cm.
 Includes bibliographical references and indexes.
 ISBN 978-1-60741-343-1 (hbk.)
 1. Economics--Sociological aspects. 2. Culture. I. Title.
 HM548.G86 2009
 306.3--dc22

                                                        2009004756

*Published by Nova Science Publishers, Inc. ✦ New York*

謹以此书纪念我的慈母

Tämä teos on omistettu muisto äitini

Denne bog er dedikeret til mindet om min mor

Questo libro è dedicato alla memoria di mia madre

Dit boek is gewijd aan de nagedachtenis van mijn moeder

Το βιβλίο αυτό είναι αφιερωμένο στη μνήμη της μητέρας μου

Dieses Buch widmet sich der Erinnerung an meine Mutter

This book is dedicated to the memory of my mother

Denna bok är dedicerad till minnet av min mamma

Тази книга е посветена на паметта на майка ми

Este libro está dedicado a la memoria de mi madre

Aceasta carte este dedicata memoriei mamei mele

이 책은 내 어머니의 전용 메모리를합니다

Ta książka poświęcona jest pamięci mojej matki

Ova knjiga je posvećena sjećanju moje majke

Эта книга посвящена памяти моей матери

Ce livre est dédié à la mémoire de ma mère

Tato kniha je věnována památce mé matce

この本には専用のメモリを私の母のです

इस पुस्तक की स्मृति को समर्पित है मेरी मां

هذا الكتاب مكرس لذكرى امي

謹以此書紀念我的慈母赫玉花女士 (1927-2005)

# CONTENTS

# ACKNOWLEDGMENTS

This book is based on a research project supported by the East Asian Development Network (EADN). Except for a few of sections, this book is not technically complicated. Therefore, I hope that it will prove useful to researchers as well as ordinary readers and students from different cultural backgrounds to get familiar with our creative, diverse cultures and to acquire some general knowledge about and specific techniques on cross-cultural economic management.

This book includes my previously published materials. Specifically, Sections 2.1 and 2.2 of Chapter 2, Section 5.1 of Chapter 5, and Section 6.1 of Chapter 6 are based on my book "Cultural Influences on Economic Analysis" (Palgrave-Macmillan, 2006). Part of Chapter 5 was presented at the EADN's Annual Forums held in Hong Kong (2-3 November 2005) and Beijing (14-15 January 2007), respectively, and is included in a paper entitled "Linguistic and Religious Influences on Foreign Trade: Evidence from East Asia" (*Asian Economic Journal*, 2007, vol. 21, pp. 100-21).

I have benefited from many EADN experts and reviewers during the early stage of the project's implementation. They are (in the alphabetic order of surnames) Shigeyuki Abe (Doshisha University), Ammar Siamwalla (Thailand Development Research Institute), Chalongphob Sussangkarn (TDRI and EADN Coordinator), Chia Siow Yue (Singapore Institute for International Affairs), Josef T. Yap (Philippines Institute for Development Studies), and Zhang Yunling (Chinese Academy of Social Sciences). Steven Pressman (Monmouth University), Eui-Gak Hwang (Korea University), David Lim (Griffith University) as well as a number of anonymous reviewers have read the draft and provided in-depth comments and constructive suggestions at various stages when the draft was prepared.

Last but not least, I would appreciate the innovative jobs done by the editors, reviewers and readers at Nova. But all views, drawbacks and errors in this book certainly are mine and are not necessarily those of the supporter and the reviewers.

G.R.X.
Beijing
January 2009

# INTRODUCTION

Since World War II, especially since the end of the Cold War, a series of global and regional economic issues have been puzzling both theorists and practitioners. They include such important problems as: Why have nations with same or similar natural endowments and political contexts have so different economic performances? Why have trade and economic cooperation been efficient between some nations but more and more difficult between the others? These issues are very crucial to contemporary policymakers and practitioners, and many nice theories have been constructed in order to assess them. Unfortunately, it is argued that the existing theories cannot be used to deal with the above issues satisfactorily. Sometimes they might even yield conflicting information and results. The primary causes might be twofold. The first one concerns the continuing evolution of the global environment and regional institutions; the second relates to unrealistic assumptions from which some important variables have been excluded or highly simplified.[1]

If we are to explain why economic performances have been so diverse among nations, it is necessary for us to consider political and institutional influences. Institutions in economic research are analyzed as formal (laws, regulations) and informal (customs, traditions, norms) rules in a society that structure and simplify human interactions. Historically, institutions have been devised by human beings to create order and reduce uncertainty in exchange. They evolve incrementally connecting the past with the present and the future (North, 1991). According to new institutional economics, the economic system, like other production factors required in economic development, is a special kind of scarce resource and thus should be treated properly. The economic system of any nation is the mechanism that brings together natural resources, labor, technology and the necessary managerial talents. Anticipating and then meeting human needs through production and distribution of goods and services is the end purpose of every economic system. While the type of economic system applied by a nation is usually artificially decided, it is also to a large extent the result of historical experience, which becomes over time a part of political culture.

It is now increasingly accepted that one of the many reasons underlying the relative lack of success of the past economic development efforts is that culture was overlooked in development thinking and practice. This belated resurgence of interest has raised culture to a position of honor in development debates. Even conservative financial planners and technical

---

[1] As a matter of fact, all the theories that have been established are based on a number of unrealistic assumptions. The art of successfully setting up a theory lies in introducing simplifying assumptions only when it is unavoidable and the final results are not compromised.

problem-solvers now recognize that, if healthy and sustainable development is to take place culture cannot be ignored. In fact, many social scientists, particularly sociologists, human geographers and political scientists, have been undergoing a 'cultural conversion' in recent decades, evident both in method and content. As a result there has been a long-overdue dialogue with literary studies, and an increased concern with cultural phenomena (see, for example, Cateora and Graham, 1998, pp. 111-50; Kockel, 2002, ed.; Harrison, 1993 and 2000; Harrison and Huntington, 2001, ed.; Hofstede, 1980 and 2003; Harrison, 2006; Harris et al., 2004; and Guo, 2004, 2007a and 2009a).

This book will examine the economic effects of various cultural factors (including, but not limited to, ethnicity, language and religion)[2], as well as to present a methodological framework for researchers and policymakers to deal with cross-cultural economic activities that could be misinterpreted by existing theories. One of the most important goalss in this book is to clarify the conditions under which culture may not be a cause of misunderstanding and conflict, but be a source of creativity and profitability of international and intercultural cooperation. This book will also identify various cultural conditions under which economic policies can (or cannot) be optimally arranged. The theoretical and empirical results in this book are intended to supplement current studies on development economics and international economics, as well as to help policymakers to reappraise the roles of 'cultural factors' in, and to introduce optimal economic and cultural policies into, cross-cultural economic management. This book is divided into nine chapters, as follows.

Chapter 1 introduces the most important cultural elements (ethnicity, language and religion) and their implications for the study of cross-cultural trade and other economic issues. Our discussion of these cultural elements is not definitive and perhaps would not satisfy anthropologists. Nevertheless, the consideration is due to the concerns that (a) 'ethnicity' provides a genetic basis in which socioeconomic behaviors between groups of people can be easily differentiated; (b) 'language' is an effective tool of communication; and (c) 'religion' can provide the insights into the characteristics of culture.

After reviewing briefly the diversities of existing economies, Chapter 2 surveys and assesses various approaches by which to conduct a multidimensional analysis of the world economy. While geographic, political and economic approaches have their own respective advantages, the culture-area approach is particularly useful for the long-term, comparative economic analysis. In this chapter, a framework of seven culture areas – African, East Asian, Eastern Orthodox, Indian, Islamic, Latin American and Western – is suggested for multicultural economic analysis. Besides, approaches to estimating multicultural data and a variety of methods that may be applied in multicultural economic analysis are discussed in this chapter.

Chapter 3 presents a brief scenario of how such micro- and macro-economic activities as values and rules, organizational behaviors, warfare and income distribution, consumption patterns and marketing strategy are decided and influenced in different cultures. One of our empirical findings is that income re-distribution can be more easily conducted between individuals with same religious beliefs than between those with different religious beliefs. Since the end of the Cold War era the study of intercultural relations has become one of the most popular topics in the field of global politics and economics. There have been different views on cross-cultural economics, supporting both intercultural conflict and cooperation. We

---

[2] In this book, culture is treated as both a resource for and an obstacle to economic development.

argue that cultural dissimilarity may result in both conflict and cooperation, depending on the various conditions and contexts concerned. Specifically, intercultural cooperation will be very sensitive to the measures of cultural difference in countries where cultural difference leads to serious intranational and international barriers. However cultural dissimilarity would have a very small effect on conflict if the diverse groups have learned to live with each other in a politically stable and economically equitable environment.

Chapter 4 deals with multicultural economic development and policy. After briefly reviewing the efficiency and stability of existing multilateral economic organizations and treaties in which different number of cultures are involved, an analytic model of multicultural economies is contructed. In this chapter, a number of case studies will be conducted. Specifically, the four case studies (the genocide in Rwanda, the territorial disputes in Jammu and Kashmir, the struggle for fresh water in the Middle East, and the multicultural risks at the Oceania) provide empirical evidence that supports the hypothesis that culture sometimes may be an obstacle to multicultural development. In the meantime, the empirical evidence from four individual economies (Switzerland, Singapore, Hong Kong and mainland China) also suggests that (i) small, low-inequality economies could benefit from cultural diversity; (ii) small, backward economies could benefit from the radical and large-scale cultural influences from the outside world; and (iii) large, backward economies could benefit from the gradual and incremental cultural influences from the outside world.

In existing literature relating to the determinants of economic growth, explanatory variables such as income inequality and cultural diversity have been treated separately. In Chapter 5 we try to discuss their joint effects. Our task is to investigate whether there are any conditions under which income inequality and cultural diversity could encourage (or retard) economic growth. Evidence from a broad panel of nations reveals somewhat ambiguous results in that economic growth is quite independent from the variables of inequality and cultural (linguistic and religious) diversity. But for the post-Cold War era there is also an indication that religious diversity tends to retard growth in high inequality nations and to encourage growth in low inequality places. Besides, there is some evidence that supports the view that inequality tends to encourage growth in low religious diversity nations, but not in high religious diversity places. According to the estimated results, higher religious diversity could become a source of productive factors contributing to economic growth for low inequality nations; but in nations with high degrees of religious diversity, high inequality could seriously affect economic growth. In nations with low degrees of religious diversity, income inequality could generate higher economic growth since there are very few, if any, intercultural barriers within each religiously homogeneous nation.

Chapter 6 examines cultural influences on foreign trade. It is generally accepted that, given the markedly differing attitudes as well as cultural values between different cultural groups of people, the adoption of a common standard is unlikely to prove effective. However 'cultural dissimilarity' may also generate 'economic complementarities' that will have positive influences on foreign trade. As a result the final output of the cross-cultural influences should be nonlinear, subjecting to various conditions concerned. Using a modified gravity model and the cross-sectional data of East Asian economies, this chapter presents evidence that supports the view that the effect of distance-related transactions costs on trade tends to fall over time. Overall religious influence on foreign trade exists in the post-Cold War period but not during the Cold War period. The effects of language on inter-regional trade and of religion on intra-regional trade both weaken over time. In all circumstances, religion tends to have more significant influences on intra-regional trade than language, and language tends to exert more significant influences on inter-regional trade than religion. Finally, from 1985 to 1995 there is an indication that (i) English becomes more important for inter-regional trade, (ii) Bahasa, English and Khmer become less important for intra-regional trade, and (iii) Chinese plays an increasing role in both intra- and inter-regional trade.

Finally, Chapter 7 deals with cross-cultural conflict management. Because of the ethnic, linguistic and religious differences throughout the world, the intercultural relations have been differently formed, in patterns of either détente or confrontations. In this chapter various factors that could possibly result in cross-cultural conflicts are clarified in the form of sx hypotheses. Besides, four approaches, which have been successfully applied in the effective resolution of cross-cultural conflicts, will be discussed. They are: (i) round table negotiation, (ii) third-party mediation, (iii) shelving disputes strategy, and (iv) neutral, buffer and demilitarized zones.

A number of boxes are inserted where appropriate in the text. It is hoped that this will help students, researchers as well as ordinary readers from different academic backgrounds looking to gain more knowledge about the method of and tactics to cross-cultural economic management.

# Chapter 1

# CONCEPTS AND FACTS

Remember the days of old,
Understand the years of generation after generation.
Ask your father and he will tell you,
Your elders and they will say to you.

(Deuteronomy, 32:7)

## 1.1. ETHNICITY

Before dealing with the concept 'ethnicity', it is necessary to know some facts about 'race'. Genetically, race is defined as a group with genes frequently differing from those of other groups in human species. However the genes responsible for the hereditary differences between humans are few when compared with the vast number of genes common to all human beings regardless of the race to which they belong. All human groups belong to the same species and are mutually fertile. In practice, race usually refers to any of several subdivisions of mankind sharing certain physical characteristics, such as skin pigmentation, skin complexion, color and type of hair, shape of head, stature, form of eyes and nose, and so on. The differences among races are essentially biological and are marked by the hereditary transmission of physical characteristics.

General agreement is inadequate as to the classification of such people as the aborigines of Australia, the Dravidian people of Southern India, the Polynesians, the Ainu of Northern Japan and so on. Most anthropologists have agreed on the existence of three relatively distinct groups: Caucasoid, Mongoloid and Negroid.

- The Caucasoid group, found in Europe, North Africa, and from the Middle East to North India, is characterized as having skin of pale reddish white to olive brown. The hair is light blond to dark brown. The color of the eyes varies from light blue to dark brown.
- The Mongoloid group, which includes most peoples of East Asia and the American Indians, has been described as having skin of saffron to yellow or reddish brown. The hair is dark, straight. The eyes are from black to dark brown.

- The Negroid group, which includes the African peoples of Southern Sahara, the Pygmy groups of Indonesia, and the inhabitants of New Guinea and Melanesia, is characterized by a brown to brown-black complexion. The hair is dark and coarse, usually curly. The eyes are dark.

Modern genetics has shown that systematic genetic differences between people from different parts of the world, though they exist, are small when compared to the variations between people from the same place. The visible differences, such as skin color, are the result of a mere handful of genes. Racism is actually an unfortunate by-product of another phenomenon – a tendency to assign people to 'coalition groups', and to use whatever cues are available, be there clothing, accent, or skin color, to slot individuals into such groups or 'stereotype' them. The good news is that experiments done by researchers suggest such stereotypes are easily dissolved and replaced with others. Racism, in other words, can be eliminated.[1]

Unlike race, ethnicity is a social entity formed in the historical process. In practice, ethnicity is usually determined according to language rather than religion, because whereas in most cases an ethnic group uses the same or at least similar linguistic systems, it does not necessarily share religious beliefs. In brief, more than 2,000 ethnic groups have been identified in the world. The ethnic distribution of the world population, however, is rather uneven. For example, the largest ethic group (Han Chinese) has a population of more than one billion people, whereas the smallest (Andmanese in India) has a population of between dozens to a few hundreds. More specifically, there are more than ten million people in 67 ethnic groups; more than one million people in 202 ethnic groups; and from 100,000 to one million people in 293 ethnic groups (Hu and Zhang, 1982, p. 69).

In many cases, names used by ethnic groups for themselves tell the legend of their origin; some other ethnic groups are named after their customs or costumes. For example, the name Kirgiz means '40 girls'. A legend says that the ancestors of the Kirgiz people were 40 sisters. Kazak means 'swan'. The first Kazak was said to be the child of a swan who turned into a beautiful girl. In China, the Xibe people used 'Xibe' (leather belt or hooked belt) to name their ethnic group because they liked to wear a hooked leather belt. The Yi people who live in Southwest China like to wear black clothes, so they call themselves Nisu, meaning the 'black people'. But the Bai people have a preference for white, so they call themselves Baini, or the 'white people'. Ethnic names in many cases relate to the values and activities of the ethnicity. Sometimes, the names also indicate the natural and geographical conditions under which the ethnic peoples lived. For example, Ewenki means 'people living in the mountain forests'.

Members of the ethnic majority in China have traditionally referred to themselves as the Han nationality. This may well be because of the relatively long period of social, political, economic and military consolidation and stability enjoyed by the Chinese nation during the Han dynasty (206 BC—AD 220). The Han people, displaying the physical characteristics of Continental Asian Mongoloids, consist of more than 90 per cent of the population in China. The term 'Han', however, does not fully account for the cultural and ethnic origins of the Chinese people. It is, instead, an inclusive name for the various tribes that lived together on the Central China Plains much prior to the time of Christ. The trend over the ages was for many ethnic groups living adjacent to the Hua-Xia people to be assimilated at different times

---

[1] *The Economist* (2001, p. 61). Cited from Harris *et al.* (2004, p. 210).

and to different degrees into what ultimately the Chinese have termed the Han culture. The original ethnic stock for this amalgam seems to have primarily included the Hua-Xia, Eastern Yi, Chu-Wu and Baiyue groups. Other non-Han peoples who were assimilated into the evolving Chinese culture at different points in history include: for example, the Xiongnu (Huns) and Xianbei between the third and fifth centuries AD, the Eastern Hu and the Jurchens (ancesters of the Manchus) from the tenth through the early 13th century, later the Mongols toward the end of the 13th century, and the Manchus through their conquest of Central China in the 17th century.

The identification of ethnic groups may be a political issue. For the United States the Census Bureau provides a classification of racial groups as five categories: (i) white, (ii) black, (iii) American Indian, Eskimo, Aleutian, (iv) Asian, Pacific Islander, and (v) other (including Hispanic). Some studies also look at 'ancestry' or ethnic origin, most often defined in this context as the country of birth of the American individual (for in stance, Western European, Eastern European and Indian). It has been generally believed that colonial authorities were largely responsible for creating tribal identities among the Tutsis and the Hutus in Rwanda. Much has been written about the artificial birth of the Hutu-Tutsi split as part of the divide-and-conquer strategy of Belgium, the colonial power. For us, what is notable is the rich anecdotal evidence that physical attributes play a critical role in the conflict. On average, 'Tutsis' are taller and more slender; they have somewhat lighter skin and thinner noses. Before colonization the terms 'Hutu' and 'Tutsi' did not bear the same political meaning as they do today. In order to affirm their authority, colonial rulers redistributed power and privilege between the two groups. Belgian governed the region through Tutsis who, with more European features, were considered to be born to rule (Lee, 2002, p. 83).

Ethnic groups are not restricted to single countries. For example the Han Chinese can be found in (besides the mainland of China) almost all major countries (especially those in Southeastern Asia) and the Anglo-Saxons are distributed in the United Kingdom, the United States, Canada, Australia, New Zealand and so on. On the other hand, there is a great range of ethnic diversities in the world, and while there is only one single ethnic group in Japan, Korea, Hungary and Romania, in most places, a nation is not a homogeneous unit but rather a collection of areas fragmented along ethnic lines. Nigeria, for example, is divided into Hausa, Ibo and Yoruba tribes and areas, as Sri Lanka is divided into Sinhalese and Tamil areas.

There is a worrying case in point. The former Soviet Union was composed of 128 ethnic groups, each with its own language, culture, history, traditions – and grievances. For decades under the soviet state these groups lived side by side in an artificial soviet harmony imposed from above. In a very short period of time, however, the Soviet Union collapsed into 16 separate ethnic states, some of which are threatened by further ethnic divisions. The former Yugoslavia collapsed into small ethnic 'nations' and civil war broke out between divided ethnic groups. Czechoslovakia also divided along ethnic lines. This has been a continuing pattern in much of Africa as well. From Angola to Ethiopia to Sudan to Zimbabwe, tribal divisions are changing countries (Cateora and Graham, 1998, p. 142).

It is necessary to be very cautious in trying to identify the role of such cultural elements as race and ethnicity in socioeconomic affairs. According to the biological tenet that sees cooperation among animals as mainly influenced by genetic similarity, socioeconomic behaviors between various groups of people can be easily differentiated. But the term 'race' is not appropriate when applied to national, religious, geographic, linguistic or cultural groups, nor can the biological criteria of race be equated with any mental characteristics such as intelligence, personality, or character. In the 19th and early 20th centuries spurious theories, mainly expressed by those who were interested in emphasizing the supposed superiority of their own kind of culture or nationality, were developed about race, culture and nationality.

## 1.2. LANGUAGE

Ethnicity is usually represented by linguistic identities, giving rise to the term 'ethnolinguistics'. Though complex in terms of lexicon, grammar, syntax, phonetics and so on, languages may be classified either genetically or typologically. The genetic classification assumes that certain languages are related and that they have evolved from a common ancestral language; while typological classification is based on similarities in the language structure. Before classifying the world of languages, a few points on linguistic terminology should be explained.

Family is a label often used for a conservative genetic classification of language, one that can be proved only when an abundance of cognates (related words) is available. Phylum is a label for a liberal genetic classification that is proved with fewer cognates; it encompasses language families. A given phylum always has a greater extension than any of the families included in it, even though the term 'family' in practical usage is often employed to refer to a phylum.

The number of languages on earth is roughly between 4,000 and 6,000 (Pinker, 1994). Although the classification of these language groups may differ, they can be roughly distinguished through the following phylums:[2]

### Indo-European Phylum

This phylum is composed of Slavic languages (including Bulgarian, Macedonian, Russian, Slovene, Serbo-Croatian, Ukrainian and so on), Germanic languages (including English, Frisian, Netherlandic-German, Insular Scandinavian, and Continental Scandinavian), Latin languages (including Spanish, Portuguese, French, Italian, Romanian and so on), Albanian language, Celtic languages (including Irish, Wales, Scottish), Greek languages (including Greek and Cyprian) languages, Baltic languages (including Lithuanian and Latvian), and Indo-Iranian (including Hindi, Urdu, Bengali, Romany, Tajik, Persian and so on).

### Sino-Tibetan Phylum

This phylum is composed of Sino-Tai languages (including Chinese, Thai, Lao and so on), Tibetan-Burman languages (including Tibetan and Burman), Miao-Yao languages (including Miao and Yao), Zhuang-Dong languages (including Zhuang and Dong), and Karen.

## Hamio-Semitic Phylum

This phylum is composed of Semitic languages (including Arabic, Hebrew, dialects of East and West Aramenian and Modern South Arabic), Berber languages (including Guanche, Tamashek, Tamazight and so on), Cushitic languages (including Gallinya, Somali and so on), and Chadic languages (consisting of over 100 languages).

## Caucasian Phylum

This phylum is composed of South Caucasian languages (including Georgian, Laz, and Svan), and Northwest Caucasian languages (including, Kabardian, Abaza, Adyghian, Ubykh, Chechen, Ingush and so on).

## Ural-Altaic Phylum

This phylum is composed of Uralic languages (including Mansi, Khanti and so on), Turkic languages (including Azerbaijian, Kazakh, Uighur, Uzbek, Kirgiz, Turkmen, Turkish and so on), Mongolian languages (including Mongolian and so on), and Manchu-Tungus languages (including Manchu).

## Finno-Ugric Phylum

This phylum is composed of Hungarian, Norwegian, Swedish, Finnish, Russian Lapp and so on.

## Dravidian Phylum

This phylum is composed of Brahui, Telugu, Tamil, Malayalam, Kannada, Gondi, Tulu, Kurukh, Kui and so on.

## Nilo-Saharan Phylum

This phylum is composed of Eastern Sudanic languages (including more than 60 languages), Central Sudanic languages (including about 30 languages of which Sara, Lugbara and Mangbetu are the largest), Saharan languages (including Kanuri, Masalit, Songhai, Fur and so on).

---

[2] Based on Britannica Book (1996) and other sources.

## Niger-Congo Phylum

This phylum is composed of Bantu languages (including Rwanda, Shona, Kongo, Luba-Lulua, Xhosa and so on), Mande (including Bambara, Menda, Vai and so on), Gur (Voltaic) languages (including Mossi and so on), West Atlantic languages (including Fulani, Wolof, Temne, and so on), Adamawa-Eastern languages (including Sango and so on), and Kwa languages (including Twi, Yoruba, Igbo and so on).

## Khoisan Phylum

This phylum includes about four-dozen languages spoken in southern Africa and two click languages (Sandawe and Haza) spoken in Tanzania.

## Paleo-Siberian Phylum

This phylum is composed of Luorawetlan languages (including Chukchi, Kamchadal and Koryad) Yukaghir languages (including Yukaghir, Chuvantsy, and Gilyak), and Yeniseian language (including Ket, Kott, Assan and Arin).

## Austro-Asiatic Phylum

This phylum is composed of more than 50 languages (including Khmer, Mon, Vietnamese, Muong, Jahaic or Semang, Senoic or Sakai, Semelaic and so on) and sometimes 16 or so Munda languages (including Santali, Mundari, Ho, Sora, Kharia, Korku and so on).

## Austronesian Phylum

This phylum is composed of two families of approximately 500 languages, including: Western Austronesian (or Indonesian) and Eastern Austronesian (or Oceanic).

## Other Phylums

These languages include Japanese, Korean[3], Papuan, and so on.

There is a very uneven distribution of population among languages. The nine largest linguistic groups, which account for more than half of the world population, are Chinese (19.7 percent), English (9.2 percent), Hindi (7.3 percent), Spanish (5.6 percent), Arabic (3.8 percent), Portuguese (2.9 percent), Russian (2.7 percent), Japanese (2.1 percent) and Bengali

---

[3] Sometimes, Korean is also classified as a member of the Ural-Altaic phylum.

(2.1 percent). The other linguistic groups, each accounting for more than one percent of the world population, are French (1.9 percent), German (1.5 percent), Korean (1.2 percent), Vietnamese (1.1 percent) and Turkish (1.0 percent). Other languages may have very few speakers.[4]

Altogether, the five major Western languages (English, French, German, Portuguese and Spanish) are spoken by approximately one-fifth of the world population, of which the native English-speakers possess the largest part.[5] Even though the number of people with English as a first language has declined slightly during the past decades, English is still the primary language of intercultural communication, since it serves as a lingua franca for the largest group of people whose native languages are not English. The English used by different ethnic groups throughout the world is also diversified. English is indigenized and takes on local colorations which distinguish it from British or American English and which, in extreme cases, make these 'Englishes' almost unintelligible one to another. Nigerian Pidgin English, Indian English and other forms of English are being incorporated with their respective host cultures and perhaps will continue to differentiate themselves so as to become related but distinct languages.

---

### Box 1.1 Do "Z" Students Have Higher Ability?

Sorting based on "alphabetical order" is a fact of everyday life. Team members are listed in this order, including co-authors of scientific papers; students may be seated in a classroom according to their last name's position in the alphabet; competing firms are displayed alphabetically in phone and other directories. Could this systematic and omnipresent sorting provide an advantage to those positioned high in the alphabet? Based on the experience of the whole population of secondary-school graduates in 1999, Jurajda and Munich (2006, p. 22) analyze the success of application to Czech universities and find a small, but statistically significant effect of one's last-name-initial position in the alphabet on admission chances for those applications on the margin of admission.

The presence of alphabet-affected admission practices implies that among students admitted to selective schools, those with last names in the bottom part of the alphabet have on average higher ability. To see this, consider a simple model of school admission with students of three ability types (high, medium, and low) distributed independently of last name initial, where all high-ability and none of the low-ability students are admitted to selective schools, and where admission of medium-ability types is decided in a way affected by alphabetical sorting. Hence, the high-ability "Z" students admitted to highly selective programs should mix with both high and medium-ability "A" students. Jurajda and Munich (2006) test this implication using a national study-achievement test administered to the student population graduating from secondary schools in 1999 and find evidence fully consistent with the alphabet-based sorting hypothesis.

---

[4] Calculated by the author based on *Britannica Book of the Year 2001*. Notice that according to these statistics several other languages (such as Phoenician, Akkadian, Moabite, and Ugaritic of Semitic family, and Kott, Assan, and Arin of Paleo-Siberian phylum) have already become extinct.

[5] According to Huntington (1996, p. 60), the share of English-speakers in world population was 9.8 percent in 1958, and it declined gradually to 9.1 percent in 1970, 8.8 percent in 1980 and 7.6 percent in 1992.

Chinese speakers, mainly concentrated on the mainland of China, Taiwan, Hong Kong and other Chinese alien communities in Southeastern Asia, account for nearly one-fifth the world population. As a major branch of the Sino-Tibetan family of languages, Chinese is unique. Some of the outstanding characteristics include monosyllabicity and a simple phonological system, the use of tones to distinguish different meanings, and the syntax that depends on word order; it lacks inflection, grammatical gender and pluralization. Although the Mandarin is standardized nationwide as *putonghua*, each region speaks its own local version of it, usually reflecting influence from the native dialect of the area. These regional variations of Mandarin are perhaps as great as, or even greater than, those of other languages in the rest of the world. In spite of multitudinous dialects (such as Wu, Cantonese (Yue), Min, Hakka, Xiang, Gan and so on), many of which are mutually unintelligible, a shared written system unites people in China. It is generally believed that the unified Chinese characters used by people speaking different dialects makes it possible for the central government to maintain control effectively over a vast size of territory. Written Chinese is the only major modern writing system that uses thousands of ideographic-phonetic symbols rather than a phonetic alphabet or syllabary of a few dozen symbols. The writing system of Chinese characters has also inspired and profoundly influenced the writing systems in Japan and Korea, though, in terms of grammar and syntax, Japanese and Korean have nothing to do with Chinese.

In India around 800 different languages and over 1600 dialects are spoken. Hindi is a lingua franca as there are over 300 million speakers, of whom at least 200 million use it as a first language in the northern and central states (Saville, 2002, p. 203). Thanks to the central government's constitutional commitment, Hindi, as the official language, has been spread and developed throughout the nation. For example, in the early 1980s Hindi speakers accounted for less than 30 percent of the population; by the late 1990s, however, more than 50 percent of the population were using Hindi as a first language (source: *Britannica Book* 1998). As a result of its colonial associations, English is still regarded as a necessary second or 'associated' official language in India, especially in the southern and eastern states, where Hindi nationalism may be offensive to those who have a different language and religion (Ager, 2001, p. 27).

A glance at history reveals that the distribution of language speakers has reflected the distribution of economic power in the world. Latin, for example, was a universal language in Europe during the Middle Age and the Renaissance. French was once known as the universal language of diplomacy, and English today is often said to fill such a role in world commerce. During the heyday of the Soviet Union, Russian was the lingua franca from Prague to Hanoi. The decline of Russian power is accompanied by a parallel decline in the use of Russian as a second language. Since the late 20th century China's economic power has stimulated the learning of Chinese in other countries.

Physical (ethnic and linguistic) differences play a critical role in enabling members of one group to pinpoint members of some 'other' coalition. Early examples of this go literally back to biblical times, with tales of warring tribes using the pronunciation of certain words to establish who should be slaughtered. A most recent one stretches to 21st century Northern Ireland, where:

[…]a group of masked men [entered a school and] demanded that students produce identification or repeat the alphabet. Many Catholics pronounce the letter "h" differently to Protestants, with an aspiration influenced by the Irish language. Students were evacuated before it became clear what was planned for people with the wrong accent.[6]

# 1.3. RELIGION

Religion is a major determinant of societal attitudes and behavior. According to the *Oxford Advanced Learner's Dictionary*, 'religion' is defined as 'belief in the existence of a supernatural ruling power, the creator and controller of the universe, who has given to man a spiritual nature which continues to exist after the death of the body' (1974, p. 712). In addition, according to *The New Columbia Encyclopedia*, religion comprises at least three aspects: (1) a system of thought, and action that is shared by a group and that gives the members of that group an object of devotion; (2) a code of behavior by which an individual may judge the personal and social consequences of his action; and (3) a framework of reference by which an individual may relate to a group and their universe (1975, p. 2299).

The development of human civilization has been accompanied by increasing number of religions. The following religions are particularly important to our contemporary society:

- Hinduism
- Buddhism
- Christianity
- Confucianism
- Taoism,
- Islam
- Shinto
- Shamanism
- Animism

Dating from 1500 BC, Hinduism is a non-creedal religion. It is a combination of ancient philosophies and customs, animistic beliefs and legends. Since Hindu is born, not made, Hinduism is an ethnic religion and, therefore, many of its doctrines only apply to the Indian society. One important characteristics of Hinduism is the caste system. Each member of a particular caste has a specific occupational and social role, which is hereditary. Marriage is forbidden outside of the caste. Although efforts were made to weaken this system, it still has a strong hold in the Indian society. Another element is *baradari*, or the 'joint family'. After marriage, the bride goes to the groom's home. After several marriages in the family, there is a large joint family. All generations of the family live together and pool their income with little distinct between brothers and cousins. Women are completely subordinate to men, adult men are expected to do what their fathers tell them. Veneration of the cow is perhaps the best-known Hindu custom. Another element of traditional Hinduism is the restriction of freedom for women, following the belief that to be born a woman is a sign of sin in a former life.

---

[6] *The Economist* of June 15, 2002. Cited from Caselli and Coleman (2002).

Founded by Siddhartha Gautama (563 – 485 BC), Buddhism is one of the most influential religions in Asia. As a reformulation of Hinduism, it did not abolish caste but declare that Buddhists were released from caste restriction. At the heart of Buddhism are the Four Noble Truths: (1) existence is suffering; (2) suffering has a cause, namely craving and attachment; (3) there is a cessation of suffering, which is Nirvana; and (4) there is a path to the cessation of suffering, which includes the Noble Eightfold Path – that is, right view, right intention, right speech, right action, right livelihood, right effort, right mindfulness, and right concentration. Nirvana is the ultimate goal of the Buddhism. It represents the extinction of all cravings and the final release from suffering. To the extent that such ideal reflects the thinking of the mass of people, the society's values would be considered antithetical to such goals as acquisitions, achievement, or affluence. From another early school of Buddhism there developed the lines of thought that led toward the positions advocated by Mahayana Buddhism. The Mahayana (greater vehicle) gave itself from this name in polemical writings to distinguish itself from what it called the Hinayana (lesser vehicle), Theravada, and related schools. The main philosophical tenet of the Mahayana is that all things are empty, or devoid of self-nature. Geographically, the Hinayana Buddhism has followers in Southeast Asia (especially in Cambodia, Myanmar and Thailand) and in East Asia, while the Mahayana Buddhism only concentrates on Southwest and Northwest China.

Founded in Palestine by the followers of Jesus Christ in the first century, Christianity is now the most influential religion in the Western society. The central teachings of traditional Christianity – which is embodied in the Bible, especially in the *New Testament* – are that Jesus is the Son of God, the second person of the Trinity of God and Father, the Son, and the Holy Spirit; and that his life on earth, his crucifixion, resurrection, and ascension into heaven are the proofs of God's love and forgiveness of man's sins. In addition, Christians believe that by faith in Christ man may attain salvation and eternal life. In 1054 Christianity was split into two churches: Roman Catholicism and Orthodox (or Eastern Orthodox)[7]. The major differences between the two churches are that the doctrine of Orthodox Church accepts the first seven councils while Roman Catholics recognizes 21 general councils, and in rejection by the Orthodox Church of the jurisdiction of the Bishop of Rome (the pope). Eastern Orthodox Christianity has been mainly adopted in Russia and Central Europe, Roman Catholicism traditionally emphasized the Church and the sacraments as the principal elements of religion and the way to God. Since the 16th century there has been a further division of Christianity (see Figure 1.1).

The Protestant Reformation made some critical changes in emphasis but retained agreement with Catholicism on most traditional Christian doctrine. The Protestants, however, stressed that the Church, its sacraments, and its clergy were not essential to salvation; rather, 'salvation is by faith alone'. Protestantism minimized the distinction between the secular and the religious life. In history there have been four principal forms of ascetic Protestantism: (i) Calvinism, (ii) Pietism, (iii) Methodism, and (iv) Baptism. None of these movements was completely separated from the others, and even the distinction from the non-ascetic Churches of the Reformation is never perfectly clear. Calvinism assumed in the main area of its influence in Western Europe, especially in the 17th century. Pietism split off from the Calvinistic movement in England and Holland. It remained loosely connected with Orthodoxy, shading off from it by imperceptible gradations, until at the end of the 17th

---

[7] In what follows, the terms 'Orthodox Christianity' and 'Eastern Orthodox' will be used interchangeably.

century it was absorbed into Lutheranism. Baptism and Calvinism were at the beginning of their development sharply opposed to each other, but latter they were in close contact. Methodism first arose in the middle of the 18th century within the Englished Church of England. In the course of its development, especially in its extension to America, it became separate from the Anglican Church.

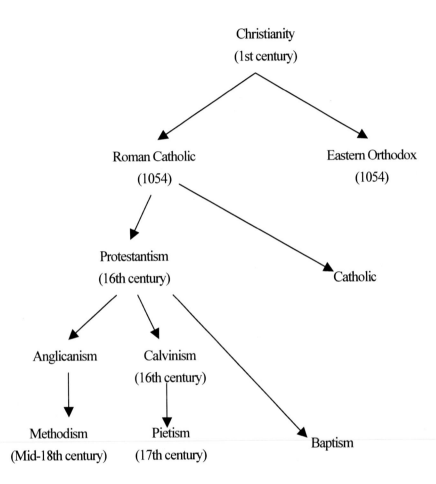

Figure 1.1. Christianity and its major sects

Founded by Kongzi or Confucius (551 – 479 BC), Confucianism was reputed to have served as the basis of the traditional Chinese culture. *Lunyu* (Analects of Confucius) records the saying and deeds of Confucius and his disciples. It covers a wide scope of subjects, ranging from politics, philosophy, literature and art to education and moral cultivation. With only 12,000 characters, it is terse but comprehensive, rich yet profound; as the major classic of Confucianism as well as the most authoritative, it has influenced Chinese society for over two thousand years. Its ideas have taken such firm root in China that all Chinese—both Han and non-Han ethnicities—have been more or less influenced by it. Since the Han dynasty, every ruler has had to pay at least some heed to this, and people also expected their ruler to act accordingly in China.[8] Confucian philosophy concerning the relationship between politics and morality serves as the basis of the Confucian school's emphasis on moral education, becoming one of the major characteristics of Confucianism. This idea also represents the distinguishing feature of the Oriental culture realm under the influence of Confucianism.

Taoism originated from sorcery, pursuit of immortality and other supernatural beliefs found in ancient China. Taoists look to the philosopher Laozi (or named Lao Tzu, born in about 600 BC) as their great leader, and take his work *The Classic of the Way and Its Power* ('Daode Jing' or 'Tao Te Ching') as their canon. Mystifying the philosophic concept of 'Dao' or 'Tao' (the way, or path), they posit that man could become one with the 'Dao' through self-cultivation and achieve immortality. As an escape from Confucianism, Taoism has been promoted by a group of scholars working against the overnice ritualism and detailed prescriptions of the classics. It has also denoted the common people's belief in certain traditional super-institutions. Applying the idea of balance in all things, Taoism argues that human moral ideas are the reflection of human depravity, that the idea of filial piety springs from the fact of impiety, that the Confucian statement of the rules of propriety is really a reflection of the world's moral disorder. Later, Taoism has developed via two directions. The first one, represented by Zhuangzi (c. 369 – 295 BC), resulted in the so-called nihilism. The second one, with the Tao as the basis of proprieties and laws, led to the founding of the Legalist school.

Founded by Muhammad (also spelled Muhammed or Mohammed) (AD 570 – 632), Islam dates back from about AD 610. Islamic adherents can be found from the Atlantic across the northern half of Africa, the Middle East, and across the most part of Asia. 'Islam' is the infinitive of the Arabic verb 'to submit'. Muslim is the present participle of the same verb, thus a Muslim is one submitting to the will of Allah – the only God of the universe – of which Mohammed is the Prophet. Muslim theology, *Tawhid*, defines the Islamic creed, whereas the law, *Shariah*, prescribes the actions of adherents. The Koran (*Qur'an*) is accepted as the ultimate guide and anything not mentioned in the Koran is quite likely to be rejected. The Five Pillars of Islam, or the duties of a Muslim, are (1) the recital of the creed, (2) prayer, (3) fasting, (4) almsgiving and (5) the pilgrimage. A Muslim must pray five times a day at definite hours. During the month of Ramadan in the midsummer in the lunar year, Muslims are required to fast from sunrise to sunset with no food, no drink and no smoking. The fast is meant to develop both self-control and sympathy for the poor. By almsgiving the Muslim shares with the poor. The pilgrimage to Mecca is a well-known aspect of Islam. There are two major groups in Islam—namely, *Sunni* and *Shia*. While they are similar in many ways, Sunni Muslims adhere to both the Koran and *Sharia*, while Shia Muslims only believe in the Koran.

The *Shinto* means in Japanese the way of the gods. Shintoism is a Japanese religion that came from the indigenous people of the country. Beginning in the late fourth century BC, it has no founder or doctrine. The beliefs of this religion center on being one with nature. Members of the Shinto belief worship the *kami*, who include native deities (including emperors and heroes), spirits of nature, and mythical objects. A perfect understanding of Shinto will enable one to have proper understanding of the Japanese nation and their culture. There is neither much grand philosophy nor complicated ritual in Shintoism. Shinto is not a

---

[8] Developing his ideas further, Confucius said: 'Regulated by the edicts and punishments, the people will know only how to stay away out of trouble, but will not have a sense of shame. Guided by virtues and the rites, they will not only have a sense of shame, but also know how to correct their mistakes of their own accord.'

religion adopted by the State. Shinto is a natural and real spiritual force, which pervades the life of the Japanese. Shinto is a creative or formative principle of life. The Shinto principle is the background of Japanese culture, code of ethics, fine arts, family and national structure. Unlike Western religions, Shinto has no scriptures or commandments. It does have customary practices, including ancestor worship adopted from Confucianism. Among the most important aspects of modern Shinto are (1) reverence for the special or divine origin of Japanese people and (2) reverence for the Japanese nation and the imperial family as head of that nation. The impact of modern Shinto on Japanese life is reflected in an aggressive patriotism. The mobilization of the Japanese and their behavior during the Second World War are examples of that patriotism.

Shamanism originated from the Evinki people of Siberia, derived from the verb scha-, 'to know', so shaman literally means 'the one who knows', is wise, a sage. Further ethnologic investigation shows that the true origin for the word shaman can be traced from the Sanskrit initially, then through Chinese-Buddhist mediation to the Manchu in northeast China. Today, in the West, 'shaman' is often taken to mean any kind of native medicine man or woman or anyone with a strong personality and an intense stare. Shamanism goes hand in hand with the animist's experience of the world: first, all that is alive, and being alive embodies a spirit; second, all that is alive is connected by these spirits. Therefore, we all – humans, trees, dogs, cats, bees, stones, mountains, seas, earth and sky – are connected. Shamans believe that there exists a medium, or 'witch', between the God and themselves. The witch, according to the shamanism, can convey the God's decrees.

As a primeval religion, the followers of animism tend to be found in remote and mountainous areas. Animists believe that hills, valleys, waterways and rocks are spiritual beings, as are the plants and animals. Furthermore, they believe that there are other, less obvious spiritual beings not commonly associated with the phenomena of everyday experience. Animists worship the natural bodies (most of which are animals) with which they have special causal relations. Magic, a key element of animism, is the attempt to achieve results through the manipulation of the spiritual world. It represents an unscientific approach to the physical world.

According to the *World Christian Encyclopedia*, edited by Barrett (1982), at the very beginning of the 20th century the religious composition of the world population was as follows: 26.9 percent Western Christians[9], 23.5 percent Chinese folk-religionists, 12.5 percent Hindus, 12.4 percent Muslims, 7.8 percent Buddhists, 7.5 percent Orthodox Christians, 6.6 percent Tribal, and 0.2 percent non-religionists. Since then, the relative numerical strength of some religions around the world has changed dramatically. At the end of the 20th century, Western Christians was still the largest number of population (27.6 percent), followed by Muslims (23.1 percent), non-religionists (17.7 percent), Hindus (15.9 percent), Buddhists (8.0 percent), Orthodox Christians (3.2 percent) and atheists (2.9 percent) (source: *Britannica Book of the Year*, 2001).

Obviously, the largest change recorded above has been the increase in the proportion of people classified as 'non-religious' or 'atheist'. This could reflect a major shift away from religion, and the religious resurgence was yet to gather full steam. Yet this increase in nonbelievers is closely matched by the decrease in those classified as adherents of 'Chinese

---

[9] Unless otherwise stated, "Western Christians" is defined to include Roman Catholics and other non-Orthodox Christians.

folk-religions' (usually mixed with elements of Confucianism, Taoism and Buddhism). The data do show increases in the proportions of the world population adhering to the two major proselytizing religions – Islam and Christianity – over the 20th century. But the Western Christians only experienced a moderate increase, while Muslims enjoyed a large expansion. In addition, due to the continuous population expansion in India, the numbers of Hindus also rose during the 20th century.

In some countries, Islam is becoming the basis for governance, legal and political system. In others, religion dominates legal and political system, such as Judaism in Israel or Roman Catholicism in the Republic of Ireland. The influence of religion is culturally weakening in some states, as with Roman Catholicism in France and Lutheranism in Sweden. Religion can be a source of divisiveness and conflict in society, for example, Northern Ireland; the former Yugoslavia (especially Bosnia and Kosovo); and Africa (including Algeria and Rwanda). Unfortunately, history demonstrates that in the name of religion, zealots and extremists may engage in culturally repressive behavior, such as religious persecutions, ethnic cleansing, terrorism of nonbelievers and even 'holy' wars (Harris et al, 2004, p. 11).

Weber (1904) argued that religious practices and beliefs had important consequences for economic development. Nevertheless, neither mainstream nor heterodox economists paid much attention to measures of culture as determinants of economic growth during the Cold War era. Since the 1990s, there has been a growing tendency for researchers such as Huntington (1996), Landes (1999) and Inglehart and Baker (2000) to use a nation's culture to explain economic growth. Recently, Barro and McCleary (2003) analyzed the influences of religious participation and beliefs on a country's rate of economic progress. They found that economic growth responds positively to the extent of religious beliefs, but negatively to church attendance. That is, growth depends on the extent of believing relative to belonging. These results accord with a perspective in which religious beliefs influence individual traits that enhance economic performance.

Some empirical research works, however, cast serious doubt on the importance of religion. For example, after examining a large cross-section of conflicts, Fox (1997) finds that in only a small minority do religious issues play more than a marginal role. Similarly, Alesina et al. (2002) find that religious fractionalization does not significantly predict the rent-seeking policy distortions usually associated to other types of ethnic fractionalization.

## 1.4. SUMMARY

During the past centuries some researchers have attempted to create exhaustive universal lists of the content of culture, while others have listed and mapped all the culture traits of particular geographic areas. The first inventory of cultural categories was undertaken in 1872 by a committee of the British Association for the Advancement of Science. The committee, which was assisted by Tylor, prepared an anthropological field manual that listed 76 culture topics, in no particular order, including such diverse items as cannibalism and language. The most exhaustive of such list is the 'Outline of Cultural Materials', first published in 1938 and still used as a guide for cataloging great masses of worldwide cultural data for cross-cultural surveys. Like the table of contents of a giant encyclopedia, the outline lists 79 major divisions and 637 subdivisions.[10]

What are the most useful attributes that a technical concept of culture should stress? There has been considerable theoretical debate by anthropologists since Tylor. In 1952, for example, Alfred Kroeber and Clyde Kluckhohn, American anthropologists, published a list of 160 different definitions of culture (Bodley, 1994). Although simplified, their list indicates the diversity of the anthropological concept of culture, including:

- **Topical** – Culture consists of everything on a list of topics, or categories, such as social organization, religion, or economy
- **Historical** – Culture is social heritage, or tradition, that is passed on to future generations
- **Behavioral** – Culture is shared, learned human behavior, a way of life
- **Normative** – Culture is ideals, values, or rules of living
- **Functional** – Culture is the way humans solve problems of adopting to the environment or living together
- **Mental** – Culture is a complex of ideas, or learned habits, that inhibit impulses and distinguish people from animals
- **Structural** – Culture consists of patterned and interrelated ideas, symbols, or behaviors
- **Symbolic** – Culture is based on arbitrarily assigned meanings that are shared by a society

Indeed, culture is too complex to define in simple terms and it can seem that each sociologist has a preferred definition. Certain agreed fundamentals, however, appear in this definition by Hoebel (1960, p. 168): 'Culture is the integrated sum total of learned behavioral traits that are shared by members of a society.' Specifically, these fundamentals are: (i) Culture is a total pattern of behavior that is consistent and compatible in its components. It is not a collection of random behaviors, but behaviors that are internally related and integrated. (ii) Culture is learned behavior. It is not biologically transmitted. It depends on environment, not heredity. Thus, it can be called the man-made part of our environment. (iii) Culture is behavior that is shared by a group of people, a society. It can be considered as the distinctive way of life of a people.[11]

The modern technical definition of culture, as socially patterned human thought and behavior, was originally proposed by a 19th-century British anthropologist, Edward Tylor. In his charter definition of the anthropological concept of culture, for example, Tylor (1871, p. 1) states 'Culture or civilization, taken in its wide ethnographic sense, is that complex whole which includes knowledge, belief, art, morals, law, customs, and any other capabilities and habits acquired by man as a member of society.' This definition is an open-ended list, which has been extended considerably since Tylor first proposed it.

Although many more complicated compositions for a culture have been suggested, we have mainly discussed the below three elements – ethnicity, language and religion. Of course,

---

[10] Cited from Bodley (1994).

[11] Cited from Cateora and Graham (1998, p. 112).

our discussion of these cultural elements is not definitive and perhaps would not satisfy anthropologists. Nevertheless, our consideration is due to the concerns that (a) 'ethnicity' provides a genetic basis in which socioeconomic behaviors between groups of people can be easily differentiated; (b) 'language' is an effective tool of communication; and (c) 'religion' can provide the insights into the characteristics of culture.

# Chapter 2

# CULTURE AND ECONOMICS

> The Tao of Buddha is hard and difficult. It takes an eon of effort, patience and hard work. How can one hope to achieve Tao with little merit and little wisdom? How can one attempt to attain Tao while feeling arrogant and thinking it is easy? If one tries to do so, one tries in vain... Drop all discursive thoughts and all attachments. Rest your mind. Like a wall, don't be influenced by internal and external factors; only then, can you enter the Buddhist Path.
>
> (Bodhidharma, 470–543 AD)

## 2.1. A WORLD OF ECONOMIES

When referring to the spatial heterogeneity of the world economy, at least two important points must be noted. First, about 134 million square kilometers of land area (excluding Antarctica) are shared by more than 200 independent economies differing greatly in size (for example, Russia has 147 thousand square kilometers, whereas Monaco has less than two square kilometers). The world economy thus is widely diversified in terms of physical environments and natural resource endowments. Second, more than 6 billions people are divided unevenly by these economies. For example, China has already a population of 1.3 billion, whereas Nauru, a small independent island, only has a population of about 10,000.

The fundamental characteristics of the contemporary economic issues are closely associated with the complexity of the world *per se*. The uneven distribution of natural and social resources have undoubtedly shaped or decisively influenced the growth pattern and process of the economic development of the world as a whole. Technically and methodologically, deeper insights into the characteristics and mechanisms of the contemporary world are difficult to achieve without finding some way of sub-dividing or classifying different regions. Methods to be used for the classification of the existing economies tend to be different, depending upon the analytical purposes. Most popular would be the six continents of

- Asia
- Africa
- Europe

- Latin America
- North America
- Oceania

This method to a large extent emphasizes the geographical over the socioeconomic features of the world. In a similar way, the World Bank (1996) classifies all the existing economies into five groups:

- Sub-Saharan Africa
- Asia
- Europe and Central Asia
- Middle East and North Africa
- Americas[1]

This also ignores the discrepancies within each group, since socioeconomic factors differ greatly between Europe and Central Asia, as well as between North and South America.

It may appear that the simplest method of dividing the world economy is to employ the concepts of North/South and East/West. But whereas 'North' and 'South' have universally accepted fixed reference points at the poles, 'East' and 'West' do not, and the use of such concepts to identify geographical areas is confusing. It all depends on where you stand. For example, 'West' and 'East' presumably originally referred to the western and eastern parts of Eurasia. From the American viewpoint, however, the Far East is actually the Far West. For most of Chinese history the West meant India, whereas in Japan the 'West' usually meant China (Naff, 1986).

None of the above classifications, however, can reflect the diversified natural and geographical conditions of the world. To this end, more technical criteria are needed. For example, the existing economies can be classified by the following climate zones:

- Humid
- Semi-humid
- Semi-arid and
- Arid
- Tropical
- Subtropical
- Frigid

They can also be classified into three extrinsically different groups, using the geographical criteria if they are:

- Landlocked
- Islands

---

[1] Specifically, the World Bank (1996, p. 394) defines the 'Sub-Saharan Africa' for East and Southern Africa; 'Asia' for 'East Asia and Pacific'; and 'Europe and Central Asia' for Eastern Europe, Central Asia, and the rest of Europe.

- Mixed

These two classification approaches are useful for researchers engaged with some specific purposes. For example, the climate-zone approach is usually applied for agricultural economics analyses while extrinsic geographical locations are important instruments for analysis of the spatial determinants of international trade. However they are not suitable for other economic comparisons and analyses.

Economies are also diversified organizationally. For example, the existing independent countries can be divided into different categories of political status in the forms of governments and ruling powers. These include:

- Republic
- Constitutional monarchy
- Parliamentary state
- Provisional military government
- Socialist republic
- Federal republic
- Monarchy
- Federal parliamentary state
- Islamic republic
- Transitional military republic
- Federal Islamic republic
- Transitional government
- Federal constitutional monarchy
- Federation of monarchy
- Monarchical–sacerdotal state
- Constitutional monarchy under military rule

During the 20th century the failure of the centrally planned economies (CPEs) to keep pace with their market-oriented counterparts demonstrated clearly enough that planning entire economies at the central government level is not a productive path to long-term development. Since the fall of the socialist system in 1990, old institutions which had provided a degree of economical and social stability to society have been rapidly destroyed and new market-oriented ideologies have spread rapidly throughout the economic environment of the former Soviet Union. By the late 1990s, however, while many elements of a market-based formal framework had been established, its implementation was often weak. The enforcement of new laws and regulations has been constrained by the presence of old informal institutions – the strong bureaucracy, the weak respect for law, informal networking and other social factors, which were historically rooted in the behavior of the Soviet society. As a result the speed and sequencing of the economic reforms, which were important at the beginning of the transition, seems to be becoming less important in comparison with the necessity of institutional transformation.

It is true that political classifications may be helpful for those who want to conduct comparative studies of international politics and other politically related economic issues. But examples of economies with the same form of government or ruling power but with different political and economic performances can be found all over the world.

Political systems can be further classified according to the extent to which an administration or governance is intrusive, or backed by the use of force. The term 'authoritarian' refers to an organization or an independent state, which enforces strong and sometimes oppressive measures against the population, generally without attempting to gain the consent of the population. In an authoritarian state, citizens are subject to state authority in many aspects of their lives, including many that other political philosophies would see as matters of personal choice. Authoritarianism may take different forms. Specifically, absolute monarchies are almost always authoritarian, and dictatorships are always so. Democracies are normally not authoritarian, but may exhibit authoritarian behavior in some respects. Totalitarian governments tend to be revolutionary, intent on changing the basic structure of society, while authoritarian ones tend to be conservative. As a result the existing economies can be roughly classified into the following types:

- Authoritarian
- Democracy
- Totalitarian

Authoritarian regimes typically grant wide powers to law enforcement agencies; at its most extreme, this leads to a police state. Authoritarian regimes may or may not have a rule of law – in the former case, laws and procedures exist and are applied, though they may seem intrusive, unjust or excessive; in the latter case, laws do not exist, or are routinely ignored, and the actions of the government are at the whim of the leadership. Dictatorships and absolute monarchies are almost always authoritarian. Authoritarianism is distinguished from totalitarianism both in degree and scope. What's more, authoritarian administration or governance is less intrusive and, in the case of groups, not necessarily backed by the use of force. The experiences of East Asia, especially of Japan, South Korea and China make clear that it is possible for a country to have an interventionist government and still enjoy extremely rapid economic growth over a period of decades. Nevertheless, certain policies that helped Japan develop in the 1950s and 1960s, generated growth in East Asia in the 1970s and 1980s, and, more recently, sparked China's economic boom from the 1980s onwards were specific to the time and place. However they may not have worked well in other countries, nor are they likely to be appropriate in the time to come.

The International Monetary Fund (IMF) classifies existing economies into three categories:

- Advanced economies
- Developing countries
- Countries in transition (IMF, 1997b, p. 147)

In addition, the following two categories are also used:

- Net creditor countries
- Net debtor countries (IMF, 1997b, p. 174)

It is noticeable that the former has no clear boundaries while the latter can only be used for the purposes of international financial analyses. The World Bank has classified existing economies into three or four groups:

- Low-income
- Middle-income, which is further divided into
  - o 'Lower-middle'
  - o 'Upper-middle'
- High-income economies[2]

Classification by income level, however, does not necessarily reflect development status. Even worse, it may not be a suitable criterion by which to conduct any consistent analyses and comparisons of different groups of economies over a longer period of time as rising and falling income levels shift economies from one category to another.

The World Bank (1996, pp. 396-7) further classifies existing economies according to an identification of the types of international trade in which major exports are those that make up 50 percent or more of the total exports of goods and services from one category. On the basis of these criteria, they arrive at the following classification:

- Exporters of manufactures
- Exporters of non-fuel primary products
- Exporters of fuels (mainly oil)
- Exporters of services
- Diversified exporters
- Not classified by export category

This kind of classification may provide clear information about the resource endowments and industrial advantages (disadvantages) for each group of economies. But it is too technical and, again, it ignores the socioeconomic differences between the various groups of the existing economies.

There is another flaw in the political and economic classifications suggested above. Economies are constantly undergoing processes of political and economic transformation. For example, politically and institutionally, the former USSR and the other economies of the Central and Eastern Europe would have been characterized as socialist states before the early 1990s. Since then, however, all of them have implemented various forms of market-oriented reforms.

## 2.2. CULTURES AND CULTURE AREAS

According to *The American Heritage Dictionary of the English Language* (2000, 4th edn, updated in 2003), 'culture' is defined as the following: (a) the totality of socially transmitted

---

[2] The World Bank (1996, pp. 394-5) defined low-income economies, lower-middle-income economies, upper-middle-income economies and high-income economies with the per capita GNPs of US$725 or less, US$726-2,895, US$2,896-8,955 and US$8,956 or more, respectively.

behavior patterns, arts, beliefs, institutions and all other products of human work and thought; (b) these patterns, traits and products considered as the expression of a particular period, class, community, or population (such as Edwardian culture, Japanese culture, the culture of poverty); (c) these patterns, traits and products considered with respect to a particular category, such as a field subject, or mode of expression (such as religious culture in the Middle Ages, musical culture, oral culture); and (d) the predominating attitudes and behavior that characterize the functioning of a group or organization.

Unlike political and economic factors, cultural factors, such as ethnicity, language and religion, keep relatively few changes over a comparatively long period of time. They can, therefore, serve as an important instrument for the comparative analysis of the world economy. However, given the great varieties of ethnic, linguistic and religious groups throughout the world (see Appendix 1 for details), the number of individual cultures is too large to be a practical tool and it would be very difficult to conduct useful multicultural economic comparisons.[3] Consequently, to facilitate cross-cultural economic analyses and comparisons, our analytical framework will be mainly based on a synthetic term – 'culture area'.

The concept of 'culture area' reflects the theoretical position that each culture, on whatever level it may be analyzed, must be examined with regards to its own history and the general principles of independent invention, culture borrowing, cultural integration and so on. In the *International Encyclopedia of the Social Sciences*, culture areas are defined as 'geographical territories in which characteristic culture patterns are recognizable through repeated associations of specific traits and, usually, through one or more modes of subsistence that are related to the particular environment' (1972, p. 563).

There usually exists a small and relatively homogeneous core in each culture area. Culture areas also have boundaries. The influence of a specific culture is always the strongest in the core and becomes weaker from the core to peripheral areas. In theory, the boundary of a culture area can be determined as the line beyond which the influence of culture comes to zero. However the boundaries between culture areas are not necessarily distinct; recognizable cultures within a given area may contrast with those of neighboring ones, and if the boundaries are not sharply delineated, zones of composite culture or blended traits may make the transition from one to another a matter of gradation. Within a single area, quite different ways of life may coexist as characteristic patterns.

Although distinction between regions based on culture are as old as mankind, the roots of the culture area concept can be traced to Europe, where the work of the German geographer Friedrich Ratzel (1844-1904) inspired the development of the *Kulturkreise* (cultural circles) school. *Kulturkreise*, which attempted to reconstruct the diffusion, or spread, of cultural traits from a few of dominant cultural clusters, was associated with the German anthropologists Leo Frobenius (1873-1938) and Fritz Graebner (1877-1934). It was not in Europe, however, but in the United States that the concept of culture area gained real social scientific cohesion. One impetus for this development was the need to make sense of the growing body of ethnographic data produced by early anthropological expeditions in the American West.

---

[3] If X, Y, and Z are used to denote the numbers of ethnic, linguistic, and religious groups, respectively, the largest number of cultures (N) that encompass different kinds of the ethnic, linguistic, and religious groups can be expressed by $N = X \cdot Y \cdot Z$.

In 1917 Clark Wissler (1870 – 1947), an anthropologist with the American Museum of Natural History, used the culture area concept to integrate what was known about Native American communities. Wissler gathered together ethnographic data from a variety of sources and used these data to group Native American tribes based on similarities and differences in their substance systems, modes of transport, textiles, artwork and religious practice. As a result of this effort, he discerned a distinct geographic pattern, with groups living in proximity, or in similar natural environments, sharing many cultural traits. Wissler eventually defined nine distinct Native American culture areas, grouping tribes that shared significant traits.[4]

Even though the pioneer and classic works on the formulation and application of the culture area concept were carried out several decades later (see, for example, Wissler, 1917), early studies on classification of culture areas may date back to the late 19th or the very early 20th century (Driver, 1962). In 1896, O.T. Mason recognized 18 culture areas or environments in the Western Hemisphere (Kroeber, 1939, p. 7). Farrand (1904) suggested a seven-part classification of North American Indians, including considerations of both geography and culture, and discussed them at some length. Holms (1903) mapped the North American Indians into 19 geo-ethnic groups, which correspond well to the groupings in the later work of both Wissler (1917) and Kroeber (1939). Thereafter, there are a number of case studies on the culture area distinctions in Asian and other cultures.[5]

Before it is possible to start an economic comparison of different culture areas, it is necessary to answer the basic question: How many culture areas are there in the world?

While scholars have generally agreed in their identification of the major cultures in history and on those that exist in the world (see Box 2.1), there have also been differences of opinions. For example, Spengler (1928) specified eight major cultures and McNeil (1963) discussed nine civilizations in the whole history. Bagby (1958, pp. 165-74) saw seven major civilizations or nine if Japan is distinguished from China and the Eastern Orthodox from the West. Rostovanyi (1993) identified for seven and Braudel (1994) nine major contemporary civilizations. Quigley (1979, pp. 77 and 88) argued for 16 clear historical cases and very probably eight others, while Toynbee (1961, pp. 546-7) raised the number to 21 or 23.

### Box 2.1 How Have the World Civilizations Evolved?

The world civilizations have evolved through different phases, since they first emerged more than three thousand years ago. Some regions witnessed two or three generations of affiliated cultures, with the demise of one culture and interregnum followed by the rise of another successor generation. A simplified chart of the relations among major Eurasian civilizations through time is shown below.

---

[4] Cited from Brown (2005).
[5] The earliest literature would include Bacon (1946), Kroeber (1947), Naroll (1950) and Patai (1951).

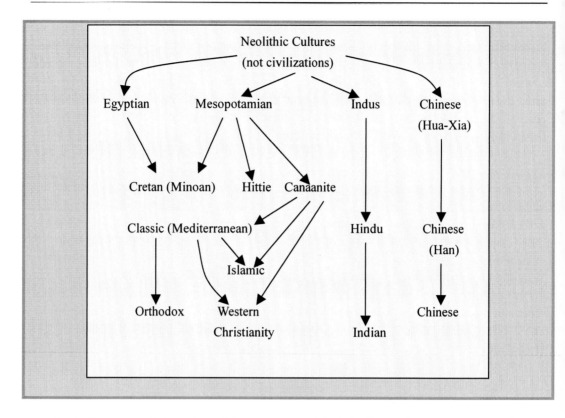

Such divergent opinions depend in part, as noted by Huntington (1996, p. 44), on whether cultural groups such as the Chinese and Indians are thought to have had a single civilization throughout history or two or more closely related civilizations, one being the offspring of the other. Despite these differences, the identity of the major civilizations is not contested. As Melko (1969, p. 133) argued, there exist at least 12 major cultures in the world, seven of which no longer exist (Mesopotamian, Egyptian, Cretan, Classical, Byzantine, Middle American and Andean) and five of which still do (Chinese, Japanese, Indian, Islamic and Western).

From the perspective of intercultural politics, Galtung (1992, pp. 23-4) and Huntington (1996, pp. 45-7) developed a similar multicultural structure of seven or eight culture areas, including:

- Sinic
- Japanese
- Hindu
- Islamic
- Western
- Orthodox
- Latin American

- Possibly, African[6]

Both Galtung and Huntington defined the Orthodox culture as separate distinct from its parent Byzantine culture and from Western Christian culture, and maintained that Japanese culture was also distinct. According to Quigley (1979, p. 83), Japan was to a large extent the offspring of the Sinic culture. Alternatively, both should be classified as parts of a larger East Asian culture area.

After taking account of the influences of anthropological differences, Sapper (1968) classified the world into 11 cultural divisions, including:

- Germanic
- Latin
- Slavic
- West Asian
- Indian
- East Asian
- The inland
- African
- Malayan
- Australian
- The North Pole

This classification only satisfies anthropologists. Political economists have usually treated Australia as part of the Western culture area and Malaysia as part of the East (or Southeast) Asian culture area. Other authors have defined a relatively small number of culture areas. For example, Kendall (1976) classified the world into six distinct culture areas, including:

- Western
- Islamic
- Indian
- East Asian
- Southeast Asian
- African

In Kendall's study, the Western culture area, which is composed of four sub-culture areas (Northwest Europe, Canada, USA, South Africa, Australia and New Zealand; the Mediterranean; Central Asia; and the former USSR), is very heterogeneous in terms of geography, political economy and culture. Quite independently, Aono (1979, pp. 48-51) developed a framework that closely parallels Kendall's (1976) on the salience to a world of six culture areas, including

---

[6] Other authors who advanced similar arguments include Lind (1990), Buzan (1991), Gilpin (1993), Lind (1992 and 1994), Rostovanyi (1993), Vlahos (1991), Puchala (1994), Elmandjra (1994) and The Economist (1994, pp. 21-3).

- East Asian
- Malayan
- South Asian
- Islamic
- African
- European

Again, the European area is assumed to include at least three economically and geographically heterogeneous cultures (or sub-cultures) – Germanic, Latin and Slavic.

In brief, since 'culture' and 'area' are both generalized terms, their use in combination gives no real clue as to precise meaning. When comparing one culture area with another, the level of abstraction must be the same. Although many factors at the base of any recognizable culture area are ecological in nature, the culture area concept is one that conforms to the doctrine of limited possibilities rather than to a simple geographic determination. Viewed with this light and assessed according to the character of the geographic units and the degree of complexity of cultural similarities within, and differences between, units, the culture area concept takes shape as a classificatory device of marked utility in describing the cultural regions of the world.

## 2.3. Cultural Division of Economies

Generally, the cultural division of the world economy may vary, usually depending on different purposes or criteria selected by researchers. Our classification of contemporary culture areas is based on the criteria by which a culture area must be contiguous (that is, one can draw line around it on a map) and must be defined by cultural (rather than geographic) similarities. There is no universal answer to the question whether similar peoples in an area must belong to the same culture area, nor to what criteria can define boundary between two culture areas. Obviously, it depends on how detailed the culture area classification is intended to be, and on which criteria are most important. Besides, the following principles are also taken into account.

First, the smallest geographical unit to be used in each culture area is country or other independent statistical area, even though different cultural identities may exist in large countries, such as India and China.[7] The reason for this is to avoid collecting large-scale sub-national (or sub-regional) data and information. Of course, the use of lower area-level data can make the analysis and comparison between different cultures more accurate and meaningful. But such a task seems likely to prove very costly and, perhaps, impossible, since in many countries few statistical data on cultural minorities are available. Second, the total number of culture areas to be defined in this research should be based on the principle that too many culture areas may leave us in doubt and too few tend to overwhelm our multicultural understanding of the world economy.

In this research, a framework of seven culture areas is considered for the subdivision of the world economy (see Figure 2.1):

- African area
- East Asian area
- Eastern Orthodox area
- Indian area
- Islamic area
- Latin American area
- Western area

Figure 2.1. The seven culture areas.

Africa as a whole is not recognized as a distinct culture, since the northern part of the African continent and its eastern coast belong to Islamic culture, while elsewhere European imperialism and settlements introduced Western languages and religions.[8] But, as observed by Braudel (1994) and Huntington (1996, p. 47), the Africans are increasingly developing a sense of African identity and, conceivably, sub-Saharan Africa could cohere into a distinct civilization, with South Africa possibly as its core state. The definition of the southern and central African economies as a separate culture area in our research is due to their unique ethnic identity, as well as their history of industrialization, which is very different from that of the Islamic and European economies, all of which are geographically proximate to each other.

---

[7] For example, Northwest India belongs to the Islamic culture; and the Muslims and Tibetans in Northwest and Southwest China have nothing to do with the Han Chinese culture.

[8] For example, Dutch, French and then English settlers created a multi-fragmented European culture in South Africa.

The African area is defined as the one that includes the southern and central Africa. It has 16.67 percent of land area and 11.13 percent of population, with an average population density of 30 persons per square kilometer.[9] The major languages used in the African area are English, French, Amharic, Portuguese, and Arabic; the religious population comes from Western Christians, Muslims, and Orthodox Christians.

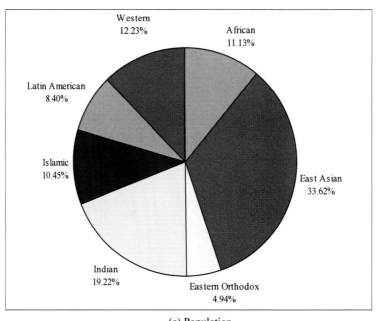

(a) Population

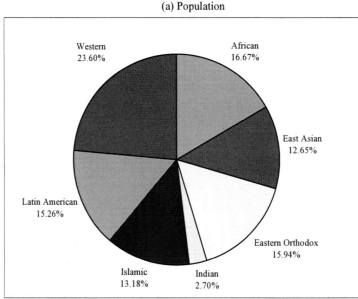

Figure 2.2. Population and land area shares by culture area.

Most scholars recognize the existence of either a single distinct Chinese culture dating back to at least 2000 BC or perhaps a thousand years earlier, or two or more Chinese cultures, one succeeding the other in the early centuries. Even though some scholars describe contemporary Japan as a distinct culture, it is also argued that Japan was to a large extent the offspring of Chinese culture, emerging during the period between AD 100 and 400, and in turn influencial to some extent on Chinese culture during its economic upsurge in the 20th century. Therefore it is reasonable to combine Japanese and Chinese culture under the heading of a single 'East Asian' culture.

The Southeast Asian economies are classified into the 'East Asian area' in view of the fact that, besides Taiwan and Singapore whose ethnic majorities are Chinese, ethnic Chinese living in other Southeast Asian economies have made considerable contributions to them. For example, during the late 20th century, the ethnic Chinese in the Philippines contributed to 35 percent of the total domestic sales with a meager 1 percent of population. With only 2-3 percent of Indonesia's total population, the ethnic Chinese held 70 percent of its domestic private capital; and in Indonesia 17 of the 25 top enterprises were controlled by the Chinese. With 10 percent of the total population in Thailand, the ethnic Chinese possessed nine of the ten largest business groups and produced half of the country's GNP. The ethnic Chinese shared about one-third of the total population but almost monopolized the economy in Malaysia.[10]

With 12.65 percent of land area, the East Asian area has 33.62 percent of population of the world. The major languages used in the East Asian area are Chinese, Japanese, Korean, Vietnamese, Thai, and English. Non-religionists account for the largest share of population[11], followed by the Buddhists, Muslims, Western Christians and atheists.

Although a part of its parent Byzantine culture and closely related to Western Christianity, the Eastern Orthodox Church has been treated as a separate religion since the 16th century. It is therefore more appropriate and useful to distinguish the Eastern Orthodox countries as a single culture area, especially for the purpose of drawing political and economic comparisons between them and Western Europe, Asia and the Islamic world.

With 15.94 percent of world land area and only 4.94 percent of world population, the Eastern Orthodox area is the least dense culture area in the world, averaging only 14 people to each each square kilometer of land. The major languages spoken in the Eastern Orthodox area are Russian, Ukrainian, Romanian, Greek, Serbo-Croatian and Armenian. Though classified as the Eastern Orthodox area, Orthodox Christianity only attracts slightly more than one-third of the believers in the area, while non-religionists make up nearly half of the total population, followed by Western Christians and Muslims.[12]

Indian culture is generally referred to as Indic or Hindu. In one form or another, Hinduism has been central to the culture of subcontinent of South Asia since the second millennium BC. Even though Indian culture is at the core of this area, some small Buddhist and Islamic communities as well as several other smaller cultural minorities are also included. The reason for this is their geographical and linguistic proximity to the Indian (but not to any other culture's) core.

---

[10] Sources: The Economist, Nov. 27, 1993, p. 33; 17 July, 1993, p. 61.

[11] It is noticeable that most of the non-religionists come from China, North Korea and Vietnam, which have adopted communist ideology.

With the smallest portion of world territory (2.70 percent) but the second largest population (19.22 percent), the Indian area is the most populous culture area in the world, for each square kilometer of land there are as many as 316 people. The major languages spoken in the Indian area are Hindi and Bengali. Western colonialism has left a legacy of some English and French speakers in this area. Hinduism is the mainstream religion, with almost two-thirds of the total population adhering to it. The other religions in this area include Islam, Western Christianity, Buddhism and Sikh.

Originating in the Arabian peninsula in the seventh century AD, Islam rapidly spread across North Africa and the Iberian peninsula and also eastward into the central Asia, the subcontinent, and Southeast Asia. The reason why we do not classify Indonesia and Malaysia as part of the Islamic area in this book is their peripheral location far from the Arabic cores and their looser Southeast Asian variety of Islam; further, their people and culture are a mixture of indigenous, Muslim, Hindu, Chinese and Christian influences; and their enterprises and businesses are largely monopolized by ethnic Chinese.

The Islamic area is defined as the northern Africa, the Middle East and adjacent Islamic states in central Asia. It has 13.18 percent of world land area and 10.45 percent of world population. The major languages spoken are Arabic, Turkish, English, French and Russian. In the Islamic area, as its name shows, Muslims account for the majority of the total population, followed by Western and Orthodox Christians.

Although an offspring of European culture, Latin America has evolved along a very different path from the Western nations. As a result Latin America has been generally recognized to have a distinct identity that differentiates it from the Western nations, especially from those that are Anglo-dominated.

The Latin American area has 15.26 percent of world land area and 8.40 percent of world population. The major languages spoken are Spanish, Portuguese and French. In terms of religion the area is homogeneous: Western Christianity accounts for the majority of the population in the Latin American area, while the remaining religions (such as Islam, Hinduism, and Judaism) and non-religion combined account for less than 5 percent of the total population.

Historical evidence suggests that Europe gradually pulled ahead of the rest of the world from the 16th century. As a result, European culture has influenced many non-European areas, some of which themselves become Westernized.[13] Mainly due to its strong influence throughout contemporary history, the Western area is the only one defined here that has a diverse geography. It includes not only the Western Hemisphere economies (except Latin America) and the traditionally defined 'West' European nations, but also those that are geographically distant from the Western core, such as Australia and New Zealand in the South Pacific, and Israel in Middle East. These countries have closer cultural linkages with the Western area than with any other areas.

Having 23.60 percent of world land area and 12.23 percent of world population, the Western area has the lowest population density. The major languages spoken are English, German, French, Italian, Spanish, Polish, Dutch, Portuguese, Hungarian, Czech and Swedish.

---

[12] It seems likely that as a result of the abandoning of communist ideology in some nations in this area, some non-religionists will transfer gradually to religious (mainly the Orthodoxy) groupings.

[13] On the role of fragments of European civilization creating new societies in North America, Latin America, South Africa and Australia, see Hartz (1964).

Western Christianity is the largest religion in the Western area, with more than 80 percent of the total population adhering to it, followed by non-religionists, Muslims, Jews and Orthodox Christians.

Tables 2.1 and 2.2 show the matrices of the linguistic and religious similarity indexes of these seven culture areas, respectively.

**Table 2.1. Linguistic similarity matrices by culture areas**

| Culture area | African | East Asian | Eastern Orthodox | Indian | Islamic | Latin American | Western |
|---|---|---|---|---|---|---|---|
| African | 1.000 | 0.019 | 0.001 | 0.053 | 0.071 | 0.032 | 0.555 |
| East Asian | 0.019 | 1.000 | 0.000 | 0.030 | 0.020 | 0.013 | 0.025 |
| Eastern Orthodox | 0.001 | 0.000 | 1.000 | 0.000 | 0.004 | 0.020 | 0.002 |
| Indian | 0.053 | 0.030 | 0.000 | 1.000 | 0.051 | 0.037 | 0.074 |
| Islamic | 0.071 | 0.020 | 0.004 | 0.051 | 1.000 | 0.039 | 0.077 |
| Latin American | 0.032 | 0.013 | 0.020 | 0.037 | 0.039 | 1.000 | 0.050 |
| Western | 0.555 | 0.025 | 0.002 | 0.074 | 0.077 | 0.050 | 1.000 |

**Table 2.2. Religious similarity matrices by culture areas**

| Culture area | African | East Asian | Eastern Orthodox | Indian | Islamic | Latin American | Western |
|---|---|---|---|---|---|---|---|
| African | 1.000 | 0.148 | 0.110 | 0.132 | 0.271 | 0.373 | 0.422 |
| East Asian | 0.148 | 1.000 | 0.396 | 0.103 | 0.094 | 0.077 | 0.149 |
| Eastern Orthodox | 0.110 | 0.396 | 1.000 | 0.069 | 0.073 | 0.041 | 0.105 |
| Indian | 0.132 | 0.103 | 0.069 | 1.000 | 0.123 | 0.023 | 0.029 |
| Islamic | 0.271 | 0.094 | 0.073 | 0.123 | 1.000 | 0.020 | 0.030 |
| Latin American | 0.373 | 0.077 | 0.041 | 0.023 | 0.020 | 1.000 | 0.689 |
| Western | 0.422 | 0.149 | 0.105 | 0.029 | 0.030 | 0.689 | 1.000 |

## 2.4. DATA AND METHODOLOGY

A problem for multicultural analysis is that the world economy has been organized according to various different statistical systems. In many market economies, national income statistics have been compiled according to the United Nations' System of National Accounts (SNA). As a key indicator derived from the SNA, gross national product (GNP) is the total value of the entire final products and services generated during a defined period of time. GNP is the sum of two components: gross domestic product (GDP) and net income from abroad. GDP measures the final output of goods and services produced by the domestic economy. Net income from abroad is income in the form of compensation of employees, interest on loans, profits and other factor payments that residents receive from abroad, less payments made for labor and capital. Most countries have estimated their GDP indicators by production method. This method sums the final outputs of the various sectors of the economy (for example, agriculture, manufacturing, and services), from which the value of the inputs to production has been subtracted.

However, in most centrally planned economies (CPEs), the national accounts were based on the material product system (MPS) whose most important aggregate is net material product (NMP) and national income (NI). NMP comprehensively covers value added in the 'material' sectors of production during a defined period of time; while NI is the total of all incomes received by all factors in productive activities carried out in their territories. The sum of the outputs of all separately enumerated production units multiplied by the relevant prices of outputs is called gross value of social product (GVSP). As GVSP also includes the values of intermediate products that are simply the material costs for consecutive production units, values of products were counted more than once. Obviously, the use of the GVSP concept could result in a series of negative effects. This is particularly true when using the GVSP as an indicator to evaluate the sizes and efficiencies of the economies, as a part of it is contributed by the intermediate products and is thus irrelevant to the social welfare.

The estimation of the GDP data left many unpersuaded in economies that are under transition from the centrally planned system to a market system. With the exception of the data on the tertiary sector, the transformation of NMP data to the corresponding GDP data were simply devised and, therefore, some question whether the GDP data may be arrived at by multiplying the NMP by some conversion factors. In fact, since a socialist accounting system does not take account of the output value of the service sector, historical records of this sector were very fragmentary. The GDP data at constant prices are inextricably linked to the real NMP data collected by the old system. Unlike the market economies in which real GDP is derived using a system of price indices, the basic production units at the lowest level of the statistical reporting system are responsible for computing the real output value based on a catalogue of fixed prices given from above. Even though they were prepared by analysts who were attempting to make measures of GDP with the same criteria as those used for Western countries, it seems likely that the GDP growth figures of Bulgaria, Romania and former Yugoslavia from 1950 till the mid-1980s have exaggerated the economic performance of these countries (Maddison, 1996, p. 125). Since the late 1980s, during which time the socialist economies were undergoing major transition, their growth may be understated because the authorities have not found it easy to monitor all the new private activities.[14]

The application of the multifarious monetary systems in different economies is another hurdle in the study of multicultural economic issues. In general, there are three options for converting the nominal values of GNP or GDP into the comparable ones. The first, and also the simplest, option is to use exchange rates. But exchange rates are mainly a reflection of purchasing power over internationally tradeable items. For these goods inter-country price differences are reduced because of possibilities for trade and specification. For example, in poor countries where wages are low, non-tradeable items, like haircuts, building construction or other services are generally cheaper than in high-income countries, so that there is a general tendency for their exchange rates to understate purchasing power. The other problem with exchange rates is that they are often powerfully influenced by capital movements, and in the past decades have been too volatile to serve as reliable indicators of purchasing power.

---

[14] In 1998 the Technical Assistance in Statistics Team of the World Bank Development Economics Data Group conducted a survey to assess the quality of statistics in a number of transition countries. The findings suggest that in many countries the basic data are well below satisfactory level, with a strong correlation between average data quality and per capita dollar GDP in these countries. More details in this regard may be found in Belkindas et al. (1999).

The second methodology appears in the World Bank Atlas. According to the World Bank Atlas method, the GNP estimates of one year proceed in the following steps. First, the GNP in constant market prices and national currency units is converted to one measured in constant average prices for the year and the two preceding years. This is done by multiplying the original constant price series by the weighted-mean domestic GNP deflator for the base period (that is, by the ratio of total GNP in current prices to total GNP in constant prices for the three-year period). In the second step, the GNP measured in constant three-year average prices in national currency is converted to one in US dollars by dividing that GNP by the weighted-mean exchange rate for the base period. The weighted-mean exchange rate is the ratio of the sum of GNP in current prices to the sum of the GNP divided by the annual average exchange rate in national currency per US dollar for the three years. The last step is to convert the GNP measured in constant average three-year US dollars to one measured in current US dollars by multiplying that GNP by the implicit US GNP deflator for the base period. In general, the Atlas method of averaging three years of exchange rates smoothes fluctuations due to the currency market and provides a more reliable measure, over time, of overall income than do estimates based on a single year's exchange rate. But it, again, does not overcome the obstacles for international economic comparisons.

The last approach is to use the purchasing power parity (PPP) converters. The PPP approach was developed by cooperative research of some national statistical offices and international agencies in the past few decades.[15] GDP and GDP per capita using PPP are GDP estimates based on the purchasing power of currencies rather than on current exchange rates. This conversion factor, the PPP, is defined as the number of units of a country's currency required to buy the same amounts of goods and services in the domestic market as one US dollar can buy in the United States. The computation involves deriving implicit quantities from national accounts expenditure data and specially collected price data and then revaluing the implicit quantities in each country at a single set of average prices. Because the same international price averages are used for every country, cross-country comparisons reflect differences in quantities of goods and services free of price-level differences. This procedure is designed to bring cross-country comparisons in line with cross-time real value comparisons that are based on constant price series.

Although considerable progress has been made to standardize the cross-national economic data, one should be very careful when interpreting internationally the economic indicators. Inter-country and inter-temporal comparisons using economic data involve complicated technical problems that are not easily resolved; therefore, readers are urged to read these data as characterizing major differences between economies rather than as precise, quantitative measurements. For example, the UK and the USA place major reliance on information on income flows, which is derived from tax sources, whereas Germany relies more on output information from industrial surveys. Measurement of output in high-tech industries can also be tackled in different ways. For example, when a country introduces a hedonic index for computers, which takes much better account of characteristics such as

---

[15] There are alternative options for the PPP approach, which are usually based on either binary or multilateral comparisons. With regards to the latter, the Geary-Khamis approach (which was initiated by R. S. Geary in 1958 and developed by S. H. Khamis in 1970) is preferred by Maddison (1996; 2001 and 2003) whose estimates on the cross-national data of GDP will be employed in my multicultural comparison of the world economy from 1950 to 2000 later in this chapter.

memory capacity and speed of operation, the new price index fell much more sharply than its predecessor.[16] As a result the GDP growth rates differ accordingly.

### 2.4.1. Estimating Multicultural Data

In theory, multicultural data can be collected directly from various statistical agencies or on the basis of relevant surveys. However, many statistical agencies only provide very few data related to cultural groups, it is very costly and, sometimes, almost impossible to conduct any meaningful multicultural surveys due to the large number of cultural (ethnic, linguistic, religious, etc.) groups concerned. In this book, we try to introduce a simple method by which to estimate multicultural data. Technically, this method is based on either one of the following two assumptions:

1.  The homogeneity of socioeconomic indiators can be found at each statistical region.
2.  There is only a single cultural group in each statistical region.

If assumption 1 exists, we can derive the multicultural data directly from multiregional data by using a weighted-mean approach. To illustrate this mathematical framework, let's have an example. Suppose that there are two homogeneous regions ($R_1$ and $R_2$), each having two ethnic groups ($E_1$ and $E_2$), in a target country. The composition of population (in persons) is shown in the following table:

| Ethnic group / Region | $E_1$ | $E_2$ |
|---|---|---|
| $R_1$ | 20 | 50 |
| $R_2$ | 40 | 30 |

If per capita income is \$3000 for $R_1$ and \$4000 for $R_2$, the average levels of per capita income of the two ethnic groups ($E_1$ and $E_2$) are

$$3000 \times \frac{20}{20+40} + 4000 \times \frac{40}{20+40} \approx 3667 \ (\$) \text{ and}$$

$$3000 \times \frac{50}{50+30} + 4000 \times \frac{30}{50+30} = 3375 \ (\$), \text{ respectively.}$$

If gross value of output is 3000 thousand \$ for $R_1$ and thousand 4000 \$ for $R_2$, the average levels of gross value of output of the two ethnic groups ($E_1$ and $E_2$) are

$$3000 \times \frac{20}{20+50} + 4000 \times \frac{40}{40+30} \approx 3143 \text{ (thousand \$) and}$$

---

[16] This approach, which treats goods as providing a collection of characteristics – here speed, memory, and so on – each with an implicit price, is called hedonic pricing ('hedonic' means pleasure in Greek) (Blanchard, 1997, p. 25).

$$3000 \times \frac{50}{20+50} + 4000 \times \frac{30}{40+30} \approx 3857 \text{ (thousand \$), respectively.}$$

The above mechanisms of derivation from multi-regional data to multi-ethnic data are not technically complicated, even if the number of regions and ethnic groups increase. Suppose $L$ and $M$ are the total numbers of the nations (or regions) and the total number of cultures, respectively. For each economic indicator, $x(i)$ and $X(i)$ denote the per capita and absolute values of the $i$th nation (or region), respectively ($i$=1, 2, 3,..., and $L$); and $y(j)$ and $Y(j)$ denote the per capita and absolute values of the $j$th culture, respectively ($j$=1, 2, 3,..., and $M$). If the number of population in the $j$th culture of the $i$th nation (or region) is expressed by $n(i, j)$, the transformation of multinational (multiregional) data to multicultural data can be conducted via the following formulas:

$$y(j) = \sum_{i=1}^{L} \frac{n(i, j)}{\sum_{i=1}^{L} n(i, j)} x(i), \text{ for per capita indicators} \qquad (2.1)$$

$$Y(j) = \sum_{i=1}^{L} \frac{n(i, j)}{\sum_{j=1}^{M} n(i, j)} X(i), \text{ for absolute indicators} \qquad (2.2)$$

It should be noted that greater intraregional economic differences usually suggest, *ceteris paribus*, larger estimation errors derived from Equations 2.1 and 2.2. In theory, the intraregional differences can be eliminated when the regions selected are reduced to smaller and culturally homogeneous ones. However, smaller regions will also result in higher costs and other possible difficulties in data collection, when the number of regions and, naturally, the amount of regional data to be collected also increases accordingly.

Although Assumption 1 does not exist in practice, we still can make some progress towards the application of Equations 2.1 and 2.2. As a matter of fact, it is not difficult to understand that the estimation errors are positively related to the number of cultures involved in Equations 2.1 and 2.2. In the case of only one culture ($M$=1), for example, there doesn't exist any estimation errors in Equations 2.1 and 2.2, since the socioeconomic indicators of each region also represent completely those of the monopolized culture involved in that region.[17] On the other hand, if the cultural diversity increases, given the existence of intranational (intraregional) differences, so do the errors produced.

After having clarified the factors by which the derivation of multicultural data from multinational (multiregional) data may be affected, we can go further to take measures so as to increase the accuracy. Specifically, we stipulate that:

- Only nations (or regions) with high intranational (or intraregional) economic divergencies may affect the estimated results and, therefore, the choice of sub-national (sub-regional) data of these nations (regions) is desirable.

---

[17] As a matter of fact, when $L$=1, Equation 2.1 becomes $y(j)=x(1)$; when $M$=1, Equation 2.2 becomes $Y(1)=$ $x(1)+x(2)+...+x(L)$.

- Only nations (regions) with great cultural diversities may affect the estimated results and, therefore, the choice of the sub-national (sub-regional) data of those nations (or regions) is desirable.

We have found that the estimation errors are positively related to both intranational (intraregional) economic difference and cultural diversity. In come cases, the indexes of intranational (intraregional) economic difference and cultural diversity are contradictory with each other. We thus meet difficulties in judging which nation (region) can produce large estimation errors. To this end, we need a comprehensive index to express the potential of estimation errors (PEE). In the simplest case, if PEE is equally contributed by cultural diversity (CD) and intranational (intraregional) economic difference (ED), we have the following formula:[18]

$$PEE = CD \times ED \qquad (2.3)$$

The quality of the multicultural data estimated using Equations 2.1 and 2.2 can be affected by three factors: (i) the falsified sample surveys and official data (released from various statistical bureaus at national and sub-national levels), (ii) the estimation errors, and (iii) the rounding errors. In practice, decreasing the size of statistical regions could result in, besides the additional rounding errors it produces, further difficulties and costs in collecting and reconstructing multi-regional data. Given the existence of spatial economic differences, the art of successfully transforming multicultural data from the multinational (multiregional) data lies in that the size of the statistical region selected can be minimized at which the spatial data are collected without difficulties and to which the accuracy of the estimated results is not sensitive.

Lastly, let us have a brief assessment of the data on multicultural composition of population (as denoted by $n(i, j)$ in Equations 2.1 and 2.2). At present, the *Encyclopedia Britannica* is the most complete data source for existing cultural groups. However, its data on language speakers need to be evaluated with care. Since some countries collect data on ethnic or 'national' groups only, the ethnic distribution was often assumed to conform roughly to the linguistic distribution. However, this approach should be viewed with caution, because a minority population is not always free to educate its children in its own languages and because better economic opportunities often draw minority group members into majority-language communities (Encyclopedia Britannica, 1998, p. 770). The Britannica's data on religious adherents are relatively more fragmentary and less reliable than the data on language speakers. This is because the nature of affiliation with an organized religion differs greatly from country to country, so does the social context of religious practice. For example, a country in which a single religion has long been predominant will often show more than 90 percent of its population to be affiliated, while in actual fact, no more than 10 percent may actually practise that religion on a regular basis (Britannica Book of the Year, 1998, p. 775). Such a situation often leads to the under-representation of minority religions, blurring of

---

[18] However, in most cases, cultural diversity and intranational (intraregional) difference do not produce the same marginal effect on the estimation errors. Due to the complicated features, we would rather leave the detailed clarification for future research.

distinctions seen to be significant elsewhere, or double counting in countries where an individual may conscientiously practise more than one 'religion' at a time.

## 2.4.2. Tips in Methodology for Comparative Analysis

Researchers have employed a variety of approaches to comparative analysis. Some of them can be applied in the cross-cultural economic analysis. Specifically, they are:

### (i) 'Patterns of Development' Analysis

Since the pioneering studies of Simon Kuznets (University of Pennsylvania, the 1971 Nobel Prize in Economics) in the 1950s, economists have sought patterns of development in large bodies of cross-country data. This approach reached its peak in the 1970s with major contributions from Hollis Chenery (Harvard University) and Moshe Syrquin (University of Miami) and from Irma Adelman (University of California at Berkeley) and Cynthia Taft Morris (Smith College and American University) (see for example, Chenery and Syrquin 1975). Now, with the increasing availability of cross-country data, the 'patterns of development' analysis has been more or less superseded by multivariate statistical analysis. However, the visual identification of patterns may still play a useful descriptive function in comparative analysis.

### (ii) In-Depth Case Studies

Often undertaken by sociologists and political scientists the intensive study of one or a small number of countries is designed to place the individual richness of each country at the forefront of analysis. The benefits of small-sample case studies relative to the large cross-country statistical exercises have to be weighed against the inability to generalize from such small samples and to conduct tests of significance. Researchers using small samples include Robert Chambers (Sussex University), Stephan Haggard (University of California) and Robert Putnam (Harvard University).

### (iii) Large-Sample Case Studies

Larger samples of case studies seek to retain the richness arising from country-specific investigation with the possibility of generalization. Research along these lines includes a series of comparative studies conducted under the direction of Ann Krueger (World Bank), and, more recently, *Voices of the Poor* directed by Deepa Narayan (World Bank), *In Search of Prosperity* by Dani Rodrick (Princeton University) and the research projects of the Global Development Network (GDN). Most authors in these projects typically employ a technique which is called "analytic narrative". The case studies can be more or less constrained by the imposition of common frameworks or by the requirement for a common survey, focus group discussions, or open-ended interviews. Such exercises provide material for generalization, but the question still remains regarding how best to extract robust generalizations.

### (iv) Analytic Narrative Approach

There are various methodological problems that are common to all analyses of cultural influences on economic activities. First, the studies of the relations between culture and economy embrace a wide diversity of substantive backgrounds. Second, the specific context matters a lot to each of the research questions, which means that each economic process or each culture has unique characteristics. While some of the problems can be handled with methodological tools that are pretty standard, others are more difficult to address and call for relatively new methodologies. *A priori*, the most relevant advantage of the analytic narrative method is that it would allow us to model historical "one-off" processes and events that have unique characteristics. Likewise, the method would render some problems of empirical testing of hypotheses manageable. Some political and cultural events usually pose insurmountable difficulties to traditional panel data or time series methods. According to Bates *et al.* (1998, pp. 14-18), there are five steps to evaluate a narrative: (i). Do the assumptions fit the facts, as they are known? (ii). Do conclusions follow from premises? (iii). Do its implications find confirmation in data? (iv). How well does the theory stand up to comparison with other explanations? (v). How general is the explanation? Does it apply to other cases?

### *(v) Multivariate Statistical Analysis*

As an increasing supply of reasonably uniform data has become available for a range of variables, the economics literature has become inundated with cross-country regressions. Major exponents in this area include Robert Barro (Harvard University) and Xavier Sala-i-Martin (Columbia University). The strengths of this approach include its ability to marshal and interpret large quantities of data and to conduct rigorous tests of statistical significance. That said, this approach has to confront questions regarding the comparability of data and tricky issues of endogeneity and causality. And by its nature reduces the richness of country-specific experience to a single, common equation. More fundamentally, regression analysis is not appropriate for the relatively small samples.

### *(vi) Qualitative Comparative Analysis*

Recently, small-to-medium size samples of case studies have been investigated more systematically using Qualitative Comparative Analysis (QCA). First introduced to the field of qualitative research methodology by Charles Ragin in 1987; it has now been extended through more advanced variants such as the Fuzzy-Set QCA (fsQCA) and the multi-value QCA (MVQCA). The QCA, largely used by researchers in comparative politics, sociology and related fields, identifies commonalities across cases. Researchers working specifically in the area of QCA include Charles Ragin (University of Arizona), Gary Goertz (University of Arizona), David Byrne (Durham University), Benoit Dihoux (Universite Catholique de Louvain) and Wendy Olsen (University of Manchester).

### *(vii) Combining Quantitative and Quantitative Approaches*

There are strengths and weaknesses for both quantitative and quantitative approaches. The quantitative approach makes aggregation possible, provides results whose reliability is measurable, and allows simulation of different policy options. But it yields sampling and non-sampling errors, misses what is not easily quantifiable and fails to capture intra-household issues. The qualitative approach has more insight into causal processes and more accuracy and depth of information on certain questions. But its weaknesses include lack of generalizability and difficulties in verifying information. There are three ways of combining the best of qualitative and quantitative approaches: (a) integrating the quantitative and qualitative methodologies; (b) examining, explaining, confirming, refuting, and/or enriching information from one approach with that from the other; and (c) merging the findings from the two approaches into one set of policy recommendations.

## 2.5. SUMMARY

For a long period culture and economy have been treated as broadly independent areas of research. Despite the importance of culture influences on economic performances, mainstream economists have tended to ignore them. Indeed, Ruttan (1991, p. 276) summarizes well the situation: "Cultural considerations have been cast into the 'underworld' of developmental thought and practice. It would be hard to find a leading scholar in the field of developmental economics who would commit herself or himself in print to the proposition that in terms of explaining different patterns of political and economic development... a central variable is culture."[19]

Furthering the understanding of the cross-cultural economic activities promises to be one of the major research areas in the postwar era, although past analyses, especially those that are quantitatively based, are mainly focused on economic variables. Since the late 20th century, however, there have been arguments respecting an increasingly close relationship between economy and culture. With regards to the mechanism of their relationship, one should recognize that economy and culture do not impose upon one another as wholly external forces, but are always intimately associated. Despite the closeness of this association, they have different logics: the one taking account of certain intrinsic or non-instrumental values, the other relating instrumental values to external goals of reproduction. Their interactions are complex as are their effects on economic development and culture change (Guo, 2003).

The Culture area concept is a means of organizing a vast amount of variegated ethnographic data into comprehensive units within a classificatory system. It depends on a number of criteria or determinants in the isolation of units. In theory, major considerations in recognizing these areas and sub-areas are ecological zones, patterns of cultural integration and correlations between the independently diffused traits, among others. In practice, however, since the factors by which a culture is determined or influenced are so numerous, the cultural classification of diversified economies in the world is an extremely difficult task. Therefore it seems necessary to simplify the multicultural division of the world economy.

The classification of human groups into culture areas has been critiqued on the grounds that the bases for these classifications, such as similar farming systems or pottery styles, are always arbitrary. Despite this limitation, the organization of human communities into cultural areas remains a common practice throughout the social sciences. Today, the definition of culture areas is enjoying a resurgence of practical and theoretical interests as social scientists conduct research on processes of cultural globalization (Gupta and Ferguson, 1997). The most obvious drawback of culture areas is that, in reality, cultural variation tends to be continuous rather than abrupt. Cultural groups near boundary thus become 'intermediate'. Also, many traits cut across culture area boundaries: cultural variation is complex and not

---

[19] Cited from Lian and Oneal (1997, p. 61).

easily reduced to geographical patterns. Despite these problems, culture area concept is extremely useful as a device for organizing ethnographic diversity, so that it may be taken account of general patterns investigated.

Culture area analysis has been widely used by both anthropologists and cultural geographers, primarily because it facilitates comparisons between regions, assists in the historical reconstruction of economic and cultural developments and lends itself to questions about the impact of the natural environment on the form of human cultures. In this chapter, we have discussed three cultural elements – ethnicity, language and religion – and proposed a framework of seven culture areas for the cultural division of the world economy. Of course, our discussion of the cultural make-up as well as the culture areas derived therefrom is not definitive and perhaps would not satisfy anthropologists. However, ethnicity, language and religion are the most important elements in representing a culture. Besides, it has been much easier for us to collect the linguistic and religious data than the other cultural data. This information will be help in preparation of the cross-national panel data of cultural index, which are needed in the quantitative analysis of cross-cultural economic activities.

# Chapter 3

# CROSS-CULTURAL ECONOMIC DIFFERENCES

When the Son of the Man comes as King and all the angels with him, he will sit on his royal throne, and the people of all the nations will be gathered before him. Then he will divide them into two groups, just as a shepherd separates the sheep from the goats. He will put the righteous people on his right and the others on his left. Then the King will say to the people on his right, 'Come, you that are blessed by my Father! Come and possess the kingdom which has been prepared for you ever since the creation of the world." Then he will say to those on his left, "Away from me, you that are under God's curse! Away to the extended fire which has been prepared for the Devil and his Angels!"

(Matthew, 25:31-41)

## 3.1. VALUES AND RULES

Western nations have achieved considerable success in recent centuries. Unlike many other religious adherents, such as Buddhists and Taoists, Western Christians, especially the Protestants, eliminate the distinction between secular and religious life. Hard work was enjoined to glorify God; achievement was the evidence of hard work; and thrift was necessary because the produced wealth was not to be used selfishly. Accumulation of wealth, capital formation and the desire for greater production became a Christian duty. By analyzing the role of cultural factors in the Western economies, we can further track its influence elsewhere. For example, the Anglo-Saxon genotype is based on the individualistic behavior and competitive pragmatism, which is reflected in the liberal economic system of the USA, Great Britain and other European countries. Given the historic differences of the European countries, one might, however, distinguish between the 'bourgeois' culture of Germany, which implies the existence of industrial, or applied, activities and the 'aristocratic' culture of Great Britain, which reflects the significant interest of British entrepreneurs in management, law and finance. The 'bourgeois' type of economic activity also typifies the Netherlands, Sweden, Switzerland and the north of Italy, where it coincides with regions influenced by the Protestant ethic (Maslichenko, 2004).

Historical evidence suggests that the Western countries gradually pulled ahead of the rest of the world from the 16th century.[1] Specifically, Northern Italy and Flanders played the leading role from the 16th to 17th century, the Netherlands from then until the end of the 18th century, the UK and Germany in the 19th and the USA since then. The main institutional characteristics of Western society that have favored its development can be broadly summarized as follows: (1) the recognition of human capacity to transform the forces of nature through rational investigation and experiment and (2) the ending of feudal constraints on the free purchase and sale of property, followed by a whole series of developments which gave scope for successful entrepreneurship (Maddison, 1996, p. 50). However, country situations differ greatly throughout the world and it is difficult to reach any generalized conclusion about the influence of deeper layers of causality. For this we need individual country narratives. At the same time, it is also worth noting that the western style institutions may not work well in other economies, which may have different demographic, cultural and historical conditions.

There is a great body of literature hypothesizing that differences in economic prosperity can be traced to the legal systems of countries. Some research has posited that countries with a legal system originating in the English common law tradition have enjoyed better growth performance than countries whose legal systems originated in the French civil law tradition, deriving from the European civil codes, especially the Napoleonic Code (See, for example, Acemoglu and Johnson, 2005; La Porta et al., 1999 and 2008; and Messick, 2005). The World Bank's Independent Evaluation Group (IEG) explores whether legal origins have affected the 'doing business' performance.[2] The results, which are based on the sample of 135 countries, are summarized in Table 3.1. In brief, there are four indicators and 13 subindicators where common law countries perform significantly better than civil law countries. These are:

- The four subindicators that comprise the 'starting a business' indicator
- The 'director liability index' and 'shareholder suits index' that comprise 'protecting investors'
- Three of the indicators for 'employing workers' (i.e., 'difficulty of hiring index', 'rigidity of hours index', and 'difficulty of hiring index')
- The 'legal rights' subindicator under the 'getting credit' indicator

Specifically, four subindicators in 'starting a business' – 'number of procedures', 'time', 'cost and minimum capital requirement' – are significantly higher in French-origin countries. It is plausible that in the case of the first three, the differences are a result of the participation of notary publics in the business registration process. The differences in 'protecting investors' and 'getting credit' could also be attributed to legal origin, since the Napoleonic Code deals with commercial procedures, among other issues. The differences in 'employing workers' are not as easy to understand, since the Napoleonic Code does not delve into this issue. A general hypothesis could be that, on average, countries with a civil law tradition favor direct supervision of markets. In this case, civil law countries would prefer more government regulation to protect the rights of workers. In addition, the number of procedures and time

---

[1] See North and Thomas (1973), North (1981 and 1990) and Abramovitz (1986) for the varieties of European experience on the importance of institutions or differential social capability.

[2] More details can be found in World Bank (2008).

**Table 3.1. How legal origins explain the differences in doing business**

| Indicator | Common law average (1) | Civil law average (2) | Difference (3)=(2)-(1) |
|---|---|---|---|
| 1. Starting a business | | | |
| 1.1 Procedures (number) | 8.2 | 10.9 | 2.6[a] |
| 1.2 Time (days) | 37.8 | 64.2 | 26.4[b] |
| 1.3 Cost (% of income per capita) | 44.4 | 96.3 | 51.9[a] |
| 1.4 Min. capital (% of income per capita) | 16.0 | 154.1 | 138.1[a] |
| 2. Dealing with licenses | | | |
| 2.1 Procedures (Number) | 16.5 | 18.6 | 2.1[c] |
| 2.2 Time (days) | 190.8 | 231.4 | 40.6[b] |
| 2.3 Cost (% of income per capita) | 539.6 | 693.7 | 154.1[c] |
| 3. Employing workers | | | |
| 3.1 Difficulty of hiring index=0(best)–100 (worst) | 17.0 | 46.2 | 29.2[a] |
| 3.2 Rigidity of hours index=0(best)–100 (worst) | 20.7 | 48.7 | 28.0[a] |
| 3.3 Difficulty of hiring index=0(best)–100 (worst) | 20.4 | 40.0 | 19.6[a] |
| 3.4 Firing costs (weeks of wages) | 58.3 | 51.3 | -7.0[c] |
| 4. Getting credit | | | |
| 4.1 Credit information index=0(worst)–6(best) | 1.9 | 2.8 | 0.9[a] |
| 4.2 Legal rights index=0(worst)–6(best) | 5.3 | 3.4 | -1.9[a] |
| 5. Protecting investors | | | |
| 5.1 Disclosure index=0(worst)–10(best) | 4.9 | 4.8 | -0.1[c] |
| 5.2 Director liability index=0(worst)–10(best) | 5.5 | 3.3 | -2.1[a] |
| 5.3 Shareholder suits index=0(worst)–10(best) | 6.5 | 4.7 | -1.8[a] |
| 6. Paying taxes | | | |
| 6.1 Payments (number) | 28.9 | 37.2 | 8.3[b] |
| 6.2 Time (hours) | 207.1 | 314.5 | 107.4[b] |
| 6.3 Total tax rate (% of profit) | 46.9 | 57.3 | 10.4[c] |

under the 'paying taxes' and the time under 'dealing with licenses' indicators are significantly different, favoring common law countries. The only indicator that favors countries with a civil law origin is the 'credit information index' in 'getting credit'. This, according to Djankov et al. (2006), can be attributed to the presence of a public credit registry in countries with a French civil law tradition.[3]

As well as describing the content of libraries, museums, moral and religious codes of conduct, the word 'culture' is commonly used to describe social life. As such, 'culture' is the living sum of symbols, meanings, habits, values, institutions, behaviors and social artifacts which characterize a distinctive and identified human population group. It confers upon individuals' identity as members of some visible community and standards for relating to the environment, for identifying fellow members and strangers, and for deciding what is

---

[3] There is a different case study in which the French and German legal systems are found to be more favorable to the economic growth of the less-developed nations than the British and Scandinavia origin (Lin, 2001).

important and what is not important to them (Goulet, 1980, p. 2). The application of the term culture to the attitudes towards and behavior of corporations arose in business jargon during the post-Cold War era. Unlike many such locutions it spread to popular use in newspapers and magazines. However, when answering the question as to how an economy was influenced by culture, we have to remember that there was no pristine economy which was somehow later influenced by culture; rather, the economy has always been culturally influenced, from inside and outside, from the beginning (Sayer, 1997, p. 18). It is usually thought that culture influences economic outcomes by affecting personal traits such as honesty, thrift, the willingness to work hard and openness to strangers. Culture is divided into various elements that can be both a resource for and an obstacle to economic development.

## 3.2. ORGANIZATIONAL BEHAVIORS

In his famous study *The Protestant Ethic and the Sprit of Capitalism*, Weber (1904) argued that the profit-maximizing behavior so characteristic of the bourgeoisie, which could be explained under fully developed capitalist conditions by its sheer necessity to survival in the face of competition, could not be so explained under the earlier phases of capitalist development. It was the product of an autonomous impulse to accumulate far beyond the needs of personal consumption, an impulse which was historically unique.[4] Weber traced its source to the 'worldly asceticism' of reformed Christianity, with its twin imperatives to methodical work as the chief duty of life, and to the limited enjoyment of its product. The unintended consequence of this ethic, which was enforced by the social and psychological pressures on the believer to prove (but not earn) his salvation, was the accumulation of capital for investment. The larger participation of Protestants (compared with that of Catholics) in modern business life was also more striking. Among journeymen, for example, the Catholics show a strong propensity to remain in their crafts, that is they more often become master of craftsmen, whereas the Protestants are attracted to a larger extent into the factories in order to fill the upper ranks of skilled labor and administrative positions (Weber, 1904, p. 7).

Although most economies in the Latin American area are more closely related to Western culture than to any others, their economic performances have been poorer than those of the Western world. It seems very likely that the heavy-handed regulatory tendencies in government, chronic inflation, a long history of debt default and fiscal irresponsibility and long-standing political instability were important in keeping Latin American growth and levels of income well below those of North America.[5] Furthermore, Catholicism led to greater emphasis on ritualistic and contemplative approach and collectivistic action as contrasted with the more individualistic and competition-oriented approach of Protestant Reformation. The result of this was an upgrading of the role of the Church and a consequent downgrading of the role of the individual. Thus, different from that of the Western nations, a system of nation-states only emerged in far propinquity in the Latin American area, with insignificant trading relations and relatively difficult intellectual interchange in spite of their linguistic and cultural similarities. Among the major differences between the Latin American area and the

---

[4] Cited from New Palgrave: a Dictionary of Economics (1987, vol. 4, p. 887).

[5] See Maddison (1992) for an analysis of 20th century constraints on performance in Brazil and Mexico, and Maddison (1995) for a much longer-term assessment of Mexico's institutional heritage.

Anglo-dominated North American area is that the majority of Latin Americans are more culturally collectivistic than the North Americans; or, in other words, North Americans are more culturally individualistic than the Latin Americans (see Box 3.1). For example, in their comparison of Latin American (Brazil) and North American (the USA) cultures' preferences of styles of negotiation, Pearson and Stephan (1999) find that Brazilians favor styles of negotiation that express a concern for the outcomes of others, whereas Americans favor styles of negotiation that reflect a concern for their own outcomes.

## Box 3.1 Collectivism versus Individualism

Individualism and collectivism are conflicting in terms of the nature of humans, society and the relationship between them. Collectivism is the political theory that states that the will of the people is omnipotent, an individual must obey; that society as whole, not the individual, is the unit of moral value. Individualism, as the antipode of collectivism, holds that the individual is the primary unit of reality and the ultimate standard of value. This view does not deny that societies exist or that people benefit from living in them, but is sees society as a collection of individuals, not something over and above them.

Collectivism holds that a group – such as a nation, a community and a race – is the primary unit of reality and the ultimate standard of value. This view stresses that the needs and goals of the individual must be subordinate to those of the group. Unlike collectivism, which requires self-sacrifice, individualism holds that every person is an end in himself and that no person should be sacrificed for the sake of another. While not denying that one person can build on the achievements of others, individualism points out that the individual is the unit of achievement. Individualism holds that achievement goes beyond what has already been done; it is something new that is created by the individual. Collectivism, on the other hand, holds that achievement is a product of society.

It is worth noting that the Eastern Orthodox area enjoyed some record growth before the 1980s, when a series of economic difficulties interrupted the progress of many Orthodox economies toward transition from the centrally planned system to a market-oriented one. While some economies in this area have returned to the normal path of growth, the substantial recovery of the Eastern Orthodox area as a whole will need more time.[6] It would be true to say that the material and industrial success of the modern West had its basis in certain natural, historical and cultural conjunctures. The natural and geographical advantage (such as adequate water and temperate climate) that gave most of the Western nations an economic advantage was also available in the Eastern Orthodox area. According to current growth theories an economy will tend to grow (or at least stop declining) as soon as all of its necessary production factors are properly arranged. This should have been true for many Eastern Orthodox economies, given their rich natural resources and well-educated manpower that they inherited from the Soviet Union. However many Eastern Orthodox economies have been critically entangled in problems in geopolitics, ethnicity and religion during the process of economic transition. It appears more and more likely that it is these factors that have blocked the social and economic development agendas of some, if not all, of these nations since the end of the Cold War.

The ethical beliefs of Confucianism have consistently remained within the bounds of a set of orthodox principles governing interpersonal relationships in most East Asian economies. They have been officially applied to all strata of society: loyalty, filial piety, benevolence, righteousness, love, faith, harmony and peace. As a result, East Asia has developed a different culture in relation to economic development from the rest of the world, in response to its own particular environment and social conditions. For instance, unlike the majority of Westerners, East Asians in general care more about their spiritual interests (including the richness of spiritual life and harmonization of feeling) than material ones. All of these have determined or at least partially influenced East Asia's economic life and structure, the result of which is a particular economic culture (see Table 3.2). Since the late 20th century, same intellectual and

**Table 3.2. Eastern versus Western cultures: values and organizational patterns**

| | Western views | Eastern views |
|---|---|---|
| **Values** | Democracy | Hierarchy |
| | Equality | Inequality |
| | Self-determination | Fatalism |
| | Individualism | Collectivism |
| | Human rights | Acceptance of status |
| | Equality for women | Male dominance |
| | Status through achievement | Status through birth or wealth[a] |
| | Facts and figures | Relationships[a] |
| | Social justice | Power structures |
| | New solutions | Good precedents |
| | Vigor | Wisdom |
| | Linear time | Cyclic time |
| | Results orientation | Harmony orientation |
| **Organizational patterns** | Individual as a unit | Company and society as a unit |
| | Promotion by achievement | Promotion by age and seniority[a] |
| | Horizontal or matrix structures | Vertical structures |
| | Profit orientation | Market share priority |
| | Contracts as binding | Contracts as renegotiable |
| | Decisions by competent individuals | Decisions by consensus |
| | Specialization | Job rotation |
| | Professional mobility | Fixed loyalty |

*Source*: based on Lewis (2003). ([a]): Some of the East Asian views have to some extent changed or westernized, especially in newly industrialized economies.

---

[6] For the recent literature on the comparisons between the transition economies in the former USSR and Eastern Europe and the market and other former centrally planed economies, one can see Desai (1997, ed.), Hardt and Kaufman (1995), Kaminski (1996), Lavigne (1999), Rumer (1996), Stephan (1999) and Woo et al. (1996).

social traditions, which were blamed for East Asia's backwardness, have subsumed into a broader concept—Asian values—and have helped explain the remarkable economic success in East Asia and prepared the region for global dominance in what was to be the 'Pacific century'.

Chinese culture is perhaps the most sophisticated in East Asia. Its religious package, aiming at a harmonious balance between Confucianism, Buddhism and Taoism, worked well for a long period. Probably because of this, the Chinese remained intoxicated by past prosperity and still proudly treated China as the zhongguo (center under heaven) of the world, even when it lagged far behind the Western nations. This kind of ethnocentrism and self-satisfaction resulted in a long period in which China was a typical autarkic society. The following were blamed for China's backwardness: the attachment to the family becomes nepotism; the importance of interpersonal relationships rather than formal legality becomes cronyism; consensus becomes wheel-greasing and corrupt politics; conservatism and respect for authority become rigidity and an inability to innovate; much-vaunted educational achievements become rote-learning and a refusal to question those in authority; and so on. With regards to the cultural differences between the Chinese and Japanese economies, Maddison (1996, p. 53) argues that:

> "In China, the foreigners appeared on the fringes of a huge country. The ruling elite regarded it as the locus of civilization, and considered the 'barbarian' intruders as an irritating nuisance. In Japan, they struck in the biggest city, humiliated the Shogun and destroyed his legitimacy as a ruler. The Japanese had already borrowed important elements of Chinese civilization and saw no shame in copying in a Western model which had demonstrated its superior technology so dramatically."

Although Japan imported not only Chinese characters but also Buddhism and Confucianism from China, the adoption of the external religions came only after the authorities decided they would not conflict with *Shinto* (the way of the gods). Unlike Western religions, Shinto has no scriptures or commandments. It does have customary practices, including ancestor worship adopted from Confucianism. The impact of modern Shinto on Japanese life is reflected in an aggressive patriotism. The mobilization of the Japanese and their behavior during the Second World War are examples of that patriotism. The economic success of the second half of the 20th century is due, at least partially, to the patriotic attitude of all those working in the Japanese enterprises. The family spirit has largely carried over to the firm, which has meant greater cooperation and productivity. Some Eastern religions (such as Buddhism and Taoism) seek virtue through passivity. Shinto, by contrast, stresses the search for progress through creative activities.[7]

The East Asian area had an incredibly high level of per capita annual labor input (947 hours), compared with the others, especially the African (608 hours), Latin American (643 hours), Western (709 hours) and Eastern Orthodox (717 hours) areas (see Table 3.3). The high labor input of the East Asian area may help us to understand, at least in part, its rapid economic growth during this period. Also noteworthy are the gender differences between culture areas. For example, the female laborers of the Indian and Islamic areas comprised

---

[7] One noticeable point lies in the fact that Shinto has coexisted with Buddhism and Confucianism in Japan, and a Japanese can embrace both of them. But despite this tolerance of diverse religious traditions, Western religions have never taken hold in Japan (Rapoport, 1989, p. 18).

only 16.5 percent and 18.3 percent of their total laborers, respectively. These figures were much lower than that of the Eastern Orthodox area (44.4 percent), the Western area (42.5 percent) and the rest. If there are no other convincing reasons for this imbalanced employment pattern between males and females it might plausibly be taken to imply that women have not been placed in a proper position of equality in the Indian and the Islamic societies.

**Table 3.3. Characteristics of human capital in the 1990s, by culture area**

| Item | African | East Asian | Eastern Orthodox | Indian | Islamic | Latin America | Western | World |
|---|---|---|---|---|---|---|---|---|
| Proportion of female labor (%)[a] | 38.1 | 37.3 | 44.4 | 16.5 | 18.3 | 26.6 | 42.5 | 36.2 |
| Ratio of employment to population (%)[a] | 39.3 | 44.0 | 42.0 | 34.6 | 30.1 | 33.1 | 44.5 | 40.5 |
| Per capita labor input (in hours)[a] | 608 | 947 | 717 | 762 | 736 | 643 | 709 | 736 |
| Gross enrolment ratios[b] | 53 | 96 | 86 | 72 | 73 | 89 | 104 | 86 |
| (1) Male | 58 | 98 | 85 | 81 | 79 | 89 | 104 | 89 |
| (2) Female | 50 | 94 | 86 | 63 | 67 | 90 | 105 | 82 |

[a]: Calculated by the author based on Maddison (1996, Table J-1).
[b]: Gross enrolment in primary education. *Source*: UNESCO (1999).

A huge labor force does not sufficiently represent an advantage in human resources for economic development, particularly when a country is undergoing transformation from the agricultural society, mainly using traditional methods of production, to an industrial society, which requires not only new and advanced technologies but also well-trained personnel. A well-educated and law-abiding population that possesses a strong work ethic is the sine qua non of modern economic growth. A striking feature of the world economy in the 20th century was the enormous increase in the average level of education. Before the 19th century the majority of the population was illiterate in almost all countries. Since then, the universal enrolment in primary education has become obligatory in the advanced countries. As a result the proportion of people receiving secondary and higher education has risen steadily. For example, the years of education per person aged 15-64 were only 3.92 for USA, 4.44 for UK and 1.50 for Japan in 1870; while they rose sharply to 18.04 for USA, 14.09 for UK and 14.87 for Japan in 1992 (Maddison, 1996, p. 37).

Education as a factor of production was first stressed by Schulz (1961) in his analysis of human capital and then has been rediscovered by 'new' growth theorists. The data on education stock should be re-adjusted before the international comparison is conducted, because educational system usually differs from country to country. Nevertheless, primary-school enrollment ratio has been often used as a crude proxy in the new growth literature, though it is sometimes not an internationally comparable measure for changes in human capital.[8] In the mid-1990s the gross primary-school enrollment ratios were 89 percent for

---

[8] For example, while many countries consider primary-school age to be 6-11 years, others do not.

males and 82 percent for females, or at the average level of 86 percent, for the total population of the primary school age (see Table 3.3). Interculturally, the Western area had the highest gross enrollment ratio (104 percent)[9], followed by the East Asian (96 percent) and Latin American (89 percent) areas; in contrast, the African area had the lowest gross enrollment ratio (only 53 percent), followed by the Indian (72 percent) and Islamic (73 percent) areas. It is also worth noting that there were larger differences of gross enrolment ratios between males and females in the Indian (81 percent for male *v.* 63 percent for female) and Islamic (79 percent for male *v.* 67 percent for female) areas than in the other culture areas.

Creativity and technological innovation have been the most fundamental element in promoting, either directly or indirectly, economic development and social change. Although it is very difficult to measure its short-term impact precisely, no one would reject the idea that technological progress is changing the world at an incredibly high rate. The most obvious contributions are transport and communications where crude means (such as horses, carriages and hand-written letters) have been superseded by superjets, telephones and faxes, as well as by increasingly efficient computer networks, including the Internet which is becoming the most important means for transmitting information. For example, people throughout most of the world now can immediately get access to the latest information about technological progress and download electronic products from the Internet. This contrasts with the intercontinental spread of technological inventions in the ancient times, which were both costly and time-consuming and could took decades or even centuries. Mobile telephones, computer networks and other technological inventions, which were once considered to be either impossible or useless, are now becoming the necessities of our daily life.

Before the early 20th century, technological innovation had been contributed mainly by individual inventors or small-scale entrepreneurs. But now the great bulk of it—such as the space shuttle and the Internet, to list but two—is conducted by prominent firms with substantial budgets, as well as by governments. As a result the process of technological innovation has become more complicated than ever before. Specifically, the technological and related products are positively related to capital stock of, and personnel engagement in, technological innovation. In addition, technological innovation is also related to the educational levels, as the content of education changes over time to accommodate to the growing stock of knowledge. There has been a proliferation of specialized intellectual disciplines to facilitate the absorption of knowledge and to promote its development through research.

There is a difference in understanding and definition of manpower and creativity between the East and the West. Creativity is the driving force behind the development of technology, economy, arts and culture as a whole. As a result it is a multi-level and complex process that covers all fields. Although Asian traditions are conservative in comparison, and the social climate and ideological make-up of the West are more liberal, each of them has valid contributions towards creativity. Western culture lays emphasis on individuals' contribution. Perhaps there may be some historical or religious reasons, but the mainstay of Western culture is individualism. This trait is manifested in the adulation of individual heroes in Western culture. The individuals' heroic exploits and contributions are placed above

---

[9] For some countries with universal primary education, the gross enrollment ratios may exceed 100 percent because some pupils are below or above the country's standard primary-school age.

collective effort. The advantage of this is that it can spur people on to greater heights. The flaw is that it results in self-centered individualism, which affects creativity indirectly (Pan, 2006). Creativity is a multi-level and complex process, involving many different factors. At a certain level, creativity requires the coordination of all sides, and the Eastern culture, which lays emphasis on collectivities, can play a positive role in this.

In China, there were great thinkers like Confucius, Mencius, Laozi and Zhuangzi. But these achievements go back to the periods of the Spring and Autumn (770 – 476 BC) and the Warring States (475 – 221 BC), and there hasn't been a likewise breakthrough for the last 1,000 years. Throughout its history, Chinese culture has two obvious historical traits. One is that it had a very long period of feudalism. The second trait is that the Imperial Examination (keju) system was too rigid and deeply entrenched. The feudal period in Europe was, by contrast, shorter and was followed by over 200 years (from the 14th to the 16th century AD) of the Renaissance, a revolutionary movement in intellectual thought and inventiveness spurred on by the call to revive the arts of classical Greece. The Enlightenment and the Industrial Revolution that followed caused a tumultuous transformation in Europe. Shaking off its feudal shackles in ideology and social systems, Europe created a brave new world for itself. Under such circumstances, Europe produced many new creations and inventions in the realms of art, science, music, architecture and so on. In the last 200 years, the United States has attracted many immigrants of high caliber and provided very favourable conditions for creativity and inventiveness, making it the only superpower in the world today.

Modern science originated from Europe. The characteristic of Western culture is reflected in making bold hypotheses followed by the meticulous search for evidence. The basis of science is the experiment. Not only can the experiment verify the soundness of the hypothesis, it can also improve or debunk it. It is due to these cultural traits that Westerners are more used to making bold hypotheses. As a result, many important and revolutionary discoveries were made. The disadvantage of this is that some of these new ideas and hypotheses may not have solid foundations, but this fault is a minor one where creativity is concerned. The traditional Eastern system emphasizes building a solid foundation, and then builds up the basic knowledge step by step. However, Eastern tradition places too much emphasis on foundations. The insistence on rote learning robbed the initiative to make bold hypotheses about new situations and new problems (Pan, 2006).

## 3.3. WEALTH AND DISTRIBUTION

The term 'cultural pattern' refers to the way in which people relate to one another. This differs to some extent from society to society. The primary kind of cultural pattern is based on kinship. In most societies, a family unit includes only the father and mother and the unmarried child (children); but it can also be larger, including more relatives, as in India and some African economies. In the Democratic Republic of Congo those who call themselves brothers include those whom would be called cousins and uncles in other parts of the world. The extended family fulfills several important social and economic roles. It provides mutual cooperation, psychological support and a kind of economic insurance or social security for its members. In a world of tribal warfare and primitive agriculture, this kind of family support was invaluable. However, in modern societies, this kind of family system becomes inefficient in promoting economic development, due to, at least in part, the lack of individual incentives for capital accumulation and controls over population growth. For example, many African and Indian economies achieved quite respectable rates of GDP growth during the 20th century, but their welfare impact was to a large extent eaten away by explosive population expansion which was faster than in the rest of the world and shows little sign of deceleration.[10] In fact, the Western family system involves controls over fertility and limited obligations to more distant kin and, as a result, reinforces the possibilities for accumulation.

In India the joint family system (*baradari*) is generally accepted as having not only stimulated population growth but also restricted capital accumulation. The caste system is another obstacle to India's economic development. In a particular caste, each member has a specific occupational and social role, which is hereditary. This hierarchical system to a large extent segregates the population into mutually exclusive groups, which prevents people from raising productivity by changing their economic activities. This gives no allowance for aptitude, intelligence or new ideas in allocating jobs and little possibility of firing someone for inefficiency. During the British rule 56,000 kilometers of railways were built and irrigation was extended eightfold in India. Conquerors of India, however, were neither absorbed into the Hindu culture nor were able to modify this caste system. Instead, they simply added themselves as another layer to a complex system of social segregation and siphoned their profits out India. Consequently, there was little growth in per capita national income in India during their rule. When the British left, most of the Indian population there were still illiterate (Maddison, 1996, p. 55$^{)}$.[11]

In a different way, but one that has in-depth economic implications is that Islamic thinkers have likewise sought dynamic approaches to the development problem-solving within the boundaries of their own value systems. Because the *Shari's* (Islamic law) prohibits the taking of interest, 'Islamic banks' neither pay nor charge it. Since the banks must remain viable, they spread the risks flowing from their borrowing and lending by receiving a share of profits from the borrowers, and distributing proportionate shares to their depositors. Technically and ethically, such payments are not considered to be interest. Islamic banks claim that they are simply facilitating the circulation of money in ways that generate productive activities. Their example shows how a religious norm can alter 'modern' practice, instead of itself being eliminated by the dictates of modernity (Shanker, 1996).

As a result of the diversified natural and social conditions, cross-cultural economic differences have virtually persisted for very many years throughout the world. It is worth noting that different methods can result in different cross-cultural scenarios. For example, when the exchange rates and *World Bank Atlas* methods are used, the Indian area is designed to have the lowest per capita GNP (that is, $396 and $373, respectively), followed by the African ($778 and $521, respectively) and Islamic ($1,877 and $1,466, respectively) areas; by contrast, when the PPP method is used, the African area becomes the poorest in terms of per capita GNP ($1499), followed by the Indian ($1,600) and Islamic ($3,597) areas. The standards of living differ greatly across all culture areas (see Table 3.4). Among all the seven culture areas, the Western area has the longest life expectancy at birth (73 years for men and

---

[10] For more analyses of the developmental dilemmas in India, see, for example, Behari (1992), Byres (1998), and Kapila (1999), and in some African economies, see, for example, Anunobi (1994), Ronald and Hope (1996) and Lewis (1998).

[11] For a detailed account of the Indian economy during the colonial period, see Roy (1999).

80 years for women), followed by the East Asian (68 years for men and 72 years for women) and Latin American (66 years for men and 73 years for women) areas; in contrast, the African area has the shortest life expectancy (50 years for men and 53 years for women) (see Table 3.4).

The inverted-U hypothesis on the relationship between income distribution and economic development was first proposed by Kuznets (1955), who suggested that inequality tends to widen during the initial stage of economic development, with a reversal of this tendency in the later stage.[12] There is mixed evidence for this hypothesis. A number of cross-sectional studies (such as Paukert, 1973; Cline, 1975; Chenery and Syrquin, 1975; Ahluwalia, 1976; Deininger and Squire, 1998) support this hypothesis. However the studies of Fields (1991), Jha (1996), and Eichera and Garcia-Penalosab (2001) show that there is no tendency for poorer countries to yield increased rather than decreased inequality or for richer countries to yield decreased rather than increased income inequality.

Based on the cross-national data from the 1980s and the 1990s (details about these data will be given in Section 5.4 of Chapter 5), we can conduct a simplified statistical test on the determinants of income inequality. Our estimated results reported in Table 3.5 reveal that income inequality is an inverse-U shaped function of income level, following the tradition of Kuznets (see Figure 3.1 for the scatter diagram). The above results do reflect an influence of growth on income distribution. Besides, our estimated result reported in Reg. (2) of Table 3.5 provides some evidence to support the view that income inequality increases with respect to religious diversity (see Figure 3.2 for the scatter diagram). This may be explained by the fact that income (re)distribution from the rich to the poor can be more easily conducted between individuals with same religious beliefs than between individuals with different religious beliefs. In fact, such issues as justice, equality and common prosperity between the rich and the poor have been mentioned in many religious scriptures. The following is an example:

> We who are strong in the faith ought to help the weak to carry their burdens. We should not please ourselves. Instead, we should all please our brothers for their own good, in order to build them up in the faith. For Christ did not please himself. Instead, as the scripture says, "The insults which are hurled at you have fallen on me." Everything written in the Scriptures was written to teach us, in order that we might have hope through the patience and encouragement which the Scriptures give us. And may God, the source of patience and encouragement, enable you to have the same point of view among yourselves by following the example of Christ Jesus, so that all of you together may praise with one voice the God and Father of our Lord Jesus Christ. (Romans, 15:1-6.)

---

[12] For an introductory literature on the empirical tests of the 'inverted-U' hypothesis, see Anand and Kanbur (1993a).

**Table 3.4. Selected socioeconomic indicators by culture areas**

| Indicator | | African area | East Asian area | Eastern Orthodox area | Indian area | Islamic area | Latin American area | Western area |
|---|---|---|---|---|---|---|---|---|
| (1) Per capita GNP | Exchange rate (US$) | 778 | 3373 | 2487 | 396 | 1877 | 4229 | 22579 |
| | World Bank Atlas | 521 | 3808 | 2363 | 373 | 1460 | 3956 | 23344 |
| | PPP rate | 1499 | 4984 | 4048 | 1600 | 3597 | 6769 | 22113 |
| (2) Daily per capita calorie supply as a percentage of total requirements (%)[a] | | 94 | 114 | 131 | 100 | 115 | 114 | 135 |
| (3) Life expectancy at birth (years)[b] | Male | 50 | 68 | 63 | 62 | 64 | 66 | 73 |
| | Female | 53 | 72 | 72 | 62 | 67 | 73 | 80 |
| (4) Population per doctor (persons)[c] | | 8203 | 1196 | 240 | 12662 | 1016 | 769 | 339 |
| (5) Population per nurse (persons)[d] | | 2298 | 1306 | 91 | 6857 | 485 | 527 | 132 |

[a] 118 economies are included in analysis for the most recent year available, within the range between 1988 and 1990;

[b] 197 economies are included in analysis for 1995-2000;

[c] 97 economies are included in analysis for the most recent year available, within the range between 1990 and 1993;

[d] 73 economies are included in analysis for the most recent year available, within the range between 1990 and 1993.

*Sources:* (1) Calculated by the author based on United Nations (2001), World Bank (2001), WRI (1999) and UNESCO (1999).

## Table 3.5. Determinants of Income inequality

| Explanatory variable | Reg. (1) | Reg. (2) | Reg. (3) |
|---|---|---|---|
| (Constant) | -0.079 (0.182) | -0.163 (0.190) | 0.041 (0.193) |
| lnGDPPC | 0.169 (0.049)[a] | 0.192 (0.051)[a] | 0.141 (0.051)[a] |
| lnGDPPC square | -0.013 (0.003)[a] | -0.015 (0.003)[a] | -0.012 (0.003)[a] |
| LANGUAGE | | -0.001 (0.002) | -0.033 (0.019)[c] |
| RELIGION | | 0.018 (0.008)[b] | |
| LANGUAGE*lnGDPPC | | | 0.005 (0.003)[c] |
| Number of observations | 164 | 164 | 164 |
| F | 31.92 | 17.41 | 16.93 |
| R sq. | 0.283 | 0.303 | 0.297 |

*Note*: The dependent variable is Gini coefficient. lnGDPPC is the natural log of GDP per capita. LANGUAGE and RELIGION are the linguistic and religious diversity indexes. The term LANGUAGE*lnGDPPC is the product of the LANGUAGE index and lnGDPPC. [a], [b] and [c] denote statistically significant at the 1%, 5% and 10% levels, respectively.

*Source*: Estimated by the author based on ordinary least squares (OLS) regressions with the data constructed in Section 5.4 of Chapter 5.

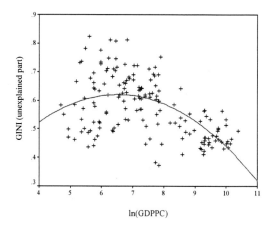

Figure 3.1. Gini coefficient versus ln(GDPPC).

Compared to religious diversity, linguistic diversity's role in the formation of income inequality is sometimes ambiguous. Our estimated result shows that the income inequality is negatively related to linguistic diversity, though it is statistically insignificant (see Reg. (2) of Table 3.5). In order words, it seems that income (re)distribution from the rich to the poor is not enhanced between people speaking a common language. Might there be a nonlinear relation between income inequality and linguistic diversity? Our regressions show that the

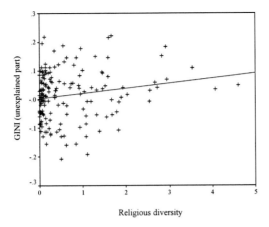

Figure 3.2. Gini coefficient versus religious diversity.

coefficients on the linguistic diversity (LANGUAGE) and on its interactive term with the natural log of GDPPC (LANGUAGE*lnGDPPC) are statistically significant at the 10% level (see Reg. (3) of Table 3.5). Specifically, linguistic diversity tends to reduce income inequality in nations represented by a value of lnGDPPC being less than the breakpoint value of 6.6[1] (see Figure 3.3a for the scatter diagram) and tends to increase income inequality in richer nations (see Figure 3.3b for the scatter diagram). This may be explained by the fact that in richer nations income (re)distribution from the rich to the poor can be more easily conducted between individuals speaking a common language than between those speaking different languages. But since the number of nations included in Figure 3.3a is quite small, we still need more detailed evidence to support the negative relationship between income inequality and linguistic diversity in poor nations.

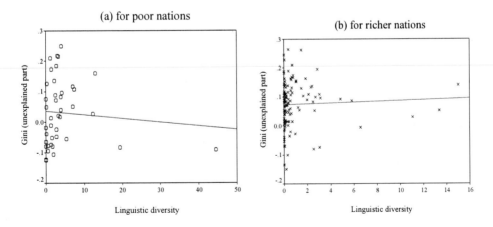

Figure 3.3. Gini coefficients versus linguistic diversity.

---

[1] After deriving the first-order differential of the dependent variable with respect to LANGUAGE and letting it be zero, we can obtain a break-point value (that is, lnGDPPC*=(0.033/0.005=6.6).

## 3.4. Consumption Patterns

Modern life has been simultaneously characterized and influenced by different cultures. When people say that 'the world is becoming smaller every day', they are referring not only to the increased speed and ease of transportation and communication but also to the increased use of international and intercultural market to buy and sell goods. The overall heightened presence of foreign goods, foreign producers and even foreign-owned assets causes many to question the impact and desirability of all international and intercultural economic transactions. An increasing number of companies are now relying on production chains that straddle many politically and culturally distinctive areas. Raw materials and components may come from different linguistic or religious areas and be assembled in another, while marketing and distribution take place in still other venues. Consumers' decisions in, for example, New York or Tokyo may become information that has an almost immediate impact on the products that are being made—and the styles that influence them—all over the world. As a result it is reasonable to assume that culture is playing an increasing important role in our contemporary economic life.

Each person is part of many different identity groups simultaneously, thus learning and becoming part of all their cultures. Each of us is culturally unique because each adopts or adapts differently the attitudes, values and beliefs of the groups to which we belong. Thus, all communication becomes intercultural because of the various group identities of those communicating (Singer, 1998). The major challenge to us is how to examine the differences that make us unique and to discover ways to be more effective in overcoming the barriers these differences have created.

Race and ethnicity – elements reflecting the primary characteristics of a culture – have direct influences on economic activities. The names of many existing ethnic groups can lead to information about their social and economic conditions. Quite a few reveal the major occupation of these peoples. For example, in the language of the Lahu people, 'Lahu' means 'roasting tiger-meat on fire', which can be gathered that the Lahu people used to live by hunting. This can also be witnessed by their neighbors in Southwest China, the Dai and the Hani, who called themselves Mushe ('the hunters'). There is a small ethnic group entitled 'Oroqen' (which has two meanings: 'people who herd tamed deer' and 'people who live on the mountains') living in the Greater and Lesser Xing'an Mountains between Mongolia, Russia and Northeast China. Another ethnic group, also living in Northeast China, call themselves the Daur (meaning 'cultivator'), indicating that these people engaged in agriculture during ancient times.

There are great disparities in consumption patterns throughout the world. According to Engel's Law, the proportion of total expenditure on food and other basic necessities drops as income level rises. Expenditure on education, leisure recreation and others, on the other hand, is seen to be more income-elastic. Nevertheless, it is necessary to be cautious in applying Engel's Law to cross-national or cross-cultural analysis. Statistical data show that some countries with same or similar income levels can have very variable consumer expenditure patterns, while some countries with different income levels may demonstrate the same or similar consumer expenditure patterns – which does not confirm Engel's Law. For example, the following is reported by the World Bank (1993, pp. 256-7):

Expenditure on food ranges from 38 percent in Kenya to 64 percent in Tanzania (both are lower-income economies) and from 25 percent in Hungary to 35 percent in Argentina and South Korea (both are upper-middle-income economies); for clothing and footwear, from 7 percent in Peru to 16 percent in Thailand (both are lower-middle-income economies); for rent, fuel and power, from 8 percent in Tanzania to 17 percent in Bangladesh (both are lower-income economies) and from 7 percent in Thailand to 23 percent in Iran (both are lower-middle-income economies); for medical care, from 2 percent in Senegal to 6 percent in Iran (both are lower-middle-income economies); for education, from 1 percent in Bangladesh to 10 percent in Kenya (both are lower-income economies); for transportation and communication, from 9 percent in Japan to 14 percent in Canada and USA (all are high-income economies), from 5 percent in Senegal to 10 percent in Peru (both are lower-middle-income economies), and from 2 percent in Tanzania to 7-8 percent in India and Peru (all are lower-income economies).

It seems very likely that only non-economic factors, including ethnic and religious ones, can account for the above variations.

Besides, the etiquette and content of food differ from culture to culture. For example, people with Latino-origin are accustomed to a diet rich in complex carbohydrates. This includes corn and corn products, beans, rice and breads. Proteins include beans, eggs, fish and shellfish, beef, pork, poultry and goat. Because frying is a common cooking method, the Mexican diet tends to be higher in fat. The type of bean depends on the culture. Cubans, Southern Mexicans, Central Americans and Venezuelans use black beans. Northern Mexicans, Dominicans and Puerto Ricans prefer pinto or pinta beans. Cubans, Central South Americans and Hispanic Caribbeans use red kidney beans. Dominicans and Puerto Ricans also use pigeon peas. Venezuelans and Brazilians use chickpeas or garbanzo beans. Latino foods are not always spicy. Oregano, tomato, garlic and black pepper are used to flavor foods by cooks from Cuba, Puerto Rico and the Dominican Republic (USDA, 2002). Cuisine for Africans, sometimes referred to as 'soul food', may include the use of collard greens and other leafy green and yellow vegetables, legumes, beans, rice and potatoes. Food preparation includes frying, barbecuing and service foods with gravy and sauces. Home-baked pies and cakes are common.

In a traditional Asian diet, rice is the mainstay and commonly eaten at every meal. Pork and poultry are the primary protein sources. Significant quantities of dried beans and nuts are also eaten. Fruits and vegetables also make up a large portion of the Asian diet. Since ancient times, the Chinese have employed many cooking methods, including braising, boiling, braising with soy sauce, roasting, baking, grilling, scalding, deep-frying, steaming, drying and salt-preserving. By contrast, the Western cuisine is much simpler. Western cuisine seldom uses the ingredients in Chinese cuisine, such as jelly fish, sea cucumbers, shark's fins, bird's nests, bean curds (tofu), oyster sauce, black bean sauce, salty shrimp paste, soy sauce and so on. Besides, Western cooking adds herbs like rosemary, dill, sage, oregano, thyme and tarragon, all of which are seldom found in the traditional Chinese food. The Chinese cuisine uses ginger, spring onions, mints, corianders, white pepper and so on but does not contain cheese, butter, cream or milk in traditional food; neither the Chinese have chocolate mousse, apple pie, cheese cakes, and fruit tarts in their diet. Besides, there is a main difference between the traditional Chinese and the Western eating habits: unlike the way in the West, where forks and knifes are used and everyone has his or her own plate of food, in China the dishes are placed on the center of a table and everybody shares with each other using chopsticks.[2]

## 3.5. MARKETING STRATEGY

Each individual human being has been socialized in a unique environment. Important aspects of the environment are shared, and these constitute a particular culture. Culture poses communication problems because there are so many variables unknown to the communicators. As the cultural variables and differences increase, communication costs and intercultural misunderstanding will appear. That is, as noted by Gudykunst (1994), "When we travel to another culture or interact with people from another culture in our culture, we cannot base our predictions of their behavior on our cultural rules and norms. This inevitably leads to misunderstanding. If we want to communicate effectively, we must use our knowledge of the other culture to make predictions. If we have little or no knowledge of the other person's culture, we have no basis for making predictions."[3]

Language, as the major tool of communication, is an obvious starting point for the exploration of differences between cultures. Every language carries a weight of values, of sensibilities, of approaches to reality – all of which insinuate themselves into the consciousness of those who speak it. To a certain extent, linguistic differences have decisively influenced global trade and marketing. Although it is not the only tool in building trusting relationships, doors usually open more quickly when knocked on by someone who speaks a familiar language. Sharing a common language, however, does not necessarily mean effective communication in technical terms. More important is the understanding of 'hidden messages', which determines the effectiveness of the communication. Proper communication takes both technical understanding of the spoken words and cultural understanding of the 'hidden meaning'. Intercultural communication is a process whereby individuals who are culturally different from each other on such important attributes as their value orientations, preferred communication codes, role expectations and perceived rules of social relationship. Although most cultural groups have their own communication styles, the differences of communication styles between the Asian and the Western worlds are most distinct (see Table 3.6). For example, when a Japanese manager says in a business negotiation 'It is very difficult' (which is a polite manner of refusal in Japanese society), the American partner would probably ask the Japanese side to find a solution, finding the expression to be more ambiguous (in American's point of view). In the contemporary Chinese society, by contrast, 'We have some difficulties' implies 'It would be O.K. under certain conditions.'

Compared to language, religion can provide more insights into the characteristics of a culture.[4] What is more important, religion can have a deep impact not only on attitudes towards economic matters but also on values that influence them. Specifically, religious attitudes and values can help to determine what we think is right or appropriate, what is important, what is desirable and so on. For example, Catholics used always to eat fish on

---

[2] See Guo (2009a, ch. 1) for an analysis of the causes for this difference.

[3] Cited from Harris, et al. (2004, p. 42).

[4] For an earlier study of the economic ethnic of the Protestantism and Catholics, see Weber (1904); and the recent one of the Jewish, Christian and Muslim, see, for example, Wilson (1997).

**Table 3.6. Eastern versus Western cultures: communication styles**

| Western styles | Eastern styles |
| --- | --- |
| Direct | Indirect |
| Blunt | Diplomatic |
| Polite | Very courteous |
| Talkative | Reserved |
| Extrovert | Introvert |
| Persuasive | Recommendations |
| Medium-strong eye contact | Weak eye contact |
| Unambiguous | Ambiguous |
| Decisive | Cautious |
| Problem solving | Accepting of the situation |
| Interrupt | Does not interrupt |
| Half listens | Listens carefully |
| Quick to deal | Courtship dance |
| Concentrates on power | Concentrates on agreed agenda |

Source: Based on Lewis (2003).

Fridays; milk products are popular among Hindus, many of whom are also vegetarians. Americans love beef, yet it is forbidden to Hindus; tabooed food in Muslim and Jewish culture is normally pork, eaten extensively by the Chinese and others. Many deluxe restaurants usually cater to diverse diets to offer 'national' dishes to meet varying cultural tastes. Besides, Luqmani *et al.* (1980) suggests a package of marketing strategies for the Muslim world, among them: 'to use religious holidays such as the end of Ramadan as the major selling time for food, clothing, and gifts'; 'to use 'excessive' profits for charitable purposes'; 'to access female consumers by saleswomen, catalogs, home demonstrations'; and so on.

Business negotiation is a process in which two or more economic entities come together to discuss common and conflicting interests in order to reach an agreement of mutual benefit. In cross-cultural business negotiations, the negotiation process differ in language, cultural conditioning, negotiating styles, approaches to problem solving, implicit assumptions and so on. Fisher (1980) addresses five considerations for analyzing cross-cultural negotiations: (i) the players and the situation; (ii) styles of decision making; (iii) national characters; (iv) cross-cultural noise; and (v) interpreters and translators. Besides, negotiators may place different values on agreements and hold different assumptions about the way contracts should be honored. The following tips will help to highlight negotiation differences in five distinct cultures:

- With Africans: Africa is a diverse continent on which to do business. According to the World Bank's annual "Doing Business" report, sub-Saharan Africa is, on average, the most difficult place to do business in the world when it comes to red tape. The notable challenge facing companies doing business includes the reality that Africans in most territories suffer from extreme poverty. There is also the further enormous challenge of language. While there are some cases of a lingua franca – such as Swahili in much of East Africa and French in parts of West Africa – there is a seemingly endless number of regional dialects in many countries. The Democratic Republic of the Congo, for example, has more than 200 ethnic groups. This reality demands a very different approach to volume customer management than that of single-language markets…

- With Arabs:[5] Junior managers enter first, followed by senior executives; take time to establish rapport and relationships; expect to mix business and personal information to establish individual support, trust and commitments; utilize a go-between in the negotiation; to gain concessions, they may try to make you feel guilty and then obligated; they like to bargain and are skilled at making deals; be patient, enjoy the process and be willing to compromise…

- With North Americans:[6] It is a good idea to prepare an agreed-upon agenda before the meeting; be prompt in starting time; prepare and pass on minutes of the meeting afterwards; the chairperson presents first; focus on issues one at a time; solicit input from all attendees; expect open discussion and debate; share problem-solving ideas; assign individual action items; be direct, assertive, involved and action oriented…

- With Latin Americans:[7] Latin American business executives tend to be extrovert, impatient, talkative, and inquisitive. Interpersonal skills are often considered more important than professional competence and experience. Latins are not very interested in schedules or punctuality. The pace of negotiations is slower in Latin America than in Europe. The best policy is to wait for your Latin counterparts to initiate any "small talk" and follow their lead in establishing rapport. Latins follow a top-down decision making process, where employees follow a trusting subservience to their superior as task orientation is dictated from above. Opinions of experienced middle-mangers and technical staff do not always carry the weight that they would in the UK. Meeting formalities must be followed; the two senior executives should sit facing each other. Be sensitive to the fact that Latins tend to stand and sit extremely close to others…

- With Chinese: Only senior members on both sides are expected to talk, unless junior members are invited to do so; do not interrupt, even if a mistake is made (take notes and share corrections in private occasions); expect a large negotiating team and long lunch breaks; "face" is important; realize that the power of the negotiator may be limited, and that sometimes assistants to and secretaries to top managers sometimes are even more useful than deputy managers; remember that there is a difference in negotiating with Chinese receiving Western educations…

- With Western Europeans. To say that the Western European market is diverse would be a gross understatement. European countries are highly receptive to new developments that improve efficiency and reduce costs and suggests there are two key opportunities to look for: products or services born out of a technological breakthrough and clever ways to serve the needs not currently recognized or acknowledged by European customers. Marketing products to Western European customers can be approached on two levels: pan-European or country-specific. However, cultural and language barriers are making it difficult to find success with

---

[5] Based on Elashmawi (2001).

[6] Based on Elashmawi (2001).

[7] Based on Castle and Carrasco (2007).

pan-European programs. To ensure messages are understood, experts recommend packaging, labeling and promotion be created for each individual country…

- With Eastern Europeans. Remember that the habits and behavior inherited from the communist period may still be in evidence. When a foreign firm invests in an Eastern European country in order to maintain their competitive advantage internationally, it must be able to quickly replicate their embedded resources within the affiliate. In addition, foreign firms have to cope with specific barriers to change inherited from the communist legacy. To make its affiliates work according to Western criteria, foreign investors have to overcome these barriers. The local firm's capacity to learn and the willingness of local workers to change skills and habits are two important factors…

- With Indians: An Indian who hesitates to say "No" may actually be trying to convey that he or she may worry whether the job can be done; aggressiveness can often be interpreted as a sign of disrespect; only the senior person might speak, and the junior members may maintain silence; Westernized Indians can be quite assertive and direct; politeness and honesty go a long way in establishing the fact that your intentions are genuine…

- With Japanese:[8] You are expected to deal with a homogeneous group of up to four, junior and middle managers; try to establish harmonious, cooperative relationships, giving time to lunch and/or dinner and entertainment; follow their rule of "etiquette", such as, token gifts called "presenta" which are exquisitely wrapped – use holidays to exchange greetings; focus on middle managers who make recommendations to senior managers who make the final decisions.

## 3.6 SUMMARY

Furthering the understanding of the determinants of economic development promises to be one of the major areas of research in the post-Cold War era. In brief, the understanding of the determinants of economic activities promises to be one of the major research areas in the postwar era. Despite the importance of culture influences on economic activities, mainstream economists have usually abstracted from them. Cultural considerations have been cast into the 'underworld' of developmental thought and practice. The past analyses, especially those that are quantitatively based, are mainly focused on economic variables. But there is no way in which economic activities could be conducted independently of human and cultural context. The economy is as much a cultural site as any other part of society, such as family, community or school.

Where culture is emphasized it is often given a purely instrumental role: culture per se can help or hamper cross-cultural economic activities (see Table 3.7). When cultural attitudes thwart economic growth, they need to be eradicated, or so the reasoning goes. Culture comes into this analysis not as something valuable in itself, but as a means to the ends of fostering and sustaining economic progress. However, culture, significant as it may be as an agent of economic activity, cannot be reduced to the position of a more promoter or impediment to

---

[8] Based on Elashmawi (2001).

economic activities. The role of culture cannot be limited to the means towards ends, rather is the social basis of the ends themselves.

**Table 3.7. Differing economic behaviors among selected religious groups**

| Religion | Competition | Thrift or save money | Profit-maximizing behavior | Inter-personal connection |
|---|---|---|---|---|
| Buddhist | ✗ | ✓ | ✓ | ✗ |
| Christian | ✓ | ✓ | ✓ | ✗ |
| Hindu | ✗ | ✗ | ✗ | ✓ |
| Jews | ✓ | ✓ | ✓ | ✓ |
| Muslim | ✗ | ✗ | ✗ | ✓ |
| Orthodox | ✓ | ✗ | ✗ | ✗ |

*Note*: "✓" and "✗" denote that the item is emphasized and is not emphasized, respectively.
*Source*: Judged by the author based on the *World Values Surveys* (1999-2002) (available from the Institute of Social Research, The University of Michigan).

In recent decades both experience and intellectual insight have pushed development thinking away from debates over the role of states and markets, and the search for a single, overarching policy prescription. Investment in physical and human capital, for example, should encourage economic growth and as a general rule, the empirical evidence presented in this chapter supports this proposition. But in a number of cases, high rates of investment and education attainment have not been enough to deliver rapid growth. It is difficult to ignore the fact that people's behavior patterns vary with distinct cultural backgrounds. Naturally, one would ask to what extent these variations are important for economic analysis in general and economic growth in particular. Are there significant influences of cultural traditions and behavioral norms on economic success and achievement? This is a subject in which much interest has been taken by sociologists and historians as well as economists. If we want to pay attention to cultural influences on economic performance in general and business behavior in particular, certain amount of skepticism toward lofty theories may not be improper. And yet the justified skepticism toward cultural theory does not give us enough reason to reject altogether the manifest influence of culture on human behavior (Sen, 2000).

Since World War II, mainstream development thinking has evolved towards a broad pragmatism. As with many subjects, a deeper understanding of development involves the recognition that sweeping beliefs are often incomplete, that layers of complexity are buried not far beneath the surface and that wisdom is often contingent on the particular conditions of time and place. Earlier analyses on the determinants of economic activities, especially those that are quantitatively based, are mainly focused on economic variables. Despite the significant existence of culture influences on economic performances, mainstream economists have failed to embrace them, although there is no way in which economic activities could be conducted independently of cultural context. The economy is as much a cultural site as any other part of society, such as family, community or school. Culture's significance for development will always be greater than that of a mere promoter of or impediment to economic growth.

*Chapter 4*

# MULTICULTURAL ECONOMIC DEVELOPMENT AND POLICY

Mankind were one community, and Allah sent (unto them) prophets as bearers of good tidings and as warners, and revealed therewith the Scripture with the truth that it might judge between mankind concerning that wherein they differed. And only those unto whom (the Scripture) was given differed concerning it, after clear proofs had come unto them, through hatred one of another. And Allah by His Will guided those who believe unto the truth of that concerning which they differed.

(Al-Baqarah, 2:213)

## 4.1. HISTORICAL REVIEW

Since the end of the Cold War, there have been serious concerns about the role of culture in the formation of bilateral and multilateral economic relations. Each culture not only provides the basis of identity (ethnicity, religion) and the mode of communication (language, ideas), but also distinguishes the motives for human behavior and the criteria of evaluation (good or bad, ugly or beautiful). For example, the comparatively smooth creation of the European Union (EU) is the product of a common European culture or some sub-European cultures that have been to some extent integrated. By contrast, the South Asian Association for Regional Cooperation (SARC), formed in 1985 and including seven Hindu, Muslim and Buddhist states, has been ineffectual, even to the point of not being able to hold meetings. Another similar example is Israel and Palestine, both of which share a narrow territory along the eastern coast of Mediterranean Sea, west of the Jordan River and the Dead Sea. Cultural and religious conflicts between the Israelis and Palestinians have always been a Gordian knot for world leaders since the founding of the state of Israel.

Founded in the 1960s, the Association of Southeast Asian Nations (ASEAN) is based to a large extent on cultural heterogeneity (which includes, among others, Buddhism, Islam, Christianity, Confucianism and atheism). In fact, the ASEAN was designed to achieve 'economic cooperation rather than economic integration'. As a result a free trade area has not been contemplated. In 1978, the ASEAN put into force a preferential trade arrangement (PTA) granting 10 to 15 percent margins of preference on 71 commodities and industrial projects. A stronger free trade proposal had been rejected during negotiations. Between 1985 and 1987 the ASEAN leaders agreed to expand the list of sectors in the PTA and to increase the margin of preferences. Until 1989, however, the fraction of goods eligible for regional preferences was still only in the order of 3 percent.[1] A series of talks beginning in the early 1990s led to the decision to create the ASEAN Free Trade Area (AFTA). Furthermore, the treatment of non-tariff barriers is vague. Even if fully implemented, the AFTA will still allow intra-bloc tariffs.

Indeed, intraregional trade performances have been much less significant in culturally diverse area than in culturally homogenous ones. For example, Africa's share of intraregional trade to total trade remained at about 2 percent from 1965 to 2000; even worse, intraregional trade as a share of total trade in ASEAN had declined before 1995, regardless of the supposedly freer trade environment. By contrast, the intraregional trade performances of many culturally homogenous trading blocs demonstrate considerable achievement. Between 1965 and 2000, for example, intraregional trade as a share of total trade in East Asia – though no trading bloc has been set up the region is primarily characterized by, or to some extent linked with, Chinese culture – rose from 32 percent to 56 percent. Even more dramatic was the intraregional trade in Mercosur (founded in 1991, including four Latin American states of Argentina, Brazil, Paraguay, and Uruguay) and Andean Community (founded in 1969, including four Latin American states of Bolivia, Ecuador, Peru, and Venezuela), which increased from 12 percent and 2 percent in 1965 to 22 percent and 13 percent in 2000, respectively (see Table 4.1).

**Table 4.1. Intraregional trade shares of total trade, selected regions, 1965-2000**

| Group | 1965 | 1970 | 1975 | 1980 | 1985 | 1990 | 1995 | 2000 |
|---|---|---|---|---|---|---|---|---|
| East Asia | 0.32 | 0.31 | 0.33 | 0.39 | 0.41 | 0.46 | 0.52 | 0.56 |
| APEC | 0.58 | 0.63 | 0.61 | 0.63 | 0.73 | 0.72 | 0.76 | 0.81 |
| ASEAN-6 | 0.22 | 0.18 | 0.14 | 0.15 | 0.18 | 0.18 | 0.22 | 0.22 |
| Europe | 0.70 | 0.73 | 0.72 | 0.72 | 0.72 | 0.76 | 0.75 | 0.78 |
| EU-15 | 0.62 | 0.65 | 0.64 | 0.64 | 0.65 | 0.69 | 0.67 | 0.68 |
| EU-12 | 0.54 | 0.58 | 0.58 | 0.58 | 0.59 | 0.64 | 0.62 | 0.65 |
| Mercosur | 0.12 | 0.10 | 0.08 | 0.13 | 0.08 | 0.11 | 0.20 | 0.22 |
| Andean Community | 0.02 | 0.03 | 0.05 | 0.05 | 0.05 | 0.06 | 0.11 | 0.13 |
| NAFTA | 0.39 | 0.42 | 0.40 | 0.36 | 0.42 | 0.39 | 0.45 | 0.48 |
| Africa | 0.02 | 0.02 | 0.01 | 0.01 | 0.02 | 0.02 | 0.02 | 0.02 |

*Notes*: (1) 'ASEAN-6' does not include Vietnam, Laos and Cambodia (as they did not join ASEAN until 1995); (2) 'EU-12' does not include Sweden, Austria, and Finland (as they did not join EU until 1995); and (3) the other groups are defined in Frankel *et al.* (1997, p. 281) and IMF (various years).
*Sources*: Frankel *et al.* (1997, p. 281) for 1965-1990 and calculation by the author based on IMF (various years) for 1995 and 2000.

In 1986 the West European nations amended the Treaty of Rome with the Single European Act. This Act provided for the removal of all remaining restrictions to the free flow

---

[1] Data source: Frankel et al. (1997, pp. 267-8), which also gives other references.

of goods, services, capital and labor among member nations, so that the member nations became a single unified market at the beginning of 1993. This was intended to produce substantial efficiency gains and other benefits for the EU. The static welfare benefits resulting from the formation of the EU are estimated to be 1 to 2 percent of GDP, while the dynamic benefits were estimated to be much larger (Cecchini, 1988). The program also induced large amounts of foreign direct investment (FDI) from the other nations, especially the Untied States and Japan, in anticipation of a new increase in EU protectionism against outsiders. However, the efforts to unify all independent economies have not been successful in the entire territory of Europe. The Organization for Security and Cooperation in Europe (OSCE), including countries from at least three cultures (Eastern Orthodox, Islam and Western Christianity) with quite different values and interests, has posed major obstacles to its developing a significant institutional identity and to a wide range of important activities.

Globalization, as an increasingly dominant force since the last decades, is shaping a new era of interaction and dependence among various economies throughout the world. It is increasing the contacts between people across various boundaries – geographical, political and cultural. Today, the interactions among people with different national and cultural identities are deeper than ever before. Generally, from the least to the most integrated, six levels of multicultural economic cooperation can be established:

- Sectoral cooperation
- Preferential trade arrangement
- Free trade area
- Customs union
- Common market
- Economic union

Obviously, 'sectoral cooperation' (SC) is the loosest form, involving straightforward cooperation in one or more selected sectors. As the most advanced form of economic cooperation, 'economic union' goes further by harmonizing or even unifying the monetary and fiscal policies of members. While separate political entities are still present, an economic union generally establishes several supranational institutions whose decisions are binding upon all members. Going beyond the free movement of goods, services and factors, economic union involves harmonizing national economic policies, typically including taxes and a common currency. For example, the decision of the European Community to change its name to the European Union in 1994 represented a determination to proceed to this higher stage of integration. The full unification of economic policies would in turn require political federalization.

The overall benefits of multicultural economic cooperation are subject to different conditions. First of all, the higher the level of pre-union tariffs and the lower the common external tariff, the more likely it is that the net effects will be positive. Along this same line, the more elastic supply and demand in the member economies are, the more likely the net results will be positive. Also, the greater the ease of switching from a higher-cost domestic source to a lower-cost member source, the greater the pre-union per-unit cost differences between the two sources; and the greater the scope for experiencing economies of scale and attracting foreign investment, the larger the potential gains from cooperation. Second, since there are markedly differing attitudes as well as different cultural values, the adoption of a common standard and the socioeconomic cooperation between different cultural groups of people is likely to be difficult (see Box 4.1). As a result the larger the number of cultural groups involved, *ceteris paribus*, the higher the consequent managerial risks and costs. Lastly, the efficiency of multicultural economic cooperation organizations may be reduced if the number of participants increases.

---

### Box 4.1 OMVS versus NBA

Within Africa there are two river-basin organizations which provide comparative examples of work on multicultural economic management. The Senegal River Authority (Organization pour La Mise en valeur de Fleuve Sénégal, or OMVS) was found in 1963 by four nations of Guinea, Mali, Mauritania and Senegal. The functions of the OMVS are navigation, promotion of irrigation and hydropower production and the authority to construct and operate joint projects (OMVS, 1988). The OMVS successfully conciliated Senegal and Mauritania on the sharing of the resources of the Senegal after the 1988 conflict in which farmers and herders on both sides of the river fought over the same land and water resources (Green Cross, 2000, p. 84). The two dams constructed by the OMVS are owned jointly by the member sates, as are the river seaports at the river mouth that the OMVS has developed and maintained.

However, as the case of the nearby river basin, the Niger, shows, good organization is not always sufficient for successful functioning. Cooperation in the Niger basin started in 1963 when seven out of the nine riparian states (Nigeria, Niger, Benin, Burkina Faso, Mali, Guinea, Sierra Leone, Algeria, and Cote d'Ivoire) signed the Act of Niamey. The structure of the Niger Basin Authority (NBA) is similar to the OMVS: secretariat, technical committee of experts and the Council of Ministers. However, unlike the OMVS, the NBA's performance was poor (Rangeley et al., 1994, pp. 43-8). The failure of the earlier multinational management organization, the Niger Commission, and its replacement, the NBA, could be the result of the heterogeneous composition of their seven member states. In 1980 this structure was reformed and an upper level of the Summit of Heads of State was added in order to improve performance, but this did not prove effective. The main reason was the fact that only a few of the nine states really shared a common interest in the joint development of that basin (Ofosu-Amaah, 1990, pp. 246-8).

---

## 4.2. A MODEL OF MULTICULTURAL ECONOMIES

In order to clarify the effects of multicultural economic influences, let us stipulate an economy with $N$ culture groups. For simplicity, the $N$ culture groups are further assumed to be represented by $N$ equally sized culture areas. All culture areas are different from each other in terms of language, religion or other cultural beliefs and values. Furthermore, to make our analysis clearer and more concrete, let us use five assumptions:

1.  All necessary production factors (such as labor force, capital, technology, natural resource and information) are both scarcely and unevenly distributed within the economy.
2.  The production factors can flow more freely within each culture area than between the $N$ culture areas of the economy when $N \geq 2$.
3.  Each of the $N$ culture areas has at least one comparatively advantageous (or disadvantageous) sector over the other(s) when $N \geq 2$.
4.  Transport and communication cost within each culture area is too small to influence the preference of the culture area in allocating its production factors.
5.  The objective of each culture area is to maximize its well-being.

In fact, assumption 1 is not *ad hoc* in the real economic world. Assumption 2 basically characterizes all economic activities in which the culture related barriers exist. Since each culture area is different and independent from the others in terms of cultural identity, intercultural economic cooperation is more difficult and costly than intracultural economic cooperation. In the real world, assumption 3 is the *sine qua non* for the culture areas to develop intercultural cooperation after the culture-related barriers are removed or reduced. Technically, assumption 4, which is commonly applied in most other economic analyses, allows the intracultural cooperation to become profitable within each of the $N$ culture areas when $N$ decreases (or, in other words, when the size of each culture area increases). Finally, assumption 5 serves as an indispensable condition under which the output levels of each culture area and of the economy as a whole can be maximized.

On the basis of the above assumptions, we can induce the following results:

## Proposition 1

Intercultural dependence within an economy usually grows with respect to the number of culture areas involved in the economy. In other words, the economic dependence of each culture area on the outside world is negatively related to its size.

### *Proof*

Suppose that the degree of economic dependence and the size of the culture area are dented by $R$ and $S$ ($S = \pi r^2$, where $r$ denotes the average radius of the culture area), respectively. Deriving the differential of $R$ with respect to $S$, we have

$$\frac{\partial R}{\partial S} = \frac{\partial R}{\partial r} \cdot \frac{\partial r}{\partial S} = \frac{1}{2\pi r} \cdot \frac{\partial R}{\partial r} \qquad (4.1)$$

It is always set in economics that the degree of economic dependence ($R$) should decrease with respect to distance, so does the latter with respect to $r$. Finally, Equation 4.1 becomes $\partial R / \partial S < 0$. As a matter of fact, since the number of culture areas ($N$) and the average size of each culture area ($S$) are negatively related to each other for the given economy, we have $\partial R / \partial N > 0$. *QED.*

## Proposition 2

Multicultural economic relations usually become less stable with respect to the number of culture areas involved. In other words, the overall stability of multicultural economic relations is negatively associated with the number of culture areas involved.

### *Proof*

While intercultural dependence may increase opportunities to promote economic development, it also raises risks and transactional costs. This totally depends on the internal and external conditions concerned. As a result some economies will inevitably face frustrations in dealing with intercultural relations, and these frustrations will be magnified for small culture areas. But such culture areas stand to gain more from intercultural trade and finance than their larger counterparts, since they face tighter resource and market-size constraints. At the same time these economies may feel any disruption the global economy generates far more intensely.[2]

Theoretically, if different groups of people have markedly differing attitudes as well as different cultural values, the adoption of a common standard and the socioeconomic coordination between them are not likely to be emphasized. From the political perspective, different culture areas may articulate their political demands by creating new parties or polarizing existing ones. As a result political systems with a small number of parties are more likely to offer moderate, comprehensive policies that reflect the interests of the nation rather than particular factions.

In order to have a concrete differentiation between economies differing in number of culture areas, let us suppose that the stability of economic relation between any pair of culture areas is expressed by $r_j$ ($0 \leq r_j < 1$). Thus, the overall stability of multicultural relations ($R$) of an economy with $N$ culture areas can be expressed by the product of all $r_j$ of the culture areas included in the economy, that is,

$$R(N) = \prod_{j=1}^{\sum_{i=1}^{N-1} i} r_j \qquad (4.2)$$

In Equation 4.2, '$\prod \ldots$' is the sign of the product of '$\ldots$'; $\sum_{i=1}^{N-1} i$ denotes the number of cultures in pairs. To make the expression simpler, let $r_j = r$ for all $j$. Then, Equation 4.2 becomes

$$R(N) = r^{\sum_{i=1}^{N-1} i} \qquad (4.3)$$

Obviously, Equation 4.3 shows that, since the value of $r$ ranges between 0 and 1, the overall stability of multicultural economic relations is negatively associated with the number of culture areas involved, that is, $R(N) < R(N-1) < \ldots R(3) < R(2)$. *QED.*

---

[2] For example, an economic shock that may feel like only a ripple to an enormous economy like the United States, or even to a large developing economy like China, is a tidal wave for an economy the size of Ghana or Bangladesh.

## Proposition 3

The output level of an economy with different culture areas usually decreases with respect to the number of culture areas involved, if the culture-related barriers exist. In more precise words, the largest output of the economy with N culture areas is lower than that of the economy with N-1 culture areas.

### *Proof*

See Annex 1 of Guo (2006).

## Proposition 4

Multicultural economic cooperation usually becomes more profitable with respect to the number of culture areas involved. In other words, after all the culture-related barriers are removed, the increase of output of an economy with $N$ culture areas is larger than that of the economy with $N$-1 culture areas.

### *Proof*

Suppose that the total output of all the $N$ sub-areas in the area now becomes $F^{**}$. Since the culture-related barriers are removed, the largest outputs of all types of cross-border areas are now the same, that is, $F_N^{**}=F_{N-1}^{**}=...F_2^{**}=F_1^*$, where $F_1^*$ (that is, the largest output of the 1-d spatial system) is defined in Guo (2006). As a result the increase of output of the area involving $N$ sub-areas becomes

$$F_N^{**}-F_N^*=F_1^*-F_N^*>0. \tag{4.4}$$

After combining Formulas 4.4 and Proposition 3, we have $F_1^*-F_N^*>F_1^*-F_{N-1}^*>...$ $F_1^*-F_i^*>...> F_1^*-F_2^*>0$. *QED.*

## 4.3. MULTICULTURAL RISKS AND CHALLENGES

Race, ethnicity, religion and language have affected the division of the world economy into separate entities as much as history, physical terrain, political fiat or conquest, resulting in sometimes arbitrary and imposed boundaries. Boundary, borderland resource and territorial disputes vary in intensity from managed or dormant to violent or militarized. Most disputes over the alignment of political boundaries concern short segments and are today less common and less hostile than borderland resource and territorial disputes. Undemarcated, indefinite, porous and unmanaged boundaries, however, encourage illegal cross-border activities, uncontrolled migration and confrontation. Territorial disputes may evolve from historical and/or cultural claims, or they may be brought on by resource competition. Regional discord directly affects the sustenance and welfare of local populations, often leaving the world community to cope with the consequent problems: refugees, hunger, disease, impoverishment, deforestation and desertification.

Scholars on international and intercultural relations worldwide employs various approaches. Much fruitful work has developed through large-scale statistical studies. Our analysis is based on an analytic narrative, rather than a large-scale statistical, approach. We intend to choose cases where disputes or conflicts are either still quite active or have been peacefully settled in order to learn from both kinds. A case-based, time-limited approach helps to explain patterns of conflict resolution.[3] In the remainder of this section, we attempt to provide empirical evidence that supports the hypothesis that culture sometimes may be an obstacle to multicultural development. In sum, four case studies will be conducted, which include (i) the genocide in Rwanda, (ii) the territorial disputes in Jammu and Kashmir, (iii) the struggle for fresh water in the Middle East, and (iv) the multicultural risks at the Oceania.

## Case Study 1

The genocide in Rwanda was unleashed on 6 April 1994, immediately following the shooting down of a plane carrying President Habyarimana and Burundi President Cyprien near the Kigali Airport. On the following day the Primer, a moderate Hutu, was assassinated and ten Belgian soldiers tortured and executed by Rwandan militiamen. The Belgian contingent (the best-equipped in the United Nations Assistance Mission for Rwanda – UNAMIR – founded on 5 October 1993, following the UN resolution 872) decided to withdraw unilaterally from the UNAMIR. The situation continued to deteriorate and killing of Tutsi civilians escalated. Nonetheless, the discussion of UN Security Council on Rwanda in April 1994 had little to do with civilian massacres, but focused on a cease-fire between the government and the Rwanda Patriotic Front (RPF) — formed in 1988 by Tutsi refugees and dissident Hutus in Uganda.

Furthermore, on 21 April 1994, the UN Security Council unanimously decided to reduce the size of UNAMIR from 2539 to 270 troops. Resolution 918 (which set a maximum of 5500 forces) was adopted on 17 May, too late to prevent the massacre since most of the killings took place between early April and mid-May. In total, the genocide lasted for about 100 days, and ended with the Tusti-dominated RPF defeating the Hutu-led government and declared a unilateral cease-fire on 18 July. At least 800,000 Rwandans were killed, mostly by *interahamwe* (those who stand together) militias – gangs of youths armed with machetes, guns and other weapons supplied by officials loyal to President Habyarimana.

It has been generally believed that colonial authorities were largely responsible for creating tribal identities among the Tutsis and the Hutus. Much has been written about the artificial birth of the Hutu-Tutsi split as part of the divide-and-conquer strategy of Belgium, the colonial power. For us, what is notable is the rich anecdotal evidence that physical attributes play a critical role in the conflict. On average, 'Tutsis' are taller and more slender; they have somewhat lighter skin, and thinner noses. Before colonization the terms 'Hutu' and 'Tutsi' did not bear the same political meaning as they do today. In order to affirm their authority, colonial rulers redistributed power and privilege between the two groups. Belgian governed the region through Tutsis who, with more European features, were considered to be born to rule (Lee, 2002, p. 83). Even during the struggle to regain independence from Belgium, Hutu-Tutsi divisions in Rwanda were apparent. Following the death of Mwami

---

[3] This is not, of course, to say that statistical analyses are unhelpful. On the contrary, they have brought out some intriguing features. Consider, for example, Hensel's findings in his fine study of patterns in territorial disputes in the Western Hemisphere between 1816 and 1992 (Hensel, 2001).

(king) Matara III in 1959, farm workers organized by the Party of the Hutu Emancipation Movement (Parmehutu) revolted against Tutsi rule and seized power in 1961. Independence was granted in July 1962, resulting in empowerment of the Hutu majority and ending the dominance of Tutsi minority. In the wake of bloody interethnic conflicts between 1963 and 1967, thousands of Tutsis were killed and tens of thousands fled into neighboring countries, mostly in Uganda.

## Case Study 2

With a total land area similar to that of Guyana or North and South Korea combined, Jammu and Kashmir has three major ethnic areas: Ladakh in the northwest, which is majority Buddhist; the Kashmir Valley (controlled by India) and the part now controlled by Pakistan, which is majority Muslim, and Jammu in the south, which is majority Hindu. Pakistan, India, and China each claim all, or part of, the former princely state of Jammu and Kashmir. A cease-fire agreement in 1949 divided the region into two sectors: the eastern part administered by India as the state of Jammu and Kashmir, and the western part administered by Pakistan and known as Azad (Free) Kashmir and the Northern Areas.

In 1947, as part of the de-colonization process, British India was divided into India and Pakistan. At the time of the partition the rulers of nearly five hundred odd princely states, which were directly under the British were advised to join either India or Pakistan, keeping in mind proximity, the demographic profile and other factors. Most states were integrated into either India or Pakistan. However there had been problems for a couple of states to be cross-nationally re-deployed. The state of Jammu and Kashmir had a Hindu Maharajah, but majority of its people were Muslims. Both India and Pakistan had contiguous borders with it. From 1947 to 1948 the state of Jammu and Kashmir was attacked by a large number of tribesmen supported by regular Pakistani troops. When Pakistani regulars and tribesmen were within gunshot of Srinagar (the capital of Jammu and Kashmir), the Maharajah sought India's assistance in exchange for acceding to India.

In 1950 China occupied the northeast portion of Kashmir, a region known as Aksai Chin. Aksai Chin is a region located at the junction of the People's Republic of China, Pakistan, and India. It is administered by China and claimed by India. Aksai Chin was part of the former princely state of Jammu and Kashmir. Accounting for about 16.9 percent of Jammu and Kashmir's land area and almost negligible population, Aksai Chin came under Chinese rule in the 1950s. In 1963 Pakistan ceded to China another 2.33 percent land claimed by India. Present distribution of land area controlled by India, Pakistan and China is as 45.62 percent, 35.15 percent and 19.23 percent, respectively.[4]

Aksai Chin is currently under the administration of the People's Republic of China, with the vast majority of it as a part of Hetian county, in the Xinjiang Uygur autonomous region. India claims the area as a part of Ladakh district of the state of Jammu and Kashmir. Aksai Chin is of strategic importance to China because it contains National Highway No. 219, a major road connecting Tibet and Xinjiang Uygur autonomous regions. In 1962 there was a short border war between China and India. The border war lasted from 20 October to 22 November, costing 1853 lives, and it ended with a Chinese victory and the birth of the Line of

Actual Control (LAC). Since 1962 the LAC has been the current, though disputable, boundary dividing Chinese and Indian occupied zones in the contested territories (Guo, 2009b).

India has repeatedly claimed the whole Jammu and Kashmir as an integral part of India. India's stand is based that the state of Jammu and Kashmir represented by the Maharajah acceded to the Union of India, and that India. By way of contrast, Pakistan has its own security concerns. If the whole area of Kashmir were to go to India then it would pose a direct threat to Pakistan's North West Frontier and Pakistani Punjab. On the other hand if Pakistan had the whole area of Kashmir it could threaten Indian Punjab. From the resource point of view all the three great rivers – Chenab Jhelun, Indus and Sutlei – flowing into Pakistan originate from Jammu and Kashmir and therefore of vital importance to Pakistan. Many attempts have been made to craft out the peace of the Jammu and Kashmir between the two warring nations. However, there had hardly been any progress on the conflict resolution.

The China-Indian relations have been shadowed by territorial disputes. India lays claim to vast territories of land that is in the possession of China. These territories are of interest to India because of its water resources. However, as called the 'White Desert', the whole region of the Aksai Chin is almost uninhabited and is considered of more importance for China than for India. In spite of many unresolved differences, both sides have instituted enough cooperative mechanisms since the 1990s to ensure peace and tranquility in the region. Hence the China-India border dispute, though important, is not an urgent question.

## Case Study 3

The Jordan River originates in the mountains of eastern Lebanon. As the Jordan flows south through the entrance to the Great Syrian Rift Valley, it is fed from underground sources and small streams at various points in Jordan, Israel, Syria, and Lebanon. The Jordan's main sources are the Hasbani River, which flows from Lebanon to Israel, the Banyas River, which flows from Syria to Israel, the Dan River, which begins and flows inside Israel, and the Yarmouk River, which begins near the Golan Heights and flows to the Jordan River. Following its flow into Lake Galilee, the Jordan River continues southward into the center of the Jordan Valley, forming the border between the western edge of Jordan and eastern side of Israel including part of the Palestinian Autonomy. The Jordan River continues flowing into the Dead Sea, and then through a smaller stream it flows eventually into the Red Sea.

The Jordan River is the largest and longest river that flows in Israel and Jordan. Moreover, it is the only river within Israel that has a permanent flow year round. The Jordan River supplies Israel and Jordan with the vast majority of their water. Inside Israel's border, over 50 percent of water sources rely on rain, which falls outside of the Israeli border. Israel depends on water supply, which either comes from rivers that originate outside the border, or from disputed lands. For the State of Jordan, the Jordan River supplies about 75 percent of its needs. In contrast to Israel, only 36 percent of the total river flow originates outside the Jordanian border. However Jordan had only 260 cubic meters per capita of water availability for the year of 1990, which is almost one-fourth less than the minimum water requirement for an industrial nation (Grunfeld, 1997).

---

[4] Based on Ramdas (2005).

The struggle for fresh water in the Middle East was a primary cause of military disputes in the region. The Syrian government, inside its borders, attempted to divert the Banyas River, which is one of the Jordan River's tributaries. This was followed by three Israeli army and air force attacks on the site of the diversion. These incidents regarding water issues led up to the outbreak of the Six-Day War in June 1967 between Israel against Syria, Jordan, and Egypt. During that war, Israel captured the Golan Heights and the site of the Banyas headwaters, which enabled Israel to prevent the diversion of the Banyas by the Syrians. Israel also gained control of the West Bank, the Jordan River as well as the northern bank of the Yarmouk (Cooley, 1984, p. 16). Like other conflicts that revolve around scarce resources, there are ways to determine the likelihood of water issues escalating into a large-scale multi-national conflict. The probability that the degree of scarcity of water to a region, the need of several nations to share one fresh water source, the military or economic power of the state that controls the water, and existence of other fresh water sources aids the ability to predict the causes and possible solutions for these conflicts.

The Middle East dispute is a multi-state one since not only Israel and Jordan have attempted to control the river, but other parties, such as Syria and the Palestinians, have also taken part in trying to control sections of the river. Israeli and Jordanian attempts to control the river were illustrated by several different constructions such as the King Talal dam, built by the Jordanians, and the National Water Carrier, built by the Israelis. These attempts led to reactions that often were followed by militant attacks. The Israeli War of Independence in 1948 and the Six-Day War in 1967 highlight this dispute as a 'war threat' conflict, in which the need for water often encouraged actual war between states.[5] Control over the cross-border resources by one party usually indicates a decrease in the amount of the resources for the other party, which can be described as a zero-sum game. For example, in the year following the Six-Day War, Israel increased its water use from the Jordan River by 33 percent (Grunfeld, 1997). As the outcomes of the war, Jordan not only lost the significant access to the water from the Jordan River, it but also had to terminate the plans to expand usage of the river and its canal system. In addition, Palestinians also took control over large sectors of the Jordan Valley that held these source waters.

The scarcity of fresh water in the Middle East is connected not only to meteorological and geographic but also to demographic factors. Throughout most of the region rainfall is irregular. The rainy season is short, between 6-8 months a year, and rainfall varies between 250-400 mm annually. This is insufficient for basic agriculture, which requires at least 400 mm of regular rainfall. Irrigated agriculture is further restricted because there are few major rivers (Grunfeld, 1997). Furthermore, there is the issue of the vastly expanding population. This population growth stems from two sources. In Jordan the population increase is due to natural birthrate but in Israel large waves of immigrants in the years following the Second World War have increased the population. The prospect of substantial increases in water demand in the coming years renders it imperative that a solution be found to Palestine's water shortage. Both the Israeli and Palestinian populations are expected to increase dramatically. This is expected to heighten demand on water resources.

The Middle East is a region of ideological, religious, economic and geo-political differences. In the past decades, Israel and Jordan have searched for alternatives to maximize the use of fresh water from the Jordan River. However each country has developed

---

[5] Based on Grunfeld (1997).

independent solutions all of which are very expensive. Both Israel and Jordan have come to realize that water resources need protection (Abu-Taleb, 1994, p. 37). Nevertheless, the two countries posses different standards of living: Israel, a first world country, concerns itself with environmental issues and sustainable solutions, while Jordan, a developing country, does not have the ability to deal with such problems (Copaken, 1996, p. 86).

The Palestinian people believe that the West Bank ought to be a part of their sovereign nation, and that the presence of Israeli military control is a violation of their right to self-determination. By contrast, Israel argues that its presence is justified because: the disputed territories have not been part of any state since the time of the Ottoman Empire and that Israel's eastern border has never been defined by anyone. According to the 1995 Israeli-Palestinian Agreement, the Israeli army should redeploy from the seven largest Palestinian towns on the West Bank, including a partial withdrawal from Hebron; and tentatively, from 450 smaller towns and villages. Together, these two areas contain the great bulk of the West Bank Palestinians – but less than 30 percent of the territory (Israel-PLO, 1995). The rest of the West Bank, which includes the Israeli settlement and so-called state land, is still under Israeli army control. The future status of the West Bank, together with the Gaza Strip on the Mediterranean shore, has been the subject of negotiation between the Palestinians and Israelis, although the current Road Map for Peace, proposed by the "Quartet" comprising the United States, Russia, the European Union, and the United Nations, envisions an independent Palestinian state in these territories living side by side with Israel.

## Case Study 4

Oceania is home to a group of peoples and cultures, with its over 14 independent small island countries being divided by three commonly recognized sub-regional constituents: Melanesia (Fiji, Papua New Guinea or PNG, the Solomon Islands and Vanuatu), Micronesia (Kiribati, Federated States of Micronesia, Marshall Island and Palau) and Polynesia (Samoa, Tonga, the Cook Islands and Tuvalu). With more than 2000 languages spoken across the region, the population of these countries is highly fragmented into various geographical, ethnic, linguistic, religious and political entities (ODN, 2006, p. 241). These characteristics have influenced the Oceania's institutional development path through two main channels. First, ethnic cleavages impinge on the political economy of reforms to the extent that the typical winners and losers of distributional struggles brought about by market reforms overlap with the inherited ethnic conflicts. Second, the cultural heritage is often at odds with the institutional changes that are necessary for the market economy to work properly.

In some countries of the Oceania region, there is a patent contradiction between the traditional definition of property rights and private property rights that are central to a market economy. Since most of the land is held under customary rights, it is not surprising that land tenure has become a key legal obstacle to reform. Customary arrangements differ from one clan to another so the drafting of national legislation to harmonize land claims within clans and between tribes, squatter encroachments and access arrangements to resources are in themselves the direct cause of disputes leading to tribal warfare, civil unrest and anarchy (the Solomon Islands and PNG); major disputes with mining and logging companies (PNG and Vanuatu); vacating plantation and arable agriculture development (PNG, Fiji and the Solomon Islands); Corruption and cronyism (PNG, the Solomon Islands, Fiji and Vanuatu);

and access to tourism infrastructure (Fiji). This has been particularly evident in the case of Fiji with regard to communal ownership of land. Indigenous groups (the majority) customarily own land and other natural resources (including marine resources) in Fiji. Fiji citizens of other ethnicity can only legitimately make use of these resources if the ethnic Fijian owners give them permission to do so. The concept of the *vanua*, inclusive of the land with its flora and fauna, rivers and adjacent seas, the people (the ancestors, those living and those yet to be born) and their customs, norms, beliefs, social organization (the way of the land or *vaka vanua*), sacred sites and sentiments continues to evoke strong emotional attachment (ODN, 2006, p. 242).

The ethnic constraints, together with geographical, political and economic features, have significantly contributed to shaping the depth, scope and sequencing of reforms, and, more often than not, the consequences have been negative concerning reform outcomes. In Fiji, for example, the privatization of government businesses was launched prior to macroeconomic stabilization and the liberalization of domestic and external markets, resulting in an unfavorable environment for business expansion. The bad timing and sequencing of reforms resulted in increased poverty and unemployment. In Fiji political and ethnic conflicts resulted in the wastage of public sector resources that severely limited the funds destined to ameliorate the consequences of reforms on employment and poverty (ODN, 2006, p. 243). The squandering of public funds by political institutions left limited funds available for the improvement of infrastructure and for the promotion of private sector participation. When funds were used to compensate the distributional effects of reforms, the allocation tended to show an ethnic bias.

## 4.4. MULTICULTURAL OPPORTUNITIES

There have been two divergent views on the development of multiculturally based economies. On the one hand, there is a concern that cultural differences would vanish under the onslaught of modernization. To this end, some pessimists simply assume that cultural beliefs and practices are incompatible with modern rationality, which demands not only secularization but also secularism. On the other hand, globalization also has been accompanied by a resurgence of local culture. As a result, optimists believe that there is or will be a growing realization that local cultures play an important part in guiding human action and holding the fabric of society together. Development, through inappropriate policies, could destroy some cultural values. However, appropriate policies, programs and projects could help cultural and economic development to benefit from each other.

The empirical evidence from modern times, as represented by four individual economies shown below, suggests that (i) small, low-inequality economies (such as Switzerland) could benefit from cultural diversity; (ii) small, backward economies (such as Singapore and Hong Kong) could benefit from the radical and large-scale cultural influences from the outside world; and (iii) large, backward economies (such as China) could benefit from the gradual and incremental cultural influences from the outside world.

## Case Study 1

Hong Kong consists of the island of Hong Kong (83 sq km), Stonecutters' Island, Kowloon Peninsula, and the New Territories on the adjoining mainland. The island of Hong Kong was ceded to Britain in 1841. Stonecutters' Island and Kowloon were annexed in 1860, and the New Territories, which are mainly agricultural lands, were leased from China in 1898 for 99 years. On 1 July 1997, Hong Kong was returned to China. The vibrant capitalist enclave retains its status as a free port, with its laws to remain unchanged for 50 years.

Western influence in China came about at the beginning of the 15th and 16th centuries due to the increased trade in Chinese products, such as silk and tea through the Silk Road that stretched from northwestern China to eastern Europe. The Europeans were interested in Hong Kong's safe harbor located on the trade routes of the Far East, thus establishing a trade enterprise between Western businessmen and China. The Portuguese were the first to reach China in 1555, but the British dominated foreign trade in the southern region of Guangdong during the early stages of Western connection in China.

Ships from the British East India Company were stationed on the Indian Coast after Emperor Kangxi (reign 1654 – 1722) of the Qing dynasty (1644 – 1911) opened trade on a limited basis in Guangzhou. Fifteen years later, the company was allowed to build a storage warehouse outside Guangzhou. The Westerners were given limited preferences and had to adhere to many Chinese rules and policies, which include "private trade and contacts between Chinese and foreign businessmen are illegal"; "foreigners' activities in China are only allowed on the conditions that 'At most ten foreigners may take a walk together near their hotel three days a month on the 8th, 18th and 28th'; "Overseas businessmen should not stay in Guangdong in winter"; and "Women from foreign countries are prohibited to enter this country", and so on.[6] Besides, Chinese rulers also banned foreigners from learning the Chinese language in fear of their potential bad influences.

Chinese commodities, namely porcelains and landscaped-furnishings, were popular among the European aristocrats. The British East India Company tried to equalize its huge purchases from China by doubling its sale of opium to the Chinese. The sale of opium saw a huge success by the beginning of the 19th Century. Fearful of the outflow of silver, the Chinese emperor banned the drug trade in 1799 but to no avail. Following the end of the first Opium War, the Treaty of Nanjing in 1842 ceded Hong Kong to Britain in perpetuity. With the involvement of the British, Hong Kong prospered. Many companies transferred from Guangzhou to Hong Kong, enabling the British colony to begin a prime Asian entrepot. Hostilities between the British and the Chinese of China continued to heighten, leading to the Second Opium War. In 1860, the "Convention of Peking", Britain gained Kowloon, Stonecutters Island and some small islands. In 1898 Britain acquired, under the "Treaty of Peking", what is known as the New Territories and 236 associated islands on a 99-year lease.

China has always maintained that the three treaties on Hong Kong were signed under pressure, and thus unjust. In 1984, the Joint Declaration signed by Britain and China agreed that the sovereignty of Hong Kong would revert back to China in 1997. On 1 July 1997 Hong Kong become a Special Administrative Region (SAR) of the People's Republic of China. The Joint Declaration also provides that for 50 years after 1997, Hong Kong's lifestyle will

---

[6] See *Guangxu Da Qing Huidian Shili* (vol. 775, p. 4 and vol. 776, p. 13)

remain unchanged. The territory will enjoy a high degree of autonomy, except in foreign and defense affairs, and China's socialist system and policies will not be practiced in the SAR.

The constant influx from China of capital and manpower led to the establishment of light manufacturing throughout the territory by the 1950s and the 1960s. At the same time, Hong Kong's tax policies began to attract growing foreign investment further adding to the territories rapid growth. In the 1950s Hong Kong began in earnest a new career as a manufacturing and industrial center. Textiles, electronics, watches, and many other low-priced goods stamped "Made in Hong Kong" flowed from the territory in ever-increasing amounts. During the 1980s Hong Kong started to work with China on a series of joint projects that brought the two closer together. Today the financial service industries have taken over from manufacturing as Hong Kong's main enterprise. This small territory was the first developing economy to enter the world's top 10 economies. And while much of the manufacturing is now likely to be done across the border and beyond, Hong Kong is still one of the world's largest exporters. Social program continue to raise the standard of living, which is comparable to that of many Western countries.

## Case Study 2

The Republic of Singapore consists of the main island of Singapore, off the southern tip of the Malay Peninsula between the South China Sea and the Indian Ocean, and 58 nearby islands, with a total land area of 624 sq km. Among Singapore's about 4.55 million populations, 76.8% are Chinese, 13.9% Malay and 7.9% Indian. Major languages include Chinese (58.8%, of which Mandarin 35.0%, Hokkien 11.4%, Cantonese 5.7%, Teochew 4.9% and other Chinese dialects 1.8%), English 23%, Malay 14.1%, Tamil 3.2%. Religions include Buddhist (43%), Islam (15%), Taoist (9%), Hindu (4%), and Christian (15%).[7]

By the 14th century, Singapore had become part of the mighty Sri Vijayan empire and was known as Temasek ("Sea Town"). Located at the natural meeting point of sea routes at the tip of the Malay Peninsula, Singapore had long known visits from a wide variety of sea craft, from Chinese junks, Indian vessels, Arab dhows and Portuguese battleships to Buginese schooners. The British, who were extending their dominion in India, and whose trade with China in the second half of the 18th century was expanding, saw the need for a port of call in this region to refit, revitalize and protect their merchant fleet, as well as to forestall any advance by the Dutch in the region. As a result, they established trading posts in Penang in 1786 and Singapore in 1819, and captured Malacca from the Dutch in 1795.

British and Dutch interest in the region grew with the spice trade, and the trading post of Singapore was founded in 1819 by Sir Stamford Raffles. Singapore proved to be a prized settlement. By 1820, it was earning revenue, and three years later, its trade surpassed that of Penang. In 1824, Singapore's status as a British possession was formalized by two new treaties by which (i) the Dutch withdrew all objections to the British occupation of Singapore; and (ii) Sultan Hussein and Temenggong Abdu'r Rahman ceded the island out right to the British in return for increased cash payments and pensions.

The policy of free trade attracted merchants from all over Asia and from as far a field as the U.S. and the Middle East. By 1824, just five years after the founding of modern Singapore,

---

[7] Source: The website of the Singaporean government.

the population had grown from a mere 150 to 10,000.[8] In 1832, Singapore became the center of government for the Straits Settlements of Penang, Malacca and Singapore. The opening of the Suez Canal in 1869 and the advent of telegraph and steamship increased Singapore's importance as a center for the expanding trade between Europe and East Asia. Singapore had been the site of military action in the 14th century when it became embroiled in the struggle for the Malay Peninsula between Siam (now Thailand), and the Java-based Majapahit Empire.

With the development of rubber planting, especially after the 1870s, it also became the main sorting and export center in the world for rubber. Before the end of the 19th century, Singapore was experiencing unprecedented prosperity and trade expanded eightfold between 1873 and 1913. The prosperity attracted immigrants from areas around the region. The peace and prosperity ended when Japanese aircraft bombed the sleeping city in 1941. It remained under Japanese occupation for three and a half years. The British forces returned in September 1945 and Singapore came under the British Military Administration. When the period of military administration ended in March 1946, the Straits Settlements was dissolved. After the war, Singapore became a Crown Colony.

The growth of nationalism led to self-government in 1959 and on 9 August 1965, Singapore became an independent republic. Independent Singapore was admitted to the United Nations on 21 September 1965, and became a member of the Commonwealth of Nations on 15 October 1965. In August 1967, Singapore joined Indonesia, Malaysia, the Philippines and Thailand to form the Association of Southeast Asian Nations. Thereafter commenced Singapore's struggle to survive and prosper on its own. It also had to create a sense of national identity and consciousness among a disparate population of immigrants.

Singapore's strategy for survival and development was essentially to take advantage of its strategic location and the favorable world economy. A massive industrialization program was launched with the extension of the Jurong industrial estate and the creation of smaller estates in Kallang Park, Tanjong Rhu, Redhill, Tiong Bahru and Tanglin Halt. The one-party Parliament emerged from the 1968 general election. Singapore's strict rules of civil obedience also drew criticism from those who said the nation's prosperity was achieved at the expense of individual freedoms. However, since the 1970s, Singapore, as a politically stable state, has enjoyed a high rate of economic growth. Singapore has developed into one of the cleanest, safest, and most economically prosperous cities in Asia.

## Case Study 3

Switzerland is a small country situated in the heart of Central Europe. Cultural connections with its neighbors (Germany, France, Italy and Austria) have resulted in a multicultural identity for Switzerland. For example, four languages (German 64%, French 20%, Italian 7% (all of which are official), and Romansch 0.5%) are spoken in different regions. The ethnic groups include German (65%), French (18%), Italian (10%), Romansch (1%) and other (6%). Major religions are Roman Catholic (42%), Protestant (35%), Muslim 4% and Orthodox (2%).[9]

---

[8] Source: www.singoriya.com/singapore_history.php. Assessed on 12 April 2009.

[9] Source: The website of the Swiss government.

The history of Switzerland has been influenced at different points by its European neighbors. Called Helvetia in ancient times, Switzerland became a league of cantons in the Holy Roman Empire in AD 1291. Fashioned around the nucleus of three German forest districts of Schwyz, Uri and Unterwalden, the Swiss Confederation slowly added new cantons. In the period between 1315 and 1388, the group of cantons that comprise Switzerland inflicted a series of crushing defeats on the armies of the Dukes of Austria, resulting in several other cantons joining the original three in the Swiss Confederation. Their location left them well placed to interfere in the interminable power struggles of the period, and their influence was backed up by the formidable reputation of their army – probably the most powerful in Europe at the end of the 15th century.

The Reformation led to a division in Swiss society between the followers of the reformer Zwingli (later, Calvin) and the Catholics. The bitter controversy considerably reduced Swiss influence in Europe and the Confederation was lucky to survive a series of defeats. In 1648 the Treaty of Westphalia gave Switzerland its independence from the Holy Roman Empire. In the following 100 years, little progress was made towards a formal union of the cantons and the religious controversy rumbled on; the dominance of the Protestants was not established until after the Second Villmergen War in 1712. In 1815, the Congress of Vienna guaranteed the neutrality and recognized the independence of Switzerland. In the revolutionary period of 1847, the Catholic cantons seceded and organized a separate union called the Sonderbund, but they were defeated and rejoined the federation. In 1848, the new Swiss constitution established a union modeled on that of the U.S. The federal constitution of 1874 established a strong central government while giving large powers of control to each canton. National unity and political conservatism grew as the country prospered from its neutrality.

Switzerland has a typically mixed economy with a bias towards light and craft-based industries. In the manufacturing sector, the machinery and equipment industry specializes in precision and advanced technology products: machine tools, printing and photographic equipment, electronic control and medical equipment. There is also a substantial chemical industry. Swiss firms have proved particularly adept at exploiting niche markets across a wide range of industries and products. The country is highly industrialized and heavily dependent on exports of finished goods. The service sector is dominated by banking, where the particular reputation of the Swiss banking community for discretion has attracted large deposits. Switzerland remains one of Europe's major financial centers.

Thanks to its multiculturalism policies towards ethnicity, language and religion, which combine many aspects of the heterogeneous European societies, Switzerland plays an important role as the headquarters of numerous international fora and serves to promote the cause of moderation between different parts of the West Europe. Strict neutrality policy enabled Switzerland to dodge two world wars in the 20th century. Geneva was the seat of the League of Nations (later the European headquarters of the United Nations) and of a number of international organizations. In 2000, the Swiss voted against a plan to cut the number of foreigners in the country to 18% of the population.[10] Since 1970, four similar anti-immigration plans have failed. Obviously, it seems unlikely that similar plans could have been approved in other rich but culturally less diversified nations (such as Japan or South Korea). In 2002, the Swiss abandoned their long-held neutrality to become the 190th member of the UN.

---

[10] In the early 2000s foreigners made up about 20%.

The principal long-term question in Swiss politics has been relations with the European Union, which accounts for 50 per cent of Switzerland's trade. The main popular concerns are the likely erosion of cantonal power (a central feature of the Swiss political system), immigration levels and the loss of the country's cherished neutrality. Switzerland is not a member of the European Union, although nearly two-thirds of its exports are sold to EU countries. In 1992, Switzerland gained admission to the IMF and World Bank. However, a referendum, held in 1992, rejected even membership of the European Economic Area – a free-trade agreement created to reduce the economic barriers between the EU and the European Free Trade Association (EFTA), to which Switzerland belongs.

Given Switzerland's continuing prosperity, economic arguments are rarely heard, although there is a broad acceptance – especially in the financial community – that the Euro will become a standard feature of commercial life in the near future. In 2001, two years after the inauguration of the Euro, the Swiss people voted – again in a referendum – to enhance links with the EU while endorsing a promise by the major parties that they would never countenance actually joining the EU.

## Case Study 4

China has a long and prosperous past. Its religious package, aiming at a harmonious balance between Confucianism, Buddhism and Taoism, worked very well for a long period. Probably because of this, the Chinese remained intoxicated by past prosperity, even when it lagged far behind the Western nations. This kind of ethnocentrism and self-satisfaction resulted in a long period in which China was a typical autarkic society. China was forced to open up to the outside world at the end of the First Opium War (1840–42). Since then, the Chinese economy has been transformed as a result of the destruction of feudalism. Foreign capital flowed gradually into the mainland, followed by the penetration of Western culture, representing the first signal for Chinese industrialization. Unfortunately, because of long civil wars as well as the Japanese invasion, Chinese economic construction had not been given priority in the first half of the 20th century.

As soon as the PRC was found on 1 October 1949, the Chinese government switched off almost all economic ties with the capitalist world. Affected by the Korean War (1950–53) and the Taiwan strait crisis, the Eastern belt stagnated, compared with most parts of the Western belt which benefited geographically to a large extent from China's close relations with the former USSR. However, it should be noted that China's foreign trade with the Soviet-type economies usually remained at a minimum level, aiming at just supplementing any gap between domestic supply and demand. Such trade reflected natural resource endowments more than anything else. Therefore, China's close ties with the socialist economies did not result in significant economic effects on the Western belt. During the period from the early 1960s to the late 1970s, China practiced autarkic socialism as a result of the Sino-USSR dispute as well as the 'self-reliance and independence' strategy.

China's economic internationalization strategy began to experience dramatic changes in the late 1970s when the top Chinese policy-makers suddenly found that the Chinese economy, after having been socialistically constructed for almost 30 years, had lagged far behind not only the Western but also those once backward economies along the western coast of the Pacific. It is now generally believed that the Chinese outward-oriented development policy has been borrowed, in part, from East Asia's newly industrialized economies such as South Korea, Taiwan, Singapore and Hong Kong. In order to attract foreign investment, China enacted the 'Law of the People's Republic of China Concerning the Joint Ventures with Chinese and Foreign Investment' in 1979. Also in this year, Guangdong and Fujian provinces were granted 'special policies and flexible measures' in foreign economic affairs. On 26 December 1979, the Guangdong provincial government proposed that a part of Shenzhen next to Hong Kong, Zhuhai next to Macau, and Santou be designed to experiment with a market-oriented economy with Chinese characteristics, namely, special economic zone (SEZ). Finally, this proposal was accepted by the National People's Congress (NPC) on 26 August 1980. At the same time, Xiamen in Southeast Fujian province *vis-à-vis* Taiwan also became a SEZ.

Thereafter, a series of open-door measures were implemented in the coastal area. In October 1983 Hainan Island, Guangdong province, was allowed to conduct some of the special foreign economic policies granted to the SEZs. In April 1984 14 coastal cities (including Tianjin, Shanghai, Dalian, Qinhuangdao, Yantai, Qingdao, Lianyungang, Nantong, Ningbo, Wenzhou, Fuzhou, Guangzhou, Ganjiang and Beihai) were designated as 'open cities'. In February 1985 three deltas of Yangtze River, Pearl River and South Fujian were approved as coastal economic development zones (EDZs). In March 1988 the EDZs of the three deltas were again approved to extensively cover larger areas while at the same time some cities and counties in Liaodong and Shandong peninsulas and Bohai Basin areas were allowed to open up economically to the outside world. In April 1988 the NPC approved the establishment of Hainan province which was organized as an SEZ with even more flexible policies than other SEZs. In April 1990 Shanghai's suggestion of speeding up the development of Pudong area using some of the SEZ's mechanisms was approved by the Chinese government.

Since the reform and open-door policies were introduced in 1978, China has basically formed a pattern featuring gradual advance from east to west, from SEZs, then to other coastal areas, and finally to the inland area. Figure 4.1 shows a spatial pattern of foreign trade in which provinces' ratios of trade to GDP are negatively related to their distances to nearest coastal port. A glance at the PRC's history reveals that China's economic stagnation and prosperity have been closely related to its policy of economic internationalization. More specifically, when an autarkic policy was implemented, economic stagnation occurred; when an outward-looking policy was introduced, economic prosperity would be achieved accordingly. China's regional economic performances have also been decided in this way.

Besides a 14,500 km coastline, China has over 22,000 km of international land boundaries through which nine frontier provinces are directly exposed to the outside world. Generally, cross-border economic cooperation and trade are naturally facilitated by the geographical factor as well as that people on both sides of the border often belong to the same minority group and share the same language and customs across the border. China's rapid border development has mainly benefited from its open-door policy and *râpprochement* with the neighboring countries since the mid-1980s. In 1984 the Chinese government promulgated the "Provisional Regulations for the Management of 'Small-volume' Border Trade" and opened hundreds of frontier cities and towns. In contrast to the eastern coastal development,

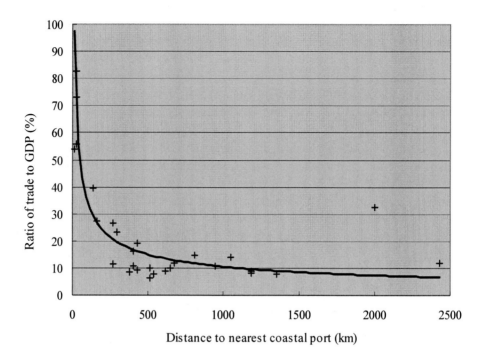

Figure 4.1. The spatial pattern of foreign trade in China.

which was mainly fueled by foreign direct investment, China's inland frontier development has been characterized by border trade with foreign neighbors. During the 1990s, China embarked on a deeper outward-looking policy in an attempt to promote the development in the frontier regions of the four provinces of Heilongjiang, Yunnan, Jilin and Liaoning and the four autonomous regions of Inner Mongolia, Xinjiang, Tibet and Guangxi. Since the early 1990s, favorable and flexible measures to manage cross-border trade and economic cooperation have been granted to those frontier provinces.

## 4.5. SUMMARY

By now, pluralism is an all-pervasive and enduring characteristic of almost all of over 200 nations and regions that make up the world community. However, ethnic, religious, and other forms of group identification can trigger a violent conflict when mobilized and manipulated to do so. Hence 'nation-building' that seeks to make all groups homogeneous, or allow one to dominate the others, is neither desirable nor feasible. A nation that depends on cultural diversity needs to create a sense of itself as a civic community, freed from any connotations of ethnic exclusivity. All its policy approaches should be grounded in this awareness. Defining and applying an effective cultural policy implies finding new ways of holding together multicultural societies based on pluralism.

The principle of pluralism, in the sense of tolerance and respect for and rejoicing over the plurality of cultures, is so important in dealings between countries that is also applies within countries, in the relations between different ethnic groups. These relations have become problematic in the course of development. In general, intercultural harmonization must follow at least two courses: (i) intercultural exchange, and (ii) mutual understanding. The intercultural contacts and exchanges are the basis for intercultural harmonization. But without mutual understanding, these contacts and exchanges would only but result in intercultural conflicts. Furthermore, more respect should be paid to the millions of indigenous peoples all over the world: it is imperative that their rights be protected, that more appropriate models be developed to promote their education, and that they have greater access to the tools of modern communication.

Intercultural conflict is usually attributed to the degree of cultural dissimilarity, since the latter implies a degree of difficulty that the disparate groups concerned have in communicating or cooperating with one another. Precisely, each culture possesses a common system of signifying and normative values, some shared basis (such as common history, language, race or ethnicity, religion) through which people identify themselves as members of a single group, and the will or decision to be primarily self-identified as a member of a given community. Ultimately, this may to some extent be traceable to a biological basis, since, in human societies, ascriptive ties are said to dampen coalition building and to inhibit compromise across groups (that cross-cutting cleavages promote), thus increasing chances for social conflict (Bollen and Jackman, 1985).

However, it is too arbitrary to say that cultural dissimilarity will inevitably result in intercultural conflicts. Where diverse groups have learned to live with each other and purse their differences within a stable political system cultural difference is likely to have a very small effect on intercultural conflict. This leads at once to the presumption that the so-called industrial democracies will be less sensitive to the measures of cultural diversity than a developing country in which cultural diversity leads to barriers to intranational contacts or, more strongly, to violence. Furthermore, as Shanker (1996) argues, since the cultural raw material for any civilization allows for various options, different patterns will emerge as people combine modern rationality with cultural heritage, economic progress with national identity. Through this process peoples and countries will come to share experience, to walk parallel rather than converging paths.

At its 26th session, in 1991, the General Conference of UNESCO adopted a resolution requesting the Director-General, in cooperation with the Secretary-General of the United Nations, to 'establish an independent World Commission on Culture and Development comprising women and men drawn from all regions and eminent in diverse disciplines, to prepare a World Report on Culture and Development and proposals for both urgent and long-term action to meet cultural needs in the context of development'. This request was endorsed by a resolution adopted by the General Assembly of the United Nations a few weeks later. The Commission began its work in the spring of 1993, focusing its international agenda on achieving a clearly defined set of goals. Foremost among them is to provide a permanent vehicle through which some of the key issues of culture and development can be explored and clarified. *Our Creative Diversity*, the Commission's first Report on Culture and Development, was designed to address a diversified audience across the world, ranging from community activists, field workers, artists and scholars to government officials and politicians. Its aim is to show them how culture shapes all our thinking, imagining and behavior. It is the transmission of behavior as well as a dynamic source of change, creativity, freedom and the awakening of innovative opportunities.

The central argument advanced in *Our Creative Diversity* is that development embraces not only access to goods and services, but also the opportunity to choose a full, satisfying, valuable and valued way of living together, thus encouraging the flourishing of human existence in all its forms and as a whole (WCCD, 1995). Even the goods and services stressed by the narrower, conventional view are valued because of what they contribute to our freedom to live in the manner to which we aspire. Culture, therefore, however important it may be as an instrument of development (or an obstacle to development), cannot ultimately be reduced to a subsidiary position as a mere promoter of (or an impediment to) economic growth. The role of culture is not exhausted as a servant of ends – though in a narrower sense of the concept this is one of its roles – but it is the social basis of the ends themselves.

In this chapter, we have argued that the cultural dissimilarity may result in both intercultural conflict and intercultural cooperation, depending on the internal and external conditions of all the cultures concerned. Specifically, intercultural cooperation will be sensitive to the measures of cultural difference in countries where cultural difference leads to serious intranational and international barriers. However, cultural dissimilarity would have a very small effect on conflict if the diverse groups have learned to live with each other in a stable political system. Rather, it even encourages cooperation for the groups intending to purse their difference through the utilization of intercultural comparative advantages.

Where there is willingness to compromise, there is still hope. The hope emerges when the peoples from all civilizations find themselves are not fundamentally so different after all. Both sides will come to understand this 'sameness' and their basic heterogeneity if they can make further progress in the worldwide dialogue and mutual understandings. It should be noted that although the various cultural groups in the world have some commonalties, it is unlikely that the cultural universalism would become a possibility in the foreseen future. Surely, it is time to learn how to let cultural diversity lead not to the clash of cultures, but to the peaceful coexistence and creativity!

# Chapter 5

# MANAGING CULTURAL
# AND ECONOMIC DIFFERENCES

Three blind men were asked to feel an elephant and report what they thought it was. The first blind person examined and manipulated the tail, noting its size and frayed end. It is a rope, he exclaimed! The second blind person concentrated on the leg, noting the knobby skin and its huge size. He concluded it was the trunk of a tree, and a large one at that. The third blind person handled the elephant's trunk the best he could because it wiggled and waggled. He reported that what was in front of him was a snake and it was pretty spry.

(An old fable)

## 5.1. LITERATURE REVIEW

### 5.1.1. Macroeconomic Effects of Cultural Diversity

A long line of assumptions have been made about the macroeconomic performances of cultural diversity. Much of it, as stated by Hagen (1986) and Cullen (1993), is attributed to the variety of competing demands on political and economic capital that must be met or on the difficulty that disparate groups have in communicating or cooperating. This hypothesis may trace back to a biological basis in which cooperation among animals is importantly influenced by genetic similarity (Wilson, 1980). There is strong empirical evidence that supports the above view. While there may be several reasons for high illiteracy (which is a clear obstacle to economic growth), it is likely that the imposition of different languages may be one of the reasons why literacy rates remain low in multicultural places. For example, In Andhra Pradesh, India's biggest state, the official language is Hindi; however, Urdu-speaking Muslims make up of at least 15 percent of the population, and constitute 50 percent more of the population in some large western cities such as Meeruta. Literacy rates in Andhra Pradesh rose from 21.2 percent to only 45.11 percent between 1961 and 1993, whereas in Kerala, where there is relatively little language conflict, the rise was from 46.8 percent to 90.59 percent (Saville, 2002, p. 203).

It is very easy to understand that culturally diverse societies are associated with political instability, which, as indicated in Nordlinger (1972) and Lijphart (1990), adversely affects economic growth. The detrimental influence of cultural diversity on economic growth may be transmitted by a proliferation of political parties, which interjects elements of political instability or political fragmentation into society. For example, Hannan and Carroll (1981) consider that the effectiveness of democratic institutions may be reduced if different groups in a society articulate their demands by creating separate political parties or by polarizing existing ones. However, there are quite different views, suggesting that a multiparty system may lead to moderation and political flexibility by allowing centrist factions to intervene as neutral arbiters (Horowitz, 1971).[1]

By way of contrast to the above hypotheses, there are also views on the positive effects of cultural diversity on economic growth. The potential benefits of heterogeneity come from variety in production (Alesina and Ferrara, 2005). Cultural diversities exist spatially and temporally, between and within nations in terms of economic availability, opportunities, access to power, resources and human existence. Although every cultural group runs the risk of being stereotyped because of shared commonalities, no group, culture, or person remains static or lives in isolation. Instead, all societies have interacted. History reveals similarities in societal structures, and differences in behavior and stages of development. Societies can and do benefit from the diversity and plurality of cultures that are discovering their own peculiarities and idiosyncrasies.

A number of scholars have empirically assessed the influence of cultural diversity on economic growth (Easterly and Levine, 1997; Bluedorn, 2001; Montalvo and Reynal-Querol, 2005; Alesina and Ferrara, 2005). The primary argument suggests that diverse states are more susceptible to development-inhibiting internal strife than their homogeneous counterparts are (Lijphart, 1977; and Lemco, 1991). Following Tocqueville (1873), Duetsch (1953), and Banks and Textor (1963), Adelman and Morris (1967) gathered the data for 74 less developed countries from 1957 to 1962 and rank each country on a 10-point ordinal scale of diversity. Their results, based on factor analysis, support their hypothesis: homogeneous countries typically had higher growth rates. Haug (1967) finds a negative correlation between per capita GNP and cultural diversity based on the data of 114 countries in 1963. Reynolds (1985) compares 37 less developed countries from 1950 to 1980 and, again, indicates that cultural diversity results in lower growth rates. He suggests that this may be due to a sense of alienation among peoples. In other words, reaching a consensus on policies favorable to economic development, especially for the long run, may be difficult when groups have different interpretations of the past and different goals for the future.

Among the existing studies on the correlation between cultural diversity and economic development, Lian and Oneal (1997) demonstrate quite a different scenario. They use the data of 98 countries from 1960 to 1985 and find that the growth rates in per capita GDP is not significantly related to ethnic, religious and linguistic differences. They then try to investigate whether the influence of cultural diversity on economic development might be indirect through the intervening factors of political instability or political fragmentation, which also shows no correlation. Obviously, their result could support an assumption that political instability and social conflict – with which economic development is closely associated – are not related to cultural difference. This assumption might be confirmed by the fact that the

---

[1] Cited from Lian and Oneal (1997).

proliferation of political groups can actually be stabilizing because it allows centrist parties to become arbiters in coalition governments (Horowitz, 1971).[2]

There are methodological reasons for the different results of the existing studies. Adelman and Morris (1967), for example, consider three indicators for cultural diversity (language, religion and ethnicity) and weigh linguistic attributes most heavily: countries where over 85 percent of the population spoke the dominant language, over 90 percent were of the same race and the society was bounded by a common religion were put in the most homogeneous group; countries in which 50 percent or fewer of the people spoke the same language were rated least homogeneous. In addition to language, race and religion, two nonascriptive characteristics (sectionalism and interest articulation) are examined in Haug (1967). Again, Haug emphasizes a country's linguistic characteristics vis-à-vis ethnic and religious divisions. Other studies, such as Hannan and Carroll (1981), Bollen and Jackman (1985) and Esman (1990), neglect one or more aspects of cultural diversity, focusing on either ethnic or ethnolinguistic cleavages. Lian and Oneal (1997) calculate each country's ethnic, linguistic and religious diversity score and then standardize the three measures of diversity by dividing each country's score by the highest score in that category to attain an average of these three standardized components.

However, there are reasons to believe that these predictions of the correlation between cultural diversity and economic development might have been misleading. One could be that the periods selected in these analyses were (or at least partly encompassed) the high tide of the Cold War, a time when global or regional economic development could only be a very special case and needs to be carefully investigated on this basis. Huntington (1996, p. 125) pointed out that countries could make choices according to their ideological preferences. It might, therefore, be wrong to apply Cold War era results to the post-Cold War period.

## 5.1.2. Macroeconomic Effects of Income Inequality

Substantial literature has analyzed the effects of income inequalities on macroeconomic performances, as reflected in rates of economic growth.[3] Most argue that greater income inequality is actually an impediment to economic growth. A seemingly plausible argument points to the existence of credit market failures such that people are unable to exploit growth-promoting opportunities for investment (see, for example, Benabou, 1996; Aghion et al., 1999; and Barro, 2000). With limited access to credit, the exploitation of investment opportunities depends on individuals' levels of assets and incomes. Specifically, poor households tend to forego human capital investments that offer relatively high rates of return. In this case, a distortion-free redistribution of assets and incomes from rich to poor tends to raise the quantity and average productivity of investment. With declining marginal products of capital, the output loss from the market failure will be greater for the poor. So the higher the proportion of poor people there are in the economy the lower the rate of growth (Ravallion, 2001).

---

[2] Similarly, Eckstein (1966) and Schattschneider (1960) propose that a two-party system is less stable than systems with more parties because decisions may appear to be zero-sum, straining the unity and peace of the society.

[3] Recent surveys of the theories on the effects of income inequality on economic growth would include Benabou (1996), Aghion et al. (1999), and Barro (2000)

A second way in which inequality could affect future growth is through political channels. The degree of inequality could affect the median voter's desired pattern of policies or it could determine individuals' ability to access political markets and participate in costly lobbying. If the mean income in an economy exceeds the median income, then a system of majority voting tends to favor redistribution of resources from rich to poor.[4] As the median voter's distance from the average capital endowment in the economy increases with the aggregate inequality of wealth, he or she will be led to approve a higher tax rate. This in turn could reduce incentives for productive investment, resulting in lower growth. If this is correct, democratic societies with a more unequal distribution of wealth should be characterized by exploitation of the rich by the poor—that is, high taxes and, consequently, low investment and growth, whereas undemocratic ones with similar characteristics would not (Deininger and Squire, 1998).

Indeed, the negative effects of income inequality might exist in almost every sphere of human life. But there also exists evidence that supports the view that income inequality could encourage economic growth – both directly and indirectly. The most intuitive thesis is that a lower degree of inequality would mean a greater amount of redistribution from rich to poor. It is this redistribution that would become an impediment to the creation of incentives for people (especially the poorest and richest groups of them) to work hard (Li and Zou, 1998). There is also a positive view for the effect of inequality on economic growth: if individual saving rates rise with the level of income, then a redistribution of resources from rich to poor tends to lower the aggregate rate of saving in an economy. Through this channel, a rise in income inequality tends to raise investment.[5] In this case, greater inequality would enhance economic growth. However, there is an argument that inequality may lead to higher fertility rates, which in turn could reduce economic growth (Perotti, 1996).

Worsening inequality of wealth and income motivates the poor to engage in crime, riots and other disruptive activities (see, for example, Hibbs, 1973; Venieris and Gupta, 1986; Gupta, 1990; and Alesina and Perotti, 1996). In a civilized world the existence of millions of starving people is not only unacceptable from an ethical point of view but can hardly be expected to lead to peace and tranquility. As a consequence, it is widely believed that inequality could become an impediment to economic development. Unfortunately, the existing empirical analyses, using data on the performance of a broad panel of countries, have yielded conflicting results. Perotti (1996) and Benabou (1996), for instance, report an overall tendency for income inequality to generate lower economic growth in cross-country regressions, whereas some panel studies, such as that of Forbes (1997) and Li and Zou (1998), find relationships with the opposite sign. Nevertheless, Deininger and Squire (1998) provide evidence in support of the view that inequality retards economic growth in poor countries but not in richer countries. Using a large bulk of time-series and cross-national data, Barro (2000) also supports this hypothesis.[6] However, other carefully conducted research

---

[4] See Perotti (1993), Alesina and Rodrik (1994), Persson and Tabellini (1994) and Benabou (1996) for detailed analyses.

[5] This effect arises if the economy is partly closed, so that domestic investment depends, to some extent, on desired national saving (Barro, 2000, p. 8).

[6] There is an indication in Barro's (2000) study that growth tends to fall with greater inequality when per capita GDP is below around $2000 (1985 US dollars) and to rise with inequality when per capita GDP is above $2000.

projects, such as Eichera and Garcia-Penalosab (2001) and Ravallion (2001), provide little evidence that supports the above views.

## 5.2. AN ANALYTICAL FRAMEWORK

Some American cities, such as New York and Los Angeles, are amongst the most troubled in terms of racial relations; at the same time they are constant producers of innovation in the arts and business. The United States itself is an economically successful melting pot, but many of its social problems are related to racial and ethnic cleavages. The "tragedy of Africa" is, according to Alesina and Ferrara (2005), largely a result of ethnic conflict, which is indeed pervasive in many parts of the developing world.

In Webster's Dictionary, 'diverse' is defined as 'the state or quality of being different or varied; a point of difference; property of being numerically different; condition capable of having various traits composed of unlike or distinct elements'. The term 'cultural diversity' used here describes a wide range of ethnic, linguistic, religious and other cultural groupings. It is generally assumed that while all persons share some traits with all others, all persons also share other traits with only some others, and all persons still have other traits, which they share with no one else. Following this assumption, each person may be described in three ways: via the universal characteristics of the species; the sets of characteristics that define that person as a member of a group; and the person's idiosyncratic characteristics. Diversity also sometimes implies clashes of values, goals and interests, which can lead to highly conflictual debates, anger, frustration, mistrust and hostility. When attempting dialogue in a conflict situation, the experience might be negative, discourage people from further interaction, and increase mistrust.

How to classify cultural groups is a difficult and politically charged issue. For example, in China only 42 ethnic groups were identified in 1953, while the number increased to 54 in 1964 and 56 in 1982, respectively.[7] All the work surveyed above shares the assumption that ethnic groups are "objective categories" into which individuals can be classified, and that such classification is commonly shared and exogenous. However, the validity of this assumption can be called into question on several grounds. First, people may not agree on what are the relevant ethnic groups into which they are supposed to "classify" others, i.e., the boundaries of these groups may not be objectively known to all. Secondly, even under the most conventional definition of cultural category (ethnic, linguistic or religious), the latter may not be determined independently of economic and policy choices at a given point in time. This can occur both because political leaders may actively pursue policies that influence (historically, often reduce) ethnic diversity, and because citizens may "choose" their identity differently in response to political and economic conditions.

Ethnic diversity does not necessarily coincide with linguistic diversity or religious diversity. For instance, most Latin American countries are relatively homogenous in terms of language but less so in terms of 'ethnicity' or 'race'. Fearon (2003) and Alesina et al. (2003) have compiled various measures of ethnic diversity which try to tackle the fact that the difference amongst groups manifests itself in different ways in different places. The two classifications are constructed differently. Alesina et al. (2003) do not take a stand on what characteristics (ethnicity, language or religion) are more salient, but adopt the country breakdown suggested by original sources, mainly the *Encyclopedia Britannica*. Fearon (2003, p. 198) instead tries to construct a list of 'relevant' ethnic groups, which 'depend on what people in the country identify as the most socially relevant ethnic groupings'.

In addition, conversion of religious groups is a widespread phenomenon. In the Middle Ages entire Central European populations switched back and fourth between Catholicism and Protestantism as the political alliances of their princes switched between the Pope and the Emperor. In Fascist Italy many Jews converted to Catholicism to escape discrimination. In modern-day India it is extremely common for lower-caste Hindus to convert to the Muslim or Catholic faiths, in which they meet with relatively less discrimination. For most people, and for most religions, the material costs of conversion are relatively modest, amounting in many cases to geographical relocation to a locality where one can easily establish a new religious identity (Caselli and Coleman, 2002).

Another noticeable fact is that each cultural element (ethnicity, language, or religion) may play a different role in the synthesized measure of cultural diversity. For example, religion may contribute a large portion to cultural diversity in the nations of Balkan and the Middle East, while ethnicity as a key factor in cultural make-up differs within South Asia and between China, Japan and Korea. Nevertheless, language is the most important index when the cultural differences within the western European nations are analyzed (see Box 5.1). There is also an argument that religion per se should be a relatively weak source of cultural diversity. For most people, and for most religions, the material costs of conversion are relatively modest, amounting in many cases to geographical relocation to a locality where one can easily establish a new religious identity (Caselli and Coleman, 2002).

## Box 5.1 A Story about the Birth of Euro

On 12 December 12 1995, leaders from the European Union were meeting in Madrid, Spain, to discuss whether or not 'ECU' was to be used as the name of the forthcoming single currency. When the meeting reached midway, German chancellor Helmut Kohl suddenly stated: "ECU as the name of the single currency is not acceptable to Germans. Its pronunciation is very similar to that of the German word 'cow'."

In December 1978, when the leaders of the European Community decided in Brussels to start the European monetary system, the European currency unit was set up in order to stabilize the exchange rates of its member states. Interestingly, the abbreviation of the European Currency Unit, or ECU, is exactly the same in both pronunciation and spelling, as the French word *ecu* (an ancient French coin). In French, 'ecu' refers to a shield used by French cavaliers in ancient times. A currency named after a shield will give people a feeling of strength. The start of the European single monetary system and the establishment of the ECU were proposed by the then French president and, therefore, worked to the particular satisfaction of France.

---

[7] Source: China Ethnic Statistical Yearbook (1997, pp. 299-300).

When the meeting came close to launch time, the Spanish premier, González said: "I have consulted with some fellows that 'EURO' is relatively acceptable." This time, the Greeks complained that the pronunciation of 'Euro' is very similar to that of 'urine' in Greek, a word that is even worse than 'Ecu' in German. But they were not able to provide better proposals. At last, with the support from Chirac, a compromise was reached: EURO was decided for the name of the EU's single currency.

A stark example of ethnicity (language) working better than religion as a coalition enforcing mechanism is recounted by Horowitz (1985, p. 43):

In seventeenth century North-America, the English were originally called "Christians," while the African slaves were described as "heathens." The initial differentiation of groups relied heavily on religion. After about 1680, however, a new dichotomy of "whites" and "blacks" supplanted the former Christian and heathen categories, for some slaves had become Christians. If reliance had continued to be placed mainly on religion, baptism could have been employed to escape from bondage. Color provided a barrier seemingly both "visible and permanent."[8]

Alesina and Ferrara (2005) highlight three 'microfoundations' underlying the nonlinear relationship between cultural (ethnic) diversity and economic performance. First, diversity can affect economic choices by directly entering individual preferences. Second, diversity can affect economic outcomes by influencing the strategies of individuals. Even when individuals have no taste for or against homogeneity, it may be optimal from an efficiency point of view to transact preferentially with members of one's own type if there are market imperfections. Finally, diversity may enter the production function. People differ in their productive skills and, more fundamentally, in the way they interpret problems and use their cognitive abilities to solve them. This can be considered the origin of the relationship between individual heterogeneity and innovation or productivity. An elegant formalization of the third microfoundation is provided by Hong and Page (1998), who prove two key results on this point. First, a group of 'cognitively diverse' problem solvers can find optimal solutions to difficult problems; second, under certain conditions a more diverse group of people with limited abilities can outperform a more homogeneous group of high-ability problem solvers. The intuition is that an individual's likelihood of improving decisions depends more on her having a different perspective from other group members than on her own high expected score.[9]

Without good reason, technological and educational advances have contributed significantly to a better understanding and appreciation of cultures that have appeared in the world. As a result '[cultural diversity will] allow all individuals to lead a life that is decent, dignified and wise, without losing their identity and sense of community, and without betraying their heritage'. (WCCD, 1995) If the WCCD's view is correct, then cultural differences do not necessarily mean violence, but something to be cherished. Consequently, native languages are beginning to be re-evaluated, traditional knowledge rediscovered, and local economies revitalized. In fact, a world without the 'Other' would be a world of

---

[8] Cited from Caselli and Coleman (2002, p. 8).

[9] Cited from Alesina and Ferrara (2005).

stagnation, for, in culture as in its nature, diversity holds the potential for innovation and creative, nonlinear solutions (Shanker, 1996).

In brief, many theories exist for assessing the macroeconomic effects of cultural diversity and of income inequality– both negative and positive (see Table 5.1 for some summarized statements of these effects). The potential benefits of heterogeneity come from variety in production, and the costs come from the inability to agree on common public goods and public policies. This is an empirically plausible implication: the benefits of skill differentiation are likely to be more relevant in more advanced and complex societies. The problem is that most of these theories tend to have offsetting effects and that the net effects on growth, which depend entirely on all the internal and external conditions and environment concerned, are ambiguous. For example, while cultural diversity raises risks and costs for economic transactions between different groups of people, including the rich and poor or those with different cultural values and religious beliefs, they may also become incentives and even productive factors contributing to technological innovations and economic development.

**Table 5.1. Theoretical effects of income inequality and cultural diversity**

|  | Negative effects | Positive effects |
|---|---|---|
| Income inequality | Inequality motivates the poor to engage in crime, riots, and other disruptive activities (Hibbs, 1973; Venieris and Gupta, 1986; Gupta, 1990; Alesina and Perotti, 1996); inequality may lead to higher fertility rates, which in turn could reduce economic growth (Perotti, 1996); rise in inequality tends to reduce the average productivity of investment (Barro, 2000). | Higher inequality tends to induce stronger incentives for people to work hard (Li and Zou, 1998); rise in inequality implies a higher level of saving rates, which tends to raise investment and to enhance economic growth (Barro, 2000). |
| Cultural diversity | Cultural diversity reduces the effectiveness of democratic institutions (Hannan and Carroll, 1981); rise in cultural diversity tends to increase the cost for intercultural communication and mistrust in economic cooperation (Bollen and Jackmam, 1985; Huntington, 1993; Montalvo and Reynal-Querol, 2003); inability to agree on common public goods and public policies (Alesina and Ferrara, 2005). | Cultural diversity holds the potential for innovation and creative, non-linear solutions (Shanker, 1996); potential benefits of heterogeneity come from variety in production (Alesina and Ferrara, 2005); comparative economic advantages usually exist between culturally dissimilar economies more often than between cultural homogeneous places (Guo, 2004). |

In this chapter, our interest will focus on the joint effects of income distribution and cultural diversity on economic growth. It is important, therefore, to explore the conditions that might diminish the negative effects of inequality and cultural factors as nations perhaps overcome barriers to intra-national economic activities or, more strongly, attain a reduction in violence, as sources of growth-inhibiting friction. The negative effects of income inequality and cultural diversity on economic development would become very small if diverse groups learned to live with each other and purse their differences peacefully. This leads to the presumption that the socially stable and economically harmonious societies will be less sensitive to the measures of income inequality and cultural diversity than those otherwise. On the evidence of the above analysis, we can summarize five hypotheses as follows:

H1   The relatively equal distribution of incomes could retard growth in culturally homogeneous nations.

H2   Cultural homogeneity could retard growth in nations with relatively equal distribution of incomes.

H3   The probability of political and economic crises usually grows with respect to the increases of cultural diversity and income inequality indexes.

H4   Higher cultural diversity could become a source of productive factors contributing growth in high income or low inequality nations.

H5   Higher inequality could help growth in high income or culturally homogeneous nations where there are very few, if any, intercultural barriers.

## 5.3. DIVERSITY AND INEQUALITY INDEXES

### 5.3.1. Cultural Diversity Indexes

There have been different ways to measure cultural diversity. The simplest method is derived from the number of cultural groups: thus, the cultural diversity of a society is positively related to the number of cultural groups involved. As shown in Table 5.2, India, the United States, China, the Philippines, Mexico and Russia are the most diversified in terms of number of linguistic groups; while South Africa, the United States, Taiwan, Canada, India, the United Kingdom and New Zealand are the most diversified in terms of number of religious groups. However, this method ignores the influence of population composition among all cultural groups. For example, given two societies having the same number of cultural groups, but that in which population is equally distributed among all cultural groups might be more culturally diverse than one in which population is unevenly distributed among a cultural *majority* and much smaller cultural minorities. To demonstrate this point, let us consider an extreme case in which the cultural majority accounts for almost 100 percent of the total population, while each of the minorities retains a tiny share. Such a society can only be defined as a culturally homogeneous, no matter how many minority groups are exist.

The second method defines cultural diversity in relation to the population ratio of the largest cultural group. In many cases, the lower the ratio of the largest cultural group, the greater the cultural diversity it implies. However, as it only takes into account one (that is, the largest) cultural group, this method may miscalculate the cultural diversity when two or more large cultural groups exist simultaneously in the country (or region). Furthermore, depending on criteria used, these methods may result in conflicting measurement on cultural diversity. As shown in Table 5.2, India, Cameroon, Togo, Zambia, France, South Africa and Uganda are defined as the most diversified in terms of population ratio of the largest linguistic group; while New Zealand, Malawi, Samoa, Australia, Suriname and Ghana are defined as the most diversified in terms of population ratio of the largest religious group.

**Table 5.2a. Economies with largest numbers of languages / religions**

| No. | Economy | By language | Economy | By religion |
|-----|---------|-------------|---------|-------------|
| 1 | India | 72 | South Africa | 30 |
| 2 | United States | 50 | United States | 15 |
| 3 | China | 49 | Taiwan | 13 |
| 4 | Philippines | 44 | Canada | 11 |
| 5 | Mexico | 38 | India | 10 |
| 6 | Russia | 36 | United Kingdom | 10 |
| 7 | Togo | 35 | New Zealand | 9 |
| 8 | Kenya | 31 | Australia | 8 |
| 9 | Zambia | 31 | Ukraine | 8 |
| 10 | Uganda | 30 | Lebanon | 8 |

*Source*: Appendix 2.

**Table 5.2b. Economies with least population shares of linguistic / religious majority (%)**

| No. | Economy | By language | Economy | By religion |
|-----|---------|-------------|---------|-------------|
| 1 | India | 10.70 | New Zealand | 21.64 |
| 2 | Cameroon | 14.86 | Malawi | 23.77 |
| 3 | Togo | 19.80 | Samoa | 26.04 |
| 4 | Zambia | 20.22 | Australia | 27.34 |
| 5 | South Africa | 22.41 | Suriname | 27.36 |
| 6 | Uganda | 24.06 | Ghana | 29.34 |
| 7 | Nigeria | 25.06 | Trinidad and Tobago | 29.39 |
| 8 | Côte d'Ivoire | 25.77 | Kenya | 29.53 |
| 9 | Gabon | 26.41 | South Africa | 29.71 |
| 10 | Chad | 27.01 | Ukraine | 30.73 |

*Source*: Appendix 2.

Although the understanding of cultural diversity may vary according to the perspective taken, the number of cultural groups and their populations should be taken into account simultaneously. To this end, the measurement of cultural diversity index (DIV) can be simplified as follows:

$$DIV = N^{(1-\rho_l)} - 1 \tag{5.1}$$

Where $N$ denotes number of cultural groups; $\rho_l$ is population ratio of the largest cultural group (that is, the majority) to the total population. In Equation 5.1, DIV is positively related to $N$ but negatively related to $\rho_l$. Specifically, when $N=1$ (or $\rho_l=1$), DIV=0.

There are a number of papers in the literature that proxy for diversity using the ethnolinguistic fractionalization index, which measures the probability that two individuals who meet at random will be from different ethnolinguistic groups (Mauro, 1995; Easterly and Levine, 1997; La Porta et al., 1999; Bluedorn, 2001; Ottaviano and Peri, 2004; Alesina and

Ferrara, 2005; and Montalvo and Reynal-Querol, 2005). Specifically, the ethno-linguistic fractionalization (ELF) measure is defined as follows:

$$\text{ELF}=1-\sum_{i=1}^{N}S_i^{2} \qquad (5.2)$$

Where $s_i$ is the share of group $i$ over the total of the population. This index represents the probability that two randomly drawn individuals from the population belong to different ethnic groups. This index reaches a theoretical maximum of 1 when every individual belongs to a different group. This measure implies that a country composed of, say, 100 equally sized groups is more fractionalized than a country with two equally sized groups.

But many hypotheses and arguments in the literature refer not just to measures of ethnic diversity like the above-mentioned one, but to more fine-grained conceptualizations of ethnic structure. For example, Horowitz (1985) and others say that ethnic conflict is more likely in countries with an ethnic majority and a large ethnic minority, as opposed to homogenous or highly heterogeneous countries. Based upon the theoretical results of Esteban and Ray (1994), Montalvo and Reynal-Querol (2002) propose the following polarization index (PI):

$$\text{PI}=1-\sum_{i=1}^{N}\left(\frac{1/2-s_i}{1/2}\right)^{2}s_i \qquad (5.3)$$

Where $s_i$ is the share of group $i$ in the population. The index PI reaches maximum when two equally sized groups face each other and declines as the configuration of groups differs more and more from this half and half split.

Lian and Oneal (1997) use a comprehensive diversity score (CDS) based on the formula developed by Molinar (1991):

$$\text{CDS}==\frac{(\sum_{i=1}^{N}\rho_i^{2})-\rho_l^{2}}{(\sum_{i=1}^{N}\rho_i^{2})^{2}} \qquad (5.4)$$

Where $\rho_i$ is the percentage of the $i$th group and $\rho_l$ is the percentage of the largest cultural group; $N$ is the total number of ethnic groups. Obviously, the larger the value of $\rho_l$, the smaller is the CDS.

Several other methods can also be used to measure cultural diversity. For example, a larger population is likely to be less homogeneous, since the average preference distance between individuals is likely to be positively correlated with the size of a country (Dahl and Tufle, 1973; and Alesina and Spolaore, 1997). But it is not effective when universally used as an index of cultural diversity.

Table 5.3 gives a few examples (labeled A—K) of how these measures work in a set of economies with differing cultural structures.

**Table 5.3. Diversity Examples**

| Type | Population structure | Eq. (5.1) | Eq. (5.2) | Eq. (5.3) | Eq. (5.4) |
|------|----------------------|-----------|-----------|-----------|-----------|
| A | Perfectly homogeneous[a] | 0 | 0 | 0 | 0 |
| B | (.95, .05) | 0.04 | 0.10 | 0.19 | 0.00 |
| C | (.8, .2) | 0.15 | 0.32 | 0.64 | 0.09 |
| D | (1/2, 1/2) | 0.41 | 0.50 | 1.00 | 1.00 |
| E | (.75, .20, .05) | 0.32 | 0.40 | 0.70 | 0.12 |
| F | (.55, .30, .15) | 0.64 | 0.59 | 0.87 | 0.65 |
| G | (1/3, 1/3, 1/3) | 1.08 | 0.67 | 0.89 | 2.00 |
| H | (.49, .17, .17, .17) | 1.03 | 0.67 | 0.78 | 0.81 |
| I | (1/4, 1/4, 1/4, 1/4) | 1.83 | 0.75 | 0.75 | 3.00 |
| J | (.48, .01, .01, .01, …) | 6.88 | 0.76 | 0.50 | 0.09 |
| K | Perfectly heterogeneous[b] | $\approx N\text{-}1$ [c] | $\approx 1$ [c] | $\approx 0$ [c] | $N\text{-}1$ |

[a] There is only one cultural group.
[b] There are $N$ cultural groups, each of which has a share of $1/N$ in population.
[c] Only when $N$ is enough large.

Montalvo and Reynal-Querol (2002) show that the PI index is highly correlated with the ELF at low levels of the ELF, uncorrelated at intermediate levels, and negatively correlated at high levels. In a cross-country regression analysis, they find that ethnic polarization has a positive impact on the likelihood that a civil war occurs, and a negative effect on a country's growth rate. They do not find an independent effect of ethnic fractionalization. Using a different data set, Alesina et al. (2003) compare the results of the polarization index PI and the fractionalization index ELF, and find that fractionalization works slightly better as a determinant of policies and economic outcomes. While the apparent inconsistency between the two sets of results may be due partly to different parameterization and partly to different data sources, it is difficult to gauge the statistical significance of the difference due to the high correlation between the two measures at low levels of fragmentation (Alesina and Ferrara, 2005).

There are arguments that the CDS is superior to the ELF because it better reflects the distance between the two largest groups without overstating the influence of the largest (Rae, 1967, p. 120; Taagepera and Shugart, 1989, p. 210; Molinar, 1991; and Lian and Oneal, 1997). However, most problematic is that the CDS formula (Equation 5.4) is not sensitive for the measures of cultural diversity in countries in which there is only one major cultural group. For example, the cases C (0.8, 0.2) and J (0.48, 0.01, 0.01, 0.01, …) in Table 5.3 have different cultural structures, but they have the same diversity score (0.09). Besides, Table 5.3 shows that the CDS index is not correlated with the other indexes.

Even though each formula has its own advantage, Equations 5.1 is the easiest in application since it does not need the data on population shares for all cultural groups. By contrast, Equations 5.2, 5.3 and 5.4 will meet difficulties in application, especially when a large number of countries are selected.

## 5.3.2. Economic Difference Indexes

Economic difference (or inequality) has several dimensions. Economists are mostly concerned with the income and consumption dimensions. Several inequality indices include the most widely used index of income inequality. Non-income inequality includes inequality in skills, education, opportunities, happiness, health, wealth and so on. Results from a review of the literature suggest a relationship between inequality in income and non-income dimensions. This indicates that one should account for the interrelationship between the different dimensions in the measurement and analyses of inequalities.

The simplest measurement for economic differences is standard error (SR). SR is a statistical approach by which economic differences are measured in absolute term, while the other approaches, such as Gini coefficient, coefficient of variation (CV) and weighed mean error ($M_W$), may be used to derive the economic differences in relative term. Usually, the results of economic differences derived from CV and Gini approaches are consistent with each other, while in some cases, an inconsistency of measurements may be generated by the two approaches. For instance, after having mathematically illustrated the Gini and CV indices with Lorenz curve, Zhou (1994, pp. 193–200) concludes that when the Gini coefficient slightly changes, it may not be consistent with CV, whereas when Gini coefficient changes at a relatively large rate, it may be consistent with CV.

Unlike Gini and CV approaches, generalized entropy (GE) is a family of measures depending on a parameter ($c$). Users may adjust the value of the parameter to suit their ethical preferences. As described in Shorrocks and Foster (1987, pp. 485–97), the parameter ($c$) determines the relative sensitivity of distribution: when $c$ is less than two, the corresponding GE is sensitive in the sense that a composite progressive-cum-regressive income transfers of the same magnitude at the upper and lower tails of the income distribution leads to an increase in inequality. In two special cases, i.e., when $c=0$ and 1, the GE family becomes two versions of Theil's entropy (TE) measure.[10]

Among the above approaches, the Gini coefficient has been most frequently applied by economists worldwide. The Gini coefficient is most prominently used as a measure of inequality of income distribution or inequality of wealth distribution. It is defined as a ratio with values between 0 and 1: A low Gini coefficient indicates more equal income or wealth distribution, while a high Gini coefficient implies more unequal distribution.[11] Mathematically, the Gini coefficient is defined as a ratio of the areas on the Lorenz curve diagram (see Figure 5.1). If the area between the line of perfect equality and the Lorenz curve is A, and the area under the Lorenz curve is B, then the Gini coefficient is A/(A+B). Since A+B=0.5, the Gini coefficient becomes A/(0.5)=2A=1-2B. If the Lorenz curve is represented by the function $y=L(x)$, the value of B can be found with integration. As a result, the Gini coefficient becomes

---

[10] In the extreme case when $c\to-\infty$, the ranking of the corresponding GE is same as that of Rawls' maximum criterion, i.e., to focus exclusively on the well-being of the worst-off province (Shorrocks, 1980, pp. 613–25).

[11] In the extreme cases, 0 corresponds to perfect equality (everyone has exactly the same income) and 1 corresponds to perfect inequality (where one person has all the income, while all the remaining persons have zero income).

$$\text{Gini}=1\text{-}2\int_0^1 L(x)\mathrm{d}x \qquad\qquad (5.5)$$

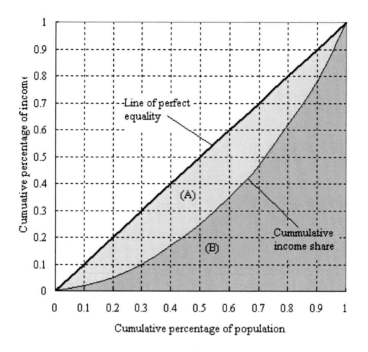

Figure 5.1. The Lorenz curve.

If an income distribution is represented by a vector of incomes, $x=(x_1, x_2, \ldots, x_n)$, where $x_i$ indicate the income of the $i$th individual in a society consisting of $n$ individuals, the Gini coefficient can be computed by the following formula:

$$\text{Gini}=\frac{\sum\sum\sqrt{(x_i-x_j)^2}}{2n^2\overline{x}} \qquad\qquad (5.6)$$

Where, $\overline{x}$ is mean for all $x$.

## 5.4. A MODEL OF GROWTH IN CULTURALLY DIVERSE ECONOMIES

Various efforts have been offered to a theoretical and empirical explanation of economic growth at the 'institutional' level.[12] It is, however, very difficult to conduct any meaningful economic comparison especially when a large number of economies with different political, historical and cultural backgrounds are taken into account. Following Gastil's (1987, p. 210)

---

[12] See, for example, Holesovsky (1977), Hwang (1993), Carson (1996), Kohler (1996), Schnitzer (1997), Gregory and Stuart (1998), McMahon and Square (2003, eds), and Rodrik (2003, ed.).

division of countries into economic systems with respect to the role of government, Barro (1991), for example, tried to differentiate quantitatively the primarily socialist, mixed between socialist and free enterprise and primarily free enterprise economies. His estimated coefficient for socialist economies is negative on growth but that for mixed systems is essentially zero. Because the division of economic systems into groups is subjective and because there are only nine 'socialist' countries in the sample, these results are not very reliable.

During the past decades the vast majority of countries in the world have undertaken 'market-oriented reforms'. Although this movement in favor of markets embraced both developed and developing countries, the changes in the developing world have been by far the most striking. However, the reform outcomes can only tell a story that establishing a full-fledged market system proved to be far more complex than had been envisaged. A global research project, launched by the Global Development Network (GDN) in 2002, presents cases of similar reforms with varied outcomes. The market reforms considered in this project are privatization, pension reform, external trade, foreign direct investment (FDI) regulations, and financial reforms. In fact, a variety of countries obtained the same 'good' outcomes applying dissimilar strategies of institutional engineering. The contrasting features of the reforms in China and India exemplify this latter point well (Fanelli and McMahon, 2006, p. 28).

Might political stability be a better factor to explain the engines for economic development than political system? To measure political stability, Barro (1991) included two variables (the number of revolutions and coups per year and the number of political assassinations per million population per year). Using Bank's (1979) data set, Barro found that each of these variables is significantly negative for economic growth. Then, what determines political stability? Naturally, economic factors, such as economic growth and income distribution, may play a very critical role. Londregan and Poole (1989), for example, found a negative association between economic growth and political instability. But what is the primary cause driving this political and economic feedback loop? In fact, although Barro's (1991) results do reflect a positive influence of growth on political stability, rather than (or in addition to) the effects of stability on growth, it still needs further statistical proofs for the hypothesis that economic growth more decisively influences political stability rather than the *vice versa*.

To conclude, existing growth theories and evidence in development experience are conflicting. Furthermore, from the standpoint of political economics, we still lack any convincing evidence to explain, for example: Why the Latin America's economic performance has been worse than the North America's. Why were the ancient civilizations of Asia so tardy in fully exploiting possibilities for growth? Why is the African area struck at the income level that most of the Western economies had more than one century ago? Nor can we find any convincing evidence for the differing economic performances between countries that have the same or similar geographical, economic or political conditions.

In past literature relating to the determinants of economic growth, income inequality and cultural diversity have been treated separately. In this section, we try to investigate their joint effects. Our task is to clarify (1) the cultural conditions under which income inequality encourages (retards) economic growth; and (2) the economic conditions under which cultural diversity encourages (retards) economic growth. Our empirical work considers average growth rates of real per capita GDP over two decades, from 1980 to 1989 and from 1990 to

1999. We define these periods as those of the Cold War and the post-Cold War, respectively. What we intend to do is to see if the determinants of economic growth are different in the two periods.[13]

Our analytical model is based on Barro's (2000) findings on the determinants of economic growth. In Barro's model, which was estimated by the three-stage least squares (3SLS) technique, 11 explanatory variables (the log of real per capita GDP and its square, the ratio of government consumption to GDP, a subjective index of the maintenance of the rule of law, a subjective for democracy (electoral rights) and its square, the ratio of inflation, the years of schooling, the log of total fertility rate, the ratio of investment to GDP, and the growth rate of the terms of trade) are used. In order to avoid possible estimation errors resulting from multicolinearity, we will only focus on how the growth rate that remains unexplained in Barro's model is related to GINI (Gini coefficient, representing income inequality) and DIVERSITY (cultural diversity, including language and religion).

As suggested in Table 5.1, the effects of income inequality and cultural diversity on economic growth, both positive and negative, may be offsetting. Consequently, the regressions might not be statistically significant. In order to clarify the conditions under which economic growth can be both positively and negatively related to income inequality and cultural diversity, we allow the influences of the DIVERSITY and GINI variables on growth to depend on each other. To this end, the DIVERSITY and GINI variables are now entered into the growth model both individually and jointly as a product. We also allow income level (measured by natural log of per capita GDP, or lnGDPPC) and DIVERSITY and GINI as joint explanatory variables in the growth model.

The dependent variable is defined as the average growth rates of real per capita GDP which remain unexplained in Barro's baseline panel regression (2000, p. 12, tab. 1).[14] The real per capita GDP, the data of which come from the World Economic Outlook of the International Monetary Fund (various years), is measured in 1985 US dollars for all sample nations. The data of the Gini coefficients come from a revised version of the World Income Inequality Database (WIID2 Beta), available at the website of the World Institute for Development Economics Research (WIDER): www.wider.unu.edu/wiid/wiid.htm. Our empirical work considers the average level for all annual Gini coefficients available within each period. Instead, when national data are absent, regional (urban or rural areas) data are used.

The data on the linguistic and religious diversity indexes are calculated based on Equation 5.1. To save the time in data collection, we will not calculate the period average data for cultural diversity indexes. Instead, we only collect the mid-period data. Specifically, we collect the cultural data for two years: 1985 for the period 1980-89 and 1995 for the period 1990-99. The framework includes countries with vastly different social, economic and

---

[13] Since 1999 is the latest year in which we have been able to assemble the panel data on all the variables employed, we have to reduce the starting year to 1980 in order to equalize the two periods (the Cold War and the post-Cold War) in length.

[14] The estimation is by three-stage least squares. Instruments are the actual values of the schooling and terms-of-trade variables, lagged values of the other variables aside from inflation, and dummy variables for prior colonial status. Since some explanatory variables employed by Barro (such as a subjective index of the maintenance of the rule of law, a subjective for democracy, the ratio of inflation, the log of total fertility rate, and the growth rate of the terms of trade) could either be influenced by cultural diversity or their data are not available, we ignore their effects on growth rates when calculating the data.

cultural conditions. The attractive feature of this broad sample is that it encompasses great variation in the explanatory variables that are to be evaluated. Our view is that it is impossible to use the experience of one or a few countries to get an accurate empirical assessment of the long-term growth implications from a set of social, economic and cultural variables. However one drawback of this kind of diverse sample is that it creates difficulties in measuring variables in a consistent and accurate way across countries and over time.

The other empirical issue, which is likely to be more important, is the sorting out of directions of causation. From a longer perspective of the human history, the extent of cultural diversities (especially in terms of religion, which appears in our model as the explanatory variable) is the final result of economic development (which appears in our model as the dependent variable). But we argue that within a shorter period of time this kind of causation is very weak.

Our baseline panel regressions don't yield any overall relation between growth and income inequality for the 1980s and 1990s as a whole (the estimated results are not reported here). But the estimated coefficients on income inequality (GINI) become statistically significant when the panel regressions are based on the data of the 1980s and the 1990s separately. Specifically, the income inequality (GINI) tends to retard growth in the 1980s and to encourage growth in the 1990s (see also Figure 5.2 for the scatter diagrams).[15] The above results are similar to Barro's (2000) findings when the full (that is, from 1980 to 1989 and from 1990 to 1999) samples are considered in a single regression, but different from with his findings when the 1980-89 and the 1990-99 samples are considered in separate regressions.

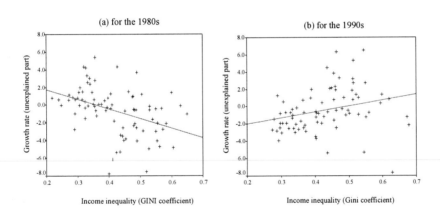

Figure 5.2. Growth rate versus income inequality.

Might there be any forms of nonlinear relation between growth and cultural diversity? Our regressions show that the coefficients on the linguistic diversity (LANGUAGE) and on its interactive term with income inequality (LANGUAGE*GINI) are statistically insignificant for both the 1980-89 and the 1990-99 periods (the regressions are omitted here). We suspect that impacts of linguistic barriers on economic activities do not exist in the 1990s, or, if they do, have at least become insignificant in contrast to the previous estimates by Alelman and Morris (1967), Haug (1967), and Reynolds (1985). The reason for this might be that

---

[15] Note that the only difference between the two panel data is that five nations (Mali, Nicaragua, Singapore, Yemen and Zambia) are missing in the 1990s' sample.

educational and technological advances have to a certain extent reduced the linguistic barriers, especially for international and intercultural economic activities in the developed economies (Guo, 2004.)

However, our regressions show that the coefficients on income inequality (GINI), religious diversity (RELIGION) and on their interactive terms are statistically significant for the 1990-99 period, though not for the 1980-89 period (the estimated results are not reported here).[16] Since the 1980s and 1990s were branded by the Cold War and the post-Cold War periods, respectively, the question arises as to whether the findings are determined to any extent by the Cold War policies. Since countries may make choices in terms of their ideological preferences (Huntington, 1996, p. 125), the determination of the economic activities during that period might be distorted, or at any rate, different from that of the post-Cold War period. Following this analytical logic, we would also believe that during the Cold War era cultural influences on economic activities might be largely reduced, if not dismissed.

More interesting results emerge in our regressions when the effect of religious diversity on economic growth is allowed to depend on the level of income inequality measured by Gini coefficient. As intuited from Figure 5.3, religious diversity tends to encourage economic growth for low inequality (represented by Gini coefficient) nations (see Figure 5.3a) and tends to retard economic growth for high inequality nations (see Figure 5.3b). This result may be supported by the following presumptions. On the one hand, the lower inequality economies will be less sensitive to the measures of cultural diversity than higher inequality economies in which cultural diversity leads to barriers to intranational trade or, more strongly, to violence. On the other hand, higher cultural diversity implies more comparative economic advantages for low inequality places.

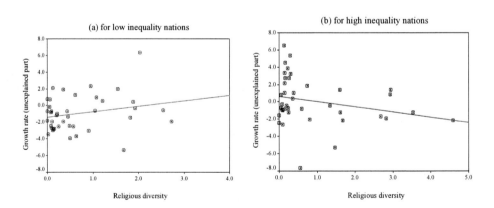

Figure 5.3. Growth rate versus religious diversity (for the 1990s).

These results have far-reaching implications. For a long time, there has been a serious concern that societal conflict arises from cultural dissimilarity (Huntington, 1993). Ultimately, this to some extent may be traceable to a biological basis, since in most circumstances cooperation among animals is importantly influenced by genetic similarity (Wilson, 1980). As a result ascriptive ties are said to dampen coalition building and to inhibit

---

[16] We have also tested other forms of regressions (including those that include the interactive term of GINI and lnGDPPC), none of which has yielded statistically meaningful results.

compromise across groups (that cross-cutting cleavages promote), thus increasing chances for social conflict (Bollen and Jackman, 1985). But our empirical evidence indicates that the above hypothesis might not be completely copied into human societies, at least during the post-Cold War period. In fact, the high level of religious diversity of a country is usually positively related to another cultural variable – religious similarity – of the country with the outside world, which usually plays an important role in foreign trade (for more discussions on the relation between cultural similarity and international trade, see Chapter 6).

The major concern here is that we are trying to identify the roles of inequality and cultural variables whose effect on economic growth is indirect. In Barro's (2000) regressions, which are based on the data of three periods (1965 to 1975, 1975 to 1985, and 1985 to 1995), higher inequality tends to retard growth in poor countries and to encourage growth in richer places. However, in our regressions, when the effect of income inequality is allowed to depend on the level of economic development, measured by the natural log of real per capita GDP, the estimated coefficients on the interactive term 'GINI*lnGDPPC' (to save space, we omit the estimated results here) are not statistically significant for the 1980s and 1990s samples.

As stated Section 5.1.2, there have been different views as to the effects of income inequality on economic growth. Our regressions suggest that for the 1990s income inequality tends to encourage economic growth for religious diversity indexes (DIVERSITY) to be low and tends to retard growth for religious diversity indexes to be high. Since there are quite few nations with a high religious diversity index (see Figure 5.4b), we still need more statistical evidence to support the view that income inequality (GINI) retards economic growth in nations with higher religious diversity indexes. Nevertheless, Figure 5.4a does provide some evidence that supports the view that income inequality (GINI) tends to encourage economic growth in nations with lower religious diversity indexes.

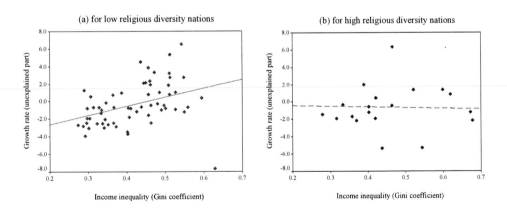

Figure 5.4. Growth rate versus income inequality (for the 1990s).

## 5.5. INTEGRATING ECONOMIC AND CULTURAL POLICIES

In our estimated results derived from the previous section, income inequality is found to be a key factor that could change the directions of the religious influences on economic growth in the 1990s (if not in the 1980s). As a summary, we can divide some typical nations in the sample into four categories according to religious diversity and income inequality (see Table 5.4):

i. Low diversity and low inequality. This category includes Morocco, Ireland, Denmark, Portugal, Greece, Belgium, Norway, and Sweden.
ii. High diversity and low inequality. This category includes New Zealand, United Kingdom; Netherlands, Canada, Germany, and South Korea.
iii. Low diversity and high inequality. This category includes Colombia, Paraguay, Ecuador, Senegal, Thailand, Algeria, Mauritania, and Turkey.
iv. High diversity and high inequality. This category includes Lesotho, Zimbabwe, Malawi, Central African Republic, Zambia, Cameroon, Kenya, Nigeria, and Malaysia.

**Table 5.4. A quadrantal classification of selected nations**

|  | Low income inequality | High income inequality |
|---|---|---|
| Low religious diversity | Morocco (0.001, 0.368); Ireland (0.059, 0.365); Denmark (0.093, 0.352); Portugal (0.055, 0.346); Greece (0.095, 0.327); Belgium (0.087, 0.297); Norway (0.085, 0.296); Sweden (0.098, 0.274) | Colombia (0.058, 0.559); Paraguay (0.084, 0.528); Ecuador (0.054, 0.513); Senegal (0.092, 0.491); Thailand (0.075, 0.481); Algeria (0.005, 0.463); Mauritania (0.003, 0.456); Turkey (0.002, 0.456); |
| High religious diversity | New Zealand (4.594, 0.370); United Kingdom (2.674, 0.358); Netherlands (1.930, 0.333); Canada (2.722, 0.316); Germany (1.210, 0.307); South Korea (1.823, 0.300) | Lesotho (1.669, 0.677); Zimbabwe (1.604, 0.672); Malawi (2.919, 0.620); Central African Rep. (1.594, 0.598); Zambia (1.522, 0.570); Cameroon (1.464, 0.544); Kenya (2.941, 0.521); Nigeria (2.032, 0.464); Malaysia (1.325, 0.463) |

*Note*: Figures within parentheses are the religious diversity indexes (in 1995) and the Gini coefficients (1990-99 averages), which are calculated based on *Britannica Book for the Year 1996* (pp. 774-7) and the World Income Inequality Database (WIID2 Beta, available at www.wider.unu.edu/wiid/wiid.htm), respectively.

According to our estimated results, higher religious diversity could become a source of productive factors contributing economic growth for low inequality nations (shown in Category II); but in nations in Category IV, high inequality could seriously affect economic growth. In Category III, income inequality could generate higher economic growth since there are very few, if any, inter-cultural barriers within each religiously homogeneous nation. But it seems that the nations listed in Category I still need stronger economic incentives (or, higher income inequality) or religious diversities in order to promote their inanimate domestic economies.

A greater diversity of religions available in a country or region is thought to promote greater competition, hence, a better quality religion product, and, hence, greater religious participation and beliefs. In Table 5.5, the presence of a state religion (SR) refers to the situation around 1970, as designated by Barrett et al. (2001, pp. 834-35). We assigned the value one only if Barrett et al. designated an individual religion, not if they classified the state as favoring religion in general. State regulation of religion (SRR) refers to a situation in which the state appoints or approves church leaders. This designation comes from discussions in Barrett (1982) and Barrett et al. (2001) and elsewhere and typically applies during the late 1970s. The countries shown are the ones included in the subsequent statistical analysis (as dictated by data availability).

**Table 5.5. A sample of economies: state religion and state regulation of religion**

| | State regulation of religion (SRR)=0 | SRR=1 |
|---|---|---|
| State religion (SR)=0 | Cameroon, Ghana, S. Africa, Canada, Mexico, U.S., Brazil, Chile, Uruguay, Hong Kong, India, Japan, S. Korea, Philippines, Singapore, Taiwan, Austria, Belgium, Cyprus, Germany, Netherlands, Poland, Switzerland, Australia, New Zealand, Bulgaria, Romania, Slovenia | China, France, Hungary, Turkey, Czech Rep., Estonia, Latvia, Lithuania, Russia, Slovak Rep. |
| SR=1 | Dom. Rep., Colombia, Israel, Malaysia, Pakistan, Denmark, Iceland, Ireland, Portugal, Spain | Argentina, Peru, Venezuela, Bangladesh, Thailand, Finland, Greece, Italy, Norway, Sweden, U.K. |

*Source*: Barrett (1982) and Barrett et al. (2001).

More fundamentally, the extent of religious diversity and competition are thought to depend on how the government regulates the market for religion. Chaves and Cann (1992) extended this argument by using empirical measures of the extent of state involvement and interference with church activities. Greater state regulation of religion—which Chaves and Cann measured by, among other things, whether the government appoints or approves church leaders—was argued to decrease the efficiency of religion providers and, therefore, to generate lower rates of church attendance. However, state religion also typically involves subsidies, such as payments to church employees, and the collection of taxes dedicated to church uses. Economic reasoning suggests that these subsidies would encourage formal religious activity – hence, the overall impact of a subsidized state church on religious participation could be positive. The opposite of subsidy is suppression, and some governments have sought to suppress religion, either specific ones or in general. For example, Communist countries, such as the Soviet Union and China, tried hard to eradicate organized religion. This oppression would be predicted to lower church attendance and religious beliefs (Barro and McCleary, 2003).

## 5.6. SUMMARY

Explaining growth is one of the most important tasks for economists. This chapter is part of an upsurge of empirical work on economic growth and tries to shed some light on the relative merit of models emphasizing the importance of cross-cultural influences. On the basis of the data of a panel of countries for the period 1980-99, we develop a model of economic growth with respect to, either individually or in an interactive term, cultural diversity and income inequality. We find that high inequality tends to retard growth in the 1980s and to encourage growth in the 1990s. Although we have not found evidence for the relation between linguistic diversity and economic growth (which is consistent with the findings of Lian and Oneal (1997)), our estimated results do suggest that the growth rate of real per capita GDP is related to religious diversity under certain circumstances.

The indication that economic development is more related to religious diversity than to linguistic diversity may be reasonable: since most governments have endeavored to popularize their official languages, fewer and fewer people – most of whom are either illiterates or economically inactive – meet linguistic difficulties in communicating nationally.[17] As a result the influence of linguistic diversity on economic development becomes less significant than that of religious diversity. If our results are correct, the make-up of cultural diversity should be much more complicated than either emphasizing language most heavily (as Alelman and Morris (1967) and Haug (1967) suggested) or treating language and religion equally (as Lian and Oneal (1997) suggested).

Our regressions provide evidence to support the view that the world economy has been more significantly influenced by religious diversity in the post-Cold War period than in the Cold War period. While it is easy to understand why the economic activities have been determined by religious diversity since the end of the Cold War, we find that, for the 1990s, religious diversity tends to retard growth in high inequality nations and to encourage growth in low inequality places. We also find some evidence to support the view that inequality tends to encourage growth in religious homogeneous nations. But we still need more statistical explanations for the negative relation between inequality and growth in nations with high religious diversity indexes.

The above evidence supports the presumption that not only the lower inequality economies will be less sensitive to the measures of cultural diversity than higher inequality places in which cultural diversity leads to barriers to intra-national trade or, more significantly, to violence, but also they can benefit from the comparative economic advantages in the existing, culturally diverse world. Furthermore, some diversity in a country may favor trade as well. For instance a certain ethnic minority in country A can be a "link" with a country B where that ethnic group is a majority, therefore facilitating trade between A and B. These results could be good news for the global and regional leaders who have been troubled by problems in dealing with cultural clashes. Hopefully, cultural diversity, if treated appropriately by all sides concerned, will come to be a positive factor for economic development.

Posner (2004) argues that the current data suffers from a 'grouping problem' at two different levels. On the one hand, many groups are aggregated into a single category while they are distinct political actors — even enemies — at national level. The most striking example of this concerns the Tutsis and the Hutus in Rwanda, which are aggregated into a single category 'Banyrwanda'. At the opposite extreme stand a number of groups that are listed as separate linguistic categories, but whose distinction has no political or economic relevance. Posner thus proposes a classification based on 'politically relevant ethnic groups', defined as groups that can influence economic policy decisions either directly or indirectly (for example, by threatening to remove politicians from power). However it is difficult to argue that the realized structure of power at a given point in time is exogenous and can be used as an underlying determinant of the definition of ethnic groups. To date, it is still unclear how to integrate linguistic or 'ethnic' differences with other dimensions that make the latter politically or economically salient.

---

[17] Barro and McCleary (2003) find that economic growth responds positively to the extent of religious beliefs.

# Chapter 6

# DOING BUSINESS ACROSS CULTURES

There is 'true' Knowledge. Learn thou it is this: to see one changeless life in all the lives, and in the separate, one inseparable. There is imperfect Knowledge: that which sees the separate existences apart, and, being separated, holds them real. There is false Knowledge: that which blindly clings to one as if 'there were all, seeking no cause, deprived of light, narrow, and dull, and dark.'

(Sankhya-Yog, the Book of Doctrines).

## 6.1. A CRITIQUE OF THEORIES ON TRADE

It has been broadly assumed that a country's economic dependence on the outside world is negatively related to its land area. For example, in an estimation of international trade, Frankel and Romer (1996, table 1) find that, for every 1 percent increase in land area, trade falls by about 0.2 percent accordingly. This may be illustrated unambiguously by the relationship between the supply and demand of some basic resources for countries differing in size (land area). Generally speaking, in comparison to large economies, small economies have a relatively limited variety of natural resources. Therefore, they have to import resources that they lack and that are essential to meeting diversified production and consumption needs. Eventually, the increased imports will stimulate exports in order to attain a balance.

Besides geographical area, a country's economic size (output) and population also influence its external economic activities. Generally, the larger the GDPs (or GNPs)[1] of trading partners, *ceteris paribus*, the larger the volume of trade between them; by contrast, population is a negative factor in the determination of international trade. This captures the well-known phenomenon that larger countries tend to be relatively less open to trade as a percentage of GDP (or GNP). Therefore, it is easy to understand that Hong Kong, Singapore and Luxembourg are more highly dependent on international trade than the United States, China or India. The former lack not only natural endowments but also room to exploit economies of scale in the domestic market, while the latter, engaging in far more trade in absolute terms (*versus* less trade as a percentage of GDP or GNP), can find more business opportunities inside their own territories.

---

[1] Linnemann (1966) and Frankel et al. (1997) have estimated the effects of both GDP and GNP on trade, but no significant difference is found.

Without considering geographical factor, it could be very difficult to understand the current patterns of both global and regional trade. For instance, bilateral trade flows across the US-Canadian border, between France, Italy, UK, Germany and the Netherlands, and along the western coast of the Pacific Ocean (including, *inter alia*, South Korea, Taiwan, Hong Kong and the mainland of China) have risen a great deal more quickly than between more remote and isolated economies. Besides distance, another proxy of geographical factor that influences international trade is adjacency. For example, bilateral trade between France and the United Kingdom will be due to their proximity, but trade between France and Germany will be further boosted by their common border.[2]

Past studies on the geographical influence on trade have raised more questions than they answered. For example, among the existing estimated results on the determinants of international trade (in logarithmic form), the statistically significant coefficients on the log of distance have ranged between –0.51 and –1.50, which demonstrates the respective decreases (in percentage) in international trade as a result of a 1 percent increase in distance.[3] No observable tendency, however, has been found for the effect of geographical proximity to fall over time. Rather, the trend seems to be upward during the courses of, among others, 1950-88 in Boisso and Ferrantino (1997) and 1965-92 in Frankel *et al.* (1997b). In their analyses on the negative correlation between distance and the interdependence for sovereign countries, Frankel *et al.* (1997a) use the data from the 1980s and obtain slightly larger coefficients (around 0.5 to 0.6) on distance compared with Eichengreen and Irwin's (1995) interwar estimates (around 0.3 to 0.6) based on the data of the 1930s. Similarly, based on the panel data from 1970, 1980 and 1990, Rauch's (1999) results show little evidence to support the decreasing tendency for trade with respect to distance from 1970 to 1990. Clearly this does not provide evidence that, as a result of declining transportation cost, there should have a decreasingly negative relation between trade and distance. Intuitively, we suspect that some powerful explanatory variables that may either resist or aid international trade must have been missing or simplified, which could in turn reduce to a greater or lesser extent the reliability of the estimated results (Guo, 2004; 2007a).

Past theories on the determinants of international trade seem controversial, or at least incomplete. The Heckscher-Ohlin (H-O), or factor-endowment, theory can be expressed in terms of two theorems. According to the H-O theorem, a nation will export the commodity produced by relatively abundant and cheap factor and import the commodity produced by relatively scarce and expensive factor (see Heckscher, 1919; and Ohlin, 1933). The factor-price equalization theorem was rigorously proved by P. A. Samuelson and therefore is also called Heckscher-Ohlin-Samuelson (H-O-S) theorem (Samuelson, 1948 and 1949). According to the H-O-S theorem, international trade will bring about equalization in the relative and absolute returns to homogeneous factors across nations. The first empirical test of the H-O model was conducted by Leontief (1954) using 1947 US data, which demonstrates that US import substitutes were about 30 percent more capital-intensive than US exports.

---

[2] Frankel *et al*'s (1997b, p. 66) estimated coefficients on 'adjacency' range between 0.5 and 0.7. Because trade is specified in natural logarithmic form in their estimates, the way to interpret the coefficients on adjacency is to take the exponent: that is to say, two countries that share a common border will, *ceteris paribus*, increase their trade by about 65-101 percent compared with two otherwise countries.

[3] For example, Linnemann (1966) puts the estimated coefficient as –0.77, Brada and Mendez (1983) and Oguledo and MacPhee (1994) as –0.76, Bikker (1987) as –0.90 to –1.1, Mansfield and Bronson (1997) as –0.51 to –0.69 (for 1950-90), and Rauch (1999) as –0.62 to –0.70 (1970-90).

Since the United States is the most capital-intensive nation, this result was the opposite of what the H-O model predicted and became known as Leontief paradox. This paradox could be explained by (1) 1947 being a nonrepresentative year, (2) the use of a two-factor (labor and capital) model, (3) the fact that US tariffs gave more protection to labor-intensive industries, and (4) the exclusion of human capital from the calculations. Some empirical studies, however, give conflicting results.[4]

A more uniform size distribution among economies is one explanation for the increase in global trade. Moreover, Helpman (1987) and Krugman (1995) predict that if the distribution of national incomes across countries becomes more equal over time, the volume of trade should increase. According to the Krugman-Helpman theory, the sum of the logs of per capita GNPs of two countries will have a positive effect on the log form of trade between the two countries. One possible explanation for the independent effect of income per capita is that exotic foreign varieties are superior goods in consumption. Low-income countries are dominated by subsistence farming. Other possibilities come out of the literature relating to endogenous theory on economic growth.[5] Even though more developed countries have more advanced transportation infrastructures, including seaports and airports, which facilitate trade, Frankel *et al.* (1997b) argue that perhaps the most important reason why industrialized countries trade more than the less developed countries is that countries tend to liberate as they develop. One reason for this pattern is that governments of poor countries depend on tariff revenue for a large portionof their budget, while more advanced countries can apply other forms of direct and indirect taxes to the domestic economy.

Till now, it seems that there should have been different hypotheses on the correlation between income level and volume of trade. Markusen (1986) and Deardorff (1998, p. 15), for example, show that if high-income consumers tend to consume larger budget shares of capital-intensive goods, which, according to the H-O theory, are produced by capital-rich countries, then it follows that (1) capital-rich countries will trade more with other capital-rich countries than with capital-poor countries, and (2) capital-poor countries will trade more with other capital-poor countries than with capital-rich countries. Obviously, these arguments support the results of Linder (1961), Helpman (1987) and, more recently, Krugman (1995) but not that of the H-O theory.

The classical theory does not offer a satisfactory explanation of why production conditions differ between countries. This is perhaps not surprising, given the nature of production at that time. Resource and cost differences were taken as given and as part of the environment in which the economic system functioned. The underlying cost differences were viewed as being determined outside the economic system for the most part, governed by the natural endowment of a country's resources. The theory does, however, make it clear that even if a country is absolutely more or less efficient in the production of all commodities, a basis for trade still exists if there is a difference in the degree of relative efficiency across commodities. Thus, there is a basis for trade between a developing country and an industrialized country that is more efficient in the production of all commodities. Both can

---

[4] See, for example, Leontief (1956), Kravis (1956a and 1956b), Keesing (1966), Kenen (1965), Baldwin (1971), Branson and Monoyios (1977), Leamer (1980; 1984; and 1993), Stern and Maskus (1981), Bowen, Leamer and Sveikauskas (1987), and Salvatore and Barazesh (1990).

[5] Frankel et al. (1997, p. 58). Of the many relevant works, some of the more important are Grossman and Helpman (1989, 1991), Rivera-Batiz and Romer (1991) and, for further references on the connections between trade and growth, Frankel et al. (1995).

benefit from specialization in production and trade of those commodities in which each has a comparative advantage.

The H-O theory has left a great deal of today's international trade unexplained. To fill up this gap, economists have put forward new theories that base international trade on economies of scale, imperfection, and cross-national differences in technological changes, among others. Even though two nations are identical in every respect, there is still a basis for mutually beneficial trade based on economies of scale. When each nation specializes in the production of one commodity, the combined total world output of both commodities will be greater than without specialization when economies of scale are present. A large portion of international trade today involves the exchange of differentiated products. Such intra-industry trade arises in order to take advantage of important economies of scale in production. Studies show that the more similar nations are in factor endowments, the greater is the importance of intra-industry relative to inter-industry trade.[6] According to the technological gap model, a firm exports a new product until imitators in other countries take its market away. In the meantime, the imitation lag allows delays in the diffusion of technology across national borders. The product cycle theory that relaxes several assumptions in the traditional trade theories defines that a product goes through five stages, including the introduction of the product, expansion of production for export, standardization and beginning of production abroad through imitation, foreign imitators underselling the nation in third markets, and foreigners underselling the innovating firms in their home markets as well (Salvatore, 1995, p. 176).

To sum up, current trade theories seem incomplete and, sometimes, controversial, especially when trade partners with different cultural characteristics are taken into account. They cannot be used to explain satisfactorily why world economic activities in the same or similar cultural environments have become increasingly more important, while the opposite is true of partners in cross-cultural environment; neither can they provide a clear and concrete methodology to explain the extraordinary trade performances within the Chinese cultural circle (Taiwan, Hong Kong, Macau, mainland China and other Chinese areas) during the post-Cold War period. Furthermore, the following are still more puzzling to the international economic theorists and practitioners: Why has Germany attracted much less foreign direct investment (FDI) than the UK? Why has France achieved a better foreign trade performance than Italy?

## 6.2. CULTURAL INFLUENCES ON FOREIGN TRADE

The emphasis on the role of cultural linkage in foreign trade can be traced back to biological analyses showing that cooperation among animals is influenced by genetic similarity (Wilson, 1980). Although it is not the only tool with which to build trusting relationships, businessmen usually make deals with whom they can understand. By contrast,

---

[6] Selected literature on the intra-industry trade can be found in Grubel and Lloyd (1975), Krugman (1980), Lancaster (1980), Greenaway and Milner (1986), Vona (1990), and Leamer (1993).

minority faces disadvantages in conducting intercultural economic activities.[7] Trade and economic cooperation are based on cultural commonality, as it is easier and more efficient for people with the same cultural identity (language, religion, or any other cultural element) to trust and communicate with each other than for those with different cultural identities.

There is a long line of thought suggesting that the adoption of a common standard between different cultural groups of people cannot be fully realized if markedly different attitudes and values exist among cultural groups. As a result, the larger the number of cultural groups involved in a multicultural society, ceteris paribus, the higher the managerial risks and costs resulting from this diversity. The problems inherent in intracultural and intercultural behaviors can be summarized as follows (Huntington, 1996, p. 129):

- Feelings of superiority (and occasionally inferiority) toward people who are perceived as being very different;
- Fear of and lack of trust in such people;
- Communication difficulties resulting from differences in language and accepted civil behavior;
- Lack of familiarity with the assumptions, motivations, relationships and social practices of other people.

For a long time since the World War II, the influences of various cultural factors on economic activities had been ignored by the mainstream development thinkers and practitioners. It seems probably that these conclusions could be correct under certain circumstances. During the Cold War, ideological preferences might have been of greatest significance in decision-making (Huntington, 1996, p. 125). Consequently, the cultural determinants of the international trade of the Cold War might be different from that of the post-Cold War period.

Since the end of the Cold War, there has been a growing concern that cultural links exhibit a trend towards increasing trade between countries that are similar to each other culturally (see Rauch and Trindade (2002), among others). Trade within the European Community constituted less than 50 percent of the community's total trade before the 1980s; by the 1990s this has grown to more than 60 percent. Trade among the ASEAN, Taiwan, Hong Kong, South Korea and the mainland of China – most of which either fall within or are closely related to the Chinese cultural circle – increased from less than 10 percent to over 30 percent of total trade from the 1950s to the 1990s. Similar shifts toward intraregional trade also occurred in Latin America in the 1990s, with trade between Brazil and Argentina tripling and Colombia-Venezuela trade quadrupling between 1990 and 1993. In 1994 Brazil replaced the United States as Argentina's principal trading partner.[8]

By way of contrast, there is a quite different viewpoint, showing that the direction of the correlation between cultural dissimilarity and international trade may change under different conditions. In order to quantitatively investigate the nonlinear effects of culture on international trade, one may build empirical models in which cultural linkage is designed not

---

[7] We define 'intercultural trade' as 'trade between countries or regions differing in one or more cultural elements'. To this end, 'intercultural trade' and 'international trade' are no longer different from each other since there are no countries that have exactly same cultural elements.

[8] Data source: IMF (various issues).

only as an individual explanatory variable but also as a product with income level. If these explanatory variables are statistically significantly when estimated simultaneously, one can further divide the full samples into two groups (that is, one with low income level trade partners, and one with high income level trade partners) under which cross-cultural influences on international trade can be estimated, respectively. On this basis and using panel data from the USA and China, cross-cultural influences on foreign trade are found to have two different directions during the 1990s: cultural dissimilarity tends to retard trade with poor countries and regions and to encourage trade with richer economies (Guo, 2004).

In the analysis of bilateral trade and economic cooperation, economists have taken account of resource endowment including quantity of arable land, quality of the soil, presence of natural resources and climate, as well as labor and managerial skills and organizational capacity. But little attention has been paid to cultural differences that would not only decide the characteristics of social resources but also influence trade patterns, either directly or indirectly. As a matter of fact, in addition to the fact that intercultural differences generate some managing risks and extra costs for bilateral trade, intercultural trade is important not only for the realization of economies of scale but also for the utilization of the culturally based complementary conditions. Although every cultural group runs the risk of being stereotyped because of shared commonalities, no group, culture, or person remains static or lives in isolation. Instead, all societies have interacted. History reveals similarities in societal structures, and differences in behavior and stages of development. The diversity and plurality of cultures can and do benefit from each other, as cultures discover their own peculiarities and idiosyncrasies.

In sum, it is reasonable to believe that culture plays differing roles in the formation of intercultural relations. On the one hand, cultural dissimilarity brings about political distrust or instability. On the other hand, it generates 'differentiation of production' or complementarity in economic terms, which in turn induces cooperation among distinctive groups of people. From the perspective of comparative economics, 'differentiation of production' implies 'comparative advantages', while the latter influences to some extent the potential benefit of trade and cooperation between different cultures. The term 'cultural monopolization of trade' is used here to denote that, since there are usually some culturally unique – both traditional and modern – commodities in each culture (see Box 6.1), intercultural exporters of these products can, at least in theory, realize a monopolized profit for each of their own. As a result, one culture's gross benefit of exporting its products to the other culture grows with greater degree of intercultural dissimilarity. As a result cultural dissimilarity is a determining source not only for intercultural conflicts but also for intercultural dependence and intercultural cooperation.

Keeping in mind that there are different viewpoints on cultural influences on trade, it is therefore noteworthy that the changing roles that culture plays in trade are very sensitive to various conditions. In order to make the analysis clearer and more concrete, some assumptions are necessary. The market structure is one of imperfect competition, with oligopolistic firms producing goods that are perfect substitutes for each other. It is assumed that the markets are segmented in different areas. Besides, we further assume that:

## Box 6.1 Culture as Economic Goods

The rise of culture as economic goods has added to the identification of culture with commodities than can be sold and traded—crafts, tourism, music, books and films. A UNESCO study (UNDP, 1999, p. 33) shows that world trade in goods with cultural content—printed matter, literature, music, visual arts, cinema and photographic, radio and television equipment—almost tripled between 1980 and 1991, form US$67 billion to US$200 billion. The vehicles for this trade in cultural goods are the new technologies. Satellite communications technology from the mid-1980s gave rise to a powerful new medium with global reach and to such global media networks as CNN. The number of TV sets per 1,000 people worldwide doubled between 1980 and 2000. The development of the Internet is spreading culture around the world, over an expanded telecommunications infrastructure of fiber optics and parabolic antennas.

At the same time, academics initiated the study of "Economics of Art and Culture" as an independent sub-discipline within the field of economics. Before the 1970s, such a subject area would have come to as a surprise even to the majority of economists. Up to that time, few economists, mainly those personally interested in the arts, had provided contribution in this area. One of them is Alan Peacock, who in 1969 had already been involved in analyzing the public promotion of arts and culture. Along with broadly based study on the performing arts in the US, the *Journal of Cultural Economics*, a specialized scholarly journal, was published in 1980s. Since then, biennial Congresses have been held under the auspices of the Association for Cultural Economics.

1. There are two factors affecting trade, that is, benefit of economic complementarity and cost of inter-political and intercultural barriers.
2. Technology is identical in all culture areas, that is, trade functions are the same in all culture areas.
3. All commodities are produced under constant returns to scale in all culture areas.
4. There is no intercultural factor mobility.
5. There are no transportation costs, tariffs, or other obstructions to the free flow of trade.
6. Trade between the culture areas concerned is balanced.

The meaning of assumption 1 is clear, and it is made to simplify the illustration. Assumption 2 means that all culture areas have access to and use the same general production techniques. Since factor prices usually differ, each culture area will use more of the relatively cheaper factor in the culture area so as to minimize its costs of production and intercultural trade. Assumption 3 means that increasing the amount of labor and capital used in the production of any commodity will increase output of that commodity in the same production. Assumption 4 means that intercultural differences in factor earnings would persist indefinitely in the absence of intercultural trade. Assumption 5 means that specialization in production proceeds until commodity prices are the same in both culture areas with trade. If we allowed for transportation costs and tariffs, specialization would proceed only until commodity prices differed by no more than the costs of transportation and the tariff on each unit of the interculturally traded commodity. Lastly, assumption 6 means that the total value of each culture area's exports equals the total value of the area's imports.

The analytical framework can be further simplified. Assume that in a pair of economically complementary nations, the size of their bilateral trade is jointly determined by only two factors: (1) the cost of intercultural transaction ($c$) and (2) the benefit of comparative advantage ($b$). Specifically, trade is supposed throughout this research to be encouraged for $b>c$ and to be retarded for other circumstances. On this basis, there is always a negative relation between the cost of intercultural transaction and cultural similarity. To enable the analytical framework concrete, we suppose that the function $c$ is monotonously related to cultural similarity ($x$), that is,

$c=c(x)$, with $c'(x)<0$ and $c''(x)=0$.

In all circumstances, $b(x)$ is positive for economically complementary nations, that is,

$b(x)>0$ for all $x$.

However, the marginal benefit of comparative advantage with respect to cultural similarity, denoted by $db/dx$, may be positive, negative or zero. Finally, we have Hypothesis 1 for the cultural conditions under which trade is encouraged or retarded:

1a) When $db/dx>0$, trade tends to be retarded for values of cultural similarity to be less than $x^*$ and to be encouraged otherwise (see Figure 6.1a).

1b) When $db/dx\leq0$, trade tends to be retarded for values of cultural similarity to be less than $x_1^*$ and to be encouraged otherwise if $|db/dx|<|dc/dx|$; it tends to be encouraged for values of cultural similarity to be less than $x_2^*$ and to be retarded otherwise if $|db/dx|>|dc/dx|$ (see Figure 6.1b).

1c) When $db/dx=dc/dx$, trade tends to be retarded if $b<c$ for all values of cultural similarity and to be encouraged if $b>c$ for all values of cultural similarity (see Figure 6.1c).

Next, let us add another explanatory variable, income level ($y$), into the system in which cultural similarity is fixed at a certain level. It is further assumed that, *ceteris paribus*, the cost of intercultural transaction is negatively related to income level. Perhaps the most obvious evidence that supports this view is the decreasing transportation cost as a result of economic development, not to mention that the higher the education attainment (which is positively related to income level), the easier is it for people from different cultural backgrounds to communicate with and understand each other. The functions of the cost of intercultural transaction and the benefit of comparative advantage, now, becomes

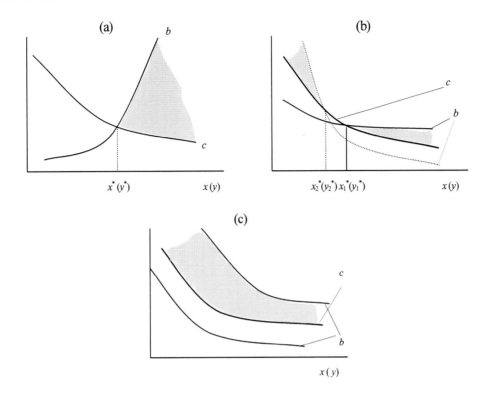

Figure 6.1. Conditions under which trade is encouraged.

$b=b(x, y)$; $c=c(x, y)$, with $\partial c/\partial y<0$.

In a check on the relation between the benefit of comparative advantage and income level, there may be different scenarios. First of all, there is an indication that the benefit of comparative advantage increases with higher income level. This viewpoint has been confirmed by the empirical analyses of, among others, Helpman (1987) and Krugman (1995), in which the sum of the logs of per capita GNPs of two countries will have a positive effect on the log form of trade between the two countries. Second, there may be a negative relation between the benefit of comparative advantage and income level, as indicated in some empirical results (Rauch, 1999).[9]

As a result, the marginal benefit of comparative advantage with respect to income level, denoted by $db/dy$, may be positive, negative or zero. Finally, Hypothesis 2 includes the following conditions under which trade is encouraged or retarded:

2a) When $\partial b/\partial y \geq 0$, trade tends to be retarded for values of income level to be less than $y^*$ and to be encouraged otherwise (see Figure 6.1a).

---

[9] As a matter of fact, a negative coefficient on per capita GDP sometimes may be found in gravity model on trade for homogeneous products if they are more agricultural and rich countries tend to have managed trade in agricultural products.

2b) When $\partial b/\partial y<0$, trade tends to be retarded for values of income level to be less than $y_1^*$ and to be encouraged otherwise if $|\partial b/\partial y|<|\partial c/\partial y|$; it tends to be encouraged for values of income level to be less than $y_2^*$ and to be retarded otherwise if $|\partial b/\partial y|>|\partial c/\partial y|$ (see Figure 6.1b).

2c) When $\partial b/\partial y=\partial c/\partial y$, trade tends to be retarded if $b<c$ for all values of income level and to be encouraged if $b>c$ for all values of income level (see Figure 6.1c).

After combining Hypotheses 1 and 2 together, we may have the cultural and economic conditions under which trade is encouraged or retarded (see Table 6.1).

**Table 6.1. Economic and cultural conditions under which trade is encouraged**

| Income level / Cultural similarity | $\partial B/\partial y\geq0$ | $\partial B/\partial y<0$ | | $\partial B/\partial y=\partial C/\partial y$ | |
|---|---|---|---|---|---|
| | | $|\partial B/\partial y|<|\partial C/\partial y|$ | $|\partial B/\partial y|>|\partial C/\partial y|$ | $B>C$ | $B<C$ |
| $\partial B/\partial x\geq0$ | $(x>x^*)$ $(y>y^*)$ | $(x>x^*)$ $(y>y_1^*)$ | $(x>x^*)$ $(y<y_2^*)$ | $(x>x^*)$ | AR |
| $\partial B/\partial x<0$  —  $|\partial B/\partial x|<|\partial C/\partial x|$ | $(x>x_1^*)$ $(y>y^*)$ | $(x>x_1^*)$ $(y>y_1^*)$ | $(x>x_1^*)$ | $(x>x_1^*)$ | AR |
| $|\partial B/\partial x|>|\partial C/\partial x|$ | $(x<x_2^*)$ $(y>y^*)$ | $(x<x_2^*)$ $(y>y_1^*)$ | $(x<x_2^*)$ | $(x<x_2^*)$ | AR |
| $\partial B/\partial x=\partial C/\partial x$  $B>C$ | $(y>y^*)$ | $(y>y_1^*)$ | $(y<y_2^*)$ | AE | AR |
| $\partial B/\partial x=\partial C/\partial x$  $B<C$ | AR | AR | AR | AR | AR |

*Notes*: (1) $x^*$, $x_1^*$ and $x_2^*$ are the values of cultural similarity at which the curves $B$ and $C$ meet; (2) $y^*$, $y_1^*$ and $y_2^*$ are the values of income level at which the curves $B$ and $C$ meet; and (3) "AE" denotes that 'trade is always encouraged", and "AR" denotes that "trade is always retarded".

Since the 1990s numerous quantitative studies have examined influences of culture on trade. Havrylyshyn and Pritchett (1991), for example, find that three languages – Portuguese, Spanish and English – are significant, in decreasing order of magnitude. In the study of poor countries, Foroutan and Pritchett (1993) find that French, Spanish and English are statistically significant. After trying supplementing the general language term and allowing each of the major languages to have an independent extra coefficient, Frankel and Wei (1995, table 2) find that two languages, English and Chinese, appear to qualify as especially important.[10] Besides, Frankel *et al.* (1997b) and Rauch (1999) use nine languages (English, Spanish, Chinese, Arabic, French, German, Japanese, Dutch and Portuguese) and treats international linguistic links as a dummy variable to represent when both countries of a pair speak a common language or had colonial links earlier in the 20th century. Frankel *et al.*'s results show a highly significant effect when all the languages are constrained to have the same coefficient.[11]

---

[10] When manufactured goods are considered alone and the individual major languages are estimated independently, Frankel et al. (1997a, table 5) found that the language coefficients lose all statistical significance.

[11] For example, the estimate fluctuates over time between 0.33 and 0.77. Pooled time-series estimates of the coefficient (in natural log) cluster around 0.44, which implies that two countries sharing linguistic/colonial links tend to trade roughly 55 percent (that is, $\exp(0.44)\approx1.55$) more than they would otherwise (Frankel *et al.*, 199b, pp. 74-5).

The above estimated coefficients on linguistic links are considerably interpreted as exhibiting a trend whereby trade in the postwar period has taken place among countries that are similar to each other linguistically. In the other words, they are interpreted as possible evidence of increased cultural barriers to economic activities. However it should be noted that linguistic variables have been highly simplified in the above studies, probably due to the fact that they are only treated as a complement variable in the determinants of economic activities. For example, the linguistic links between countries were only treated in the above studies as a dummy variable. As most countries are linguistically diversified, the international (or interregional) linguistic links should be a much more comprehensive index than as being simply expressed by '1' (for countries to share a common language) or '0' (for otherwise countries). It is worth noting that the above studies omit another important cultural variable, religion, that plays, at least in some cases, a more important role in economic development than the linguistic variable.

The economic determinants of trade seem to be controversial in the existing studies. According to the Heckscher-Ohlin theorem (see Heckscher, 1919; and Ohlin, 1933), countries with dissimilar levels of per capita income will trade more than countries with similar levels. However, a number of empirical results indicate that if the distribution of national incomes across countries becomes more equal over time, the volume of trade should increase. For example, Linder (1961) predicts that countries with similar levels of per capita income will tend to have similar preferences with somewhat differentiated marketable goods, and thus will trade more with each other. Moreover, Helpman (1987) and Krugman (1995) predict that the sum of the logs of per capita GNPs of two countries will have a positive effect on the log form of trade between the two countries.

The estimated results shown in Figure 6.2 can be used to provide various cultural and economic conditions under which the growth of trade is encouraged or retarded:

(i)   Trade between countries with dissimilar levels of per capita incomes tends to be retarded by cultural (especially religious) dissimilarity indexes; and

(ii)  Trade between countries with similar levels of per capita incomes tends to be retarded by cultural (especially religious) dissimilarity indexes when the income levels are low and tends to be encouraged by cultural (especially religious) dissimilarity indexes when the income levels are high.

## 6.3. A GRAVITY MODEL

Culture, as an informal institution, has important implications to international trade (Noland, 2005; Guo, 2007a). Although the components of culture have been variously defined, we focus on only two elements – language and religion. Of course, our discussion of these cultural elements is not definitive and perhaps would not satisfy anthropologists. Language, as the major tool of communication, is the most obvious starting point for the exploration of differences between cultures. Every language carries a weight of values, of sensibilities, of approaches to reality – all of which insinuate themselves into the consciousness of those who speak it. Although it is not the only tool to build trusting relationships, doors usually open more quickly when knocked on by someone who speaks a

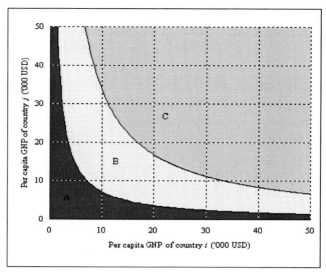

*Notes*: Area A = countries between which trade is retarded by both linguistic and religious dissimilarity indexes; Area B = countries between which trade is retarded by religious dissimilarity but is encouraged by linguistic dissimilarity; and Area C = countries between which trade is encouraged by both religious and linguistic dissimilarity indexes.

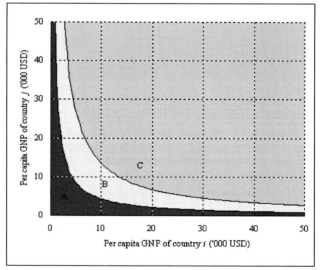

*Notes*: Area A = countries between which import is retarded by religious dissimilarity index; Area B = countries between which export is retarded by and import is encouraged by religious dissimilarity index; and Area C = countries between which import and export are encouraged by religious dissimilarity index.

Figure 6.2. Conditions under which cultural dissimilarity encourages (retards) trade.

familiar language. Compared to language, religion can provide more insights into the characteristics of a culture. What is more important, religion can have a deep impact not only on attitudes towards economic matters but also on values that influence the economic matters. Specifically, the religious attitudes and values can help to determine what we think is right or appropriate, what is important, what is desirable, and so on.

The gravity model is most commonly used by economists to study international trade.[12] The classic early application of the model was by Linnemann (1966), who continued work first reported by Tinbergen (1962) and then by Pöyhönen (1963). Some of the most recent work on the application of the model was Frankel et al. (1997a, 1997b), Rauch (1999) and Rose (2004), among others. Generally, a gravity model assumes that the volume of trade between any two economies will be directly proportional to the product of their economic masses (measured by GDP or GNP) and inversely proportional to the distance between them. Per capita incomes (measured by product of per capita GDPs or GNPs) have become a standard covariate in the gravity models of, for example, Eaton and Tamura (1994), Frankel et al. (1997a, 1997b) and Rauch (1999).

Studies such as that of Frankel *et al.* (1995, 1997b) also employ dummies for 'membership' in the geographical areas such as East Asia and the Western Hemisphere. Including these dummy variables could, as stated by Rauch (1999, fn. 6), reduce the size of estimated coefficients on distance. In this reseach, dummies for membership are excluded from analysis because they could compound the problem of interpretation that will be presented by the cultural variables employed. Adjacency is another dummy that has been used in the above studies but is also excluded from the East Asian case (to be discussed in Section 6.5) because several East Asian economies do not share a common land border with the outside world (e.g., Japan, the Philippines, Singapore and Taiwan) or their land boundaries cannot be used as efficient trade ports (such as the 38th Parallel between North and South Korea, Upper Kapuas Mts. and Iran, Kalimantan between Indonesia and Malaysia, the boundary between Myanmar and Thailand, as well as the Himalayas and the Pamirs separating China and its western neighbors).

There is a widely held view that easily observable impediments, such as transportation costs, do not adequately capture transactions costs in international trade. One response has been to directly investigate the possible role of transborder business networks or ethnic diasporas in reducing transactions costs (Rauch, 2001; Rauch and Trindade, 2002; and Combes et al., 2005). In addition, Guiso et al. (2004) and Guo (2006) suggest that more diffuse cultural affinity or similarity may be another channel. They argue that cultural distance—as proxied by, among other things, the genetic differences across national populations—is a robust determinant of the volume of international trade in the context of a conventional gravity model. In order to apply the gravity model to test the effects of the cultural influences on trade, we analyze the influences of linguistic and religious variables. The assumption here is that language is an effective tool of communication and that religion can provide the insights into the characteristics of culture. The basic form of the gravity model to be used in my empirical analysis is as the following:

$$\ln(\text{TRADE}_{ij}+1)=\alpha_0+\alpha_1\ln(\text{GDP}_i\text{GDP}_j)+\alpha_2\ln(\text{GDPPC}_i\text{GDPPC}_j)$$
$$+ \alpha_3\ln\text{DISTANCE}_{ij}+\alpha_4\text{LANGUAGE}_{ij}+\alpha_5\text{RELIGION}_{ij} \qquad (6.1)$$

In Equation 6.1, 'ln' represents natural logarithm; $\text{TRADE}_{ij}$, measured in thousand US dollars, is the sum of exports and imports between economies $i$ and $j$. In order to make the natural logarithm of TRADE become mathematically meaningful when TRADE=0,

---

[12] The earliest application of the gravity model can be traced back to the 1940s (see, e.g., Zipf, 1946; Stewart, 1948).

ln(TRADE+1) is used to approximate ln(TRADE).[13] This seems to be reasonable since the size of TRADE is, if not zero, always far larger than one thousand US dollars. $GDP_iGDP_j$ is the product of purchasing power parity (PPP)-adjusted GDP of the $i$th and $j$th economies. $GDPPC_iGDPPC_j$ is the product of PPP-adjusted GDP per capita of the $i$th and $j$th economies. $DISTANCE_{ij}$ represents the distance between the geographical centers of gravity of the $i$th and $j$th economies (in kilometers). $LANGUAGE_{ij}$ and $RELIGION_{ij}$, the measurement of which will be discussed later, denote the extents to which the $i$th and $j$th economies are linguistically and religiously linked each other, respectively.

In the East Asian case, to be discussed in Section 6.5, the data on some linguistic groups are probably subject to a wider range of error than the other variables in Equation 6.1. Therefore, the ability to use five international languages, Bahasa (Indonesian or Malay), Chinese, English, Khmer and Thai, is measured with dummy variables. Consequently the gravity model on trade is written as:

$$\ln(TRADE_{ij}+1)=\beta_0+\beta_1\ln(GDP_iGDP_j)+\beta_2\ln(GDPPC_iGDPPC_j)$$
$$+\beta_3\ln DISTANCE_{ij}+\beta_4 RELIGION_{ij}+\beta_5 BAHASA$$
$$+\beta_6 CHINESE+\beta_7 ENGLISH+\beta_8 KHMER+\beta_9 THAI \qquad (6.2)$$

In Equation 6.2, BAHASA=1, CHINESE=1, KHMER=1 and THAI=1 means that economies $i$ and $j$ both speak the language in question; otherwise these dummies take the value 0. It has been recognized that most international trade contracts and documents are processed in English, especially in East Asia where different phylums exist.[14] As a result English reading/writing ability has been an important linguistic trait that reduces trade-related transactions costs. To reflect this fact, the English dummy is defined to include not only English as a mother tongue but also lingua franca and bilingual Englishes.

Equations 6.1 and 6.2 can be estimated by using standard statistical techniques. In order to further account for the potential impacts of multicollinearity between geographical and linguistic and religious variables, additional regressions are estimated by excluding the linguistic and religious variables. Specifically, if correlation coefficients of each pair of explanatory variables are fairly large, they could suggest potential multicollinearity that can cause imprecise regression results (Greene, 2002, pp. 255-8). If cross-sectional data are used, it is also necessary to conduct tests for heteroscedasticity. More specifically, while ordinary least squares (OLS)-estimated coefficients are unbiased, weighed least squares (WLS) estimation can provide more efficient results in terms of smaller coefficient standard errors (Greene, 2002, p. 499). After each OLS run, heteroscedasticity tests are performed for each individual regression model. If heteroscedasticity is significant, WLS estimation should be performed to correct this problem.

---

[13] Note that if there are a significant number of zero values in the pair-wise trade, then Tobit regressions techniques should be used. In this research, the number of observations identified by TRADE=0 is quite small.

[14] For example, there are five main phylums in East Asia: Sino-Tibetan phylum, Ural-Altaic phylum (such as Mongolian, Manchu-Tungas, etc.), Dravidian phylum (such as Telugu, Malay, etc.), Austronesian phylum, Austro-Asiatic phylum (such as Khmer, Mon, Vietnamese, etc.) and other phylums (such as Japanese, Korean, Papuan).

## 6.4. CULTURAL SIMILARITY INDEX

Cultural similarity index can be constructed in different ways. The simplest method is to use a dummy index; i.e., using '1' for economies to be culturally linked with each other, and using '0' otherwise. Although it has been applied in a number of studies (see, for example, Havrylyshyn and Pritchett, 1991; Foroutan and Pritchett, 1993; Frankel and Wei, 1995; Frankel et al., 1997b), this method cannot precisely measure the extent to which economies are culturally linked to each other, particularly when the economies are culturally diversified.

In this research, a comprehensive method is used to construct linguistic and religious similarity indexes. Suppose that the population shares of $N$ linguistic (religious) groups are expressed by $(x_1, x_2,..., x_N)$ and $(y_1, y_2,..., y_N)$ for economies $X$ and $Y$, respectively. $x_i$ and $y_i$ (where, $x_i \geq 0$ and $y_i \geq 0$) belong to the same linguistic (religious) group. Mathematically, the linguistic and religious similarity indexes (denoted by LANGUAGE and RELIGION, respectively) between the economies $X$ and $Y$ can be measured according to the following formula:[15]

$$\sum_{i=1}^{N} \min(x_i, y_i) \tag{6.3}$$

In Equation 6.3, min (...) denotes the minimization of the variables within parentheses. The values of LANGUAGE and RELIGION range between 0 and 1. In the extreme cases, when LANGUAGE (RELIGION)=1, the two economies have a common linguistic (religious) structure (i.e., for all $i$, $x_i=y_i$); when LANGUAGE (RELIGION)=0, the two economies do not have any linguistic (religious) links with each other (i.e., for all $i$, $x_i$ (or $y_i$)=0 and $x_i \neq y_i$). In other words, greater values of LANGUAGE or RELIGION indicate greater linguistic or religious similarity between two economies. Taking East Asia as an example, let us demonstrate how to construct linguistic and religious similarity indexes.

Languages considered are Bahasa (Malay or Indonesia), Cham, Chinese, English, Japanese, Kazak, Khmer, Korean, Kyrgyz, Miao, Mongol, Thai, Yao, Uighur, and Vietnamese. Population shares of the major linguistic groups are shown in Table 6.2a. Because of data restrictions, the population shares of most linguistic groups are based on first- or native languages. In addition, both mother tongue and lingua franca and bilingual Englishes are included in the English-speaking group. For some countries where data seem to be unreliable, shares of national (official) language speakers are estimated by using literacy rates. It may be worthwhile to consider the similarity of two languages that are either within a language phylum or characterized by some form of connection. For example, many Taglog speakers in the Philippines find it relatively easy to communicate with Bahasa speakers in Indonesia or Malaysia. In addition, many Japanese and Korean business managers can read (or guess the meaning of) Chinese characters that are used in both mainland China (under the simplified form) and Taiwan and Hong Kong (under the complex form). However, these are treated as separate languages because many other languages in neighboring countries have a

---

[15] This formula has been used in Guo (2004, 2006) and Noland (2005). Several other methods can also be used to comprehensively measure linguistic and religious similarity indexes. Boisso and Ferrantino (1997), for example, use $\sum x_i y_i$ as the construct of simialirty index. However, using Equation 6.3 can prevent the index from further reduction when the values of $x_i$ and $y_i$ are small.

certain degree of similarity in East Asia. Thus, including this kind of inter-linguistic connection could result in a multicollinearity problem (with the distance variable) in Equation 6.1.

Religious groups considered are Christianity (including all western Christians, such as Anglican, Roman Catholic, Protestant, Methodist, etc.), Islam (including Sunni and Shia), Buddhism (including Mahayana and Hinayana or Theravada Buddhism), Chinese folk-religion (a mixture of Confucianism and Taoism, which still finds followers in some Southeast Asian economies as well as China), and Hinduism. Subdivisions of Christianity and Islam are not distinguished because they are not that important in East Asia (in contrast to some the Western hemisphere and the Middle East), Hinayana Buddhism, which has followers in Southeast Asia (especially in Cambodia, Myanmar and Thailand) and in East Asia, is not separated from Mahayana Buddhism, which is concentrated in Southwest and Northwest China as well as Japan and Korea. Population shares of the major religious groups are shown in Table 6.2b. Religions such as 'folk religion' ('Chinese folk-religion' is an exception), 'traditional religion', 'atheism' and 'non-religion' are not distinguished in Equation 6.3 because followers of such religions are extremely diverse compared to the other religions considered.[16] For example, 'traditional or folk religionists' from one nation (say, Togo) and 'traditional or folk religionists' form the other (say, China) do not have a common religious ground for people to trust each other. In addition, Chondogyo, which only exists in North and South Korea (two economies that have not set up formal economic and trade relations), and Shintoism, which only exists in Japan, are excluded from the analysis.

Estimates of the percentage of Japanese who are Buddhist vary widely. Perhaps 85% of the population will cite Buddhism if asked what their preferred religion is, but about 75% also claim to be nonreligious. Frequently cited and high estimates of the Buddhist share (85% or 90%) come primarily from birth records, following a longstanding practice of family lines being officially associated with a local Buddhist temple. In Japan there has been a large and thriving Buddhist community, but surveys indicate that the numbers of veritable Buddhists are far fewer than those of nominal Buddhists (Ash, 1997, pp. 160-1).

## 6.5. EVIDENCE FROM EAST ASIA

The major task of this section is to quantitatively investigate the sources for changes in East Asia's foreign trade over time. Thus, the use of the cross-sectional data from the East Asian economies in different years enables that the estimated results are not an artifact of any particular time period and to allow for changes in coefficients on the linguistic and religious variables. Generally, a decade-long period is appropriate for this kind of research because analysis for a shorter period would not reflect relevant social and economic changes, while

---

[16] Atheism and non-religion were each treated as a 'religious affiliation' in China, but they were grouped as a single religious group in North Korea (Encyclopedia Britannica, 1996, pp. 775-776).

## Table 6.2a. Shares of major linguistic groups in East Asia (%), 1985 and 1995

| Economy | Bahasa[a] 1995 | Bahasa[a] 1985 | Chinese 1995 | Chinese 1985 | English[b] 1995 | English[b] 1985 | Khmer 1995 | Khmer 1985 | Thai 1995 | Thai 1985 |
|---|---|---|---|---|---|---|---|---|---|---|
| Brunei | 82.03 | 64.73 | 9.48 | 20.54 | 3.27 | NA | | | | NA |
| Cambodia | | | 3.08 | NA | | | 88.63 | NA | | |
| China | | | 92.06 | 88.65 | | | | | | |
| Hong Kong | | | 76.56 | 98.58 | 20.29 | 20.29[c] | | | | |
| Indonesia | 85.00[d] | 77.00[d] | NA | NA | | | | | | |
| Japan | | | 0.17 | | 0.06 | | | | | |
| Korea, North | | | 0.16 | | | | | | | |
| Korea, South | | | 0.11 | | | | | | | |
| Laos | | | | 1.09 | | | 16.41[e] | 7.00[e] | | |
| Malaysia | 84.30[f] | 76.30[f] | 33.60[g] | 33.60[g] | 24.61 | 24.61[c] | | | | |
| Myanmar | | | | | | | | | | |
| Philippines | | | 0.05 | 0.25 | 29.54 | 29.54[c] | | | | |
| Singapore | 10.30 | 14.70 | 56.26 | 76.66 | 27.23 | 27.23[c] | | | | |
| Taiwan | | | 97.85 | 97.85 | | | | | | |
| Thailand | 3.65 | 3.80 | 12.13 | 11.31 | | | 1.27 | 1.40 | 80.15 | 81.36 |
| Vietnam | | | 1.40 | | | | 1.38 | 1.35 | 1.62 | 1.32 |

Notes: (1) Cham, Japanese, Kazak, Korean, Kyrgyz, Miao, Mongol, Taglog, Yao, Uighur, and Vietnamese, which are also taken in to account in the measurement of linguistic similarity index, are not shown in this table. (2) "NA" denotes data are not available. (3) Blanks denote that figures are less than 0.005% or data are not available. (4) Totals in the table may not be added up to 100 due to the existence of bilinguists.

a: Include 'Bahasa Indonesia' and 'Bahasa Malay'. In some countries populations also include second language speakers as well as other relevant linguistic groups (such as 'Malay-Chinese', 'Malay-English', 'Malay-Chinese-English', and 'Malay-others'). b: Include mother tongue, lingua franca, and bilingual Englishes. c: As of 1995 due to the data unavailability or unreliability in 1985. d: Represented by literacy rates, based on Jalal and Sardjunanu (2006). e: As for 'Mon-Khmer' or 'Lao-Theung'. f: Represented by literacy rates based on ACCU (2005). g: As of 1979. Based on Languages of the World, 14th Edition (available from www.ethnologue.com/14/show_country .asp?name=Malaysia).

Source: Calculated by the author based on Encyclopedia Britannica (1986, 1996), except those that are noted otherwise.

**Table 6.2b Shares of selected religious groups in East Asia (%), 1985 and 1995**

| Economy | Christian | | Muslim | | Buddhist | | Hindu | | Chinese folk-religion | |
|---|---|---|---|---|---|---|---|---|---|---|
| | 1995 | 1985 | 1995 | 1985 | 1995 | 1985 | 1995 | 1985 | 1995 | 1985 |
| Brunei | | | 67.21 | 63.39 | | 13.84 | | | | |
| Cambodia | | | 2.12 | | 95.00 | | | | | |
| China | 5.95 | | 1.47 | 2.40 | 8.48 | 6.00 | | | 20.13 | 20.10 |
| Hong Kong | 8.47 | 9.51 | | | 21.88[a] | 20.80[a] | | | 51.93[a] | 69.69[a] |
| Indonesia | | 7.50 | 87.21 | 83.60 | 1.03 | | 1.83 | | | |
| Japan[b] | 0.69 | 0.74 | | | 40.86[b] | 41.82[b] | | | | |
| Korea, North[c] | | | | | | | | | | |
| Korea, South[c] | 24.06[d] | 25.69 | | | 24.35 | 37.40 | | | 17.51[e] | 17.51 |
| Laos | | | | | 57.81 | 58.00 | | | | |
| Malaysia | 6.39 | | 52.92 | 52.90 | 17.33 | 17.30 | 6.99 | | 11.59 | 11.60 |
| Myanmar | 4.91 | 5.60 | 3.82 | 3.60 | 89.45 | 87.20 | 0.51 | | | |
| Philippines | 90.68 | 84.10[f] | 4.57 | | | | | | | |
| Singapore | 12.89 | 10.35 | 14.92 | 16.21 | 15.97[a] | 26.76 | 3.29 | | 37.90[a] | 29.30 |
| Taiwan | 3.45 | 7.40 | 0.23 | | 22.95 | 43.00 | | | 18.85[g] | 48.50 |
| Thailand | 0.54 | | 4.04 | 3.80 | 94.80 | 95.00 | | | | |
| Vietnam | 8.68 | 7.40 | | | 66.67 | 55.30 | | | | |

Notes: (1) Atheism, traditional religion and non-religion are not listed in this table since they cannot be taken into account in the calculation of religious similarity index. (2) 'Christian' includes all western Christians, such as Anglican, Roman Catholic, Protestant, Methodist, etc. (3) Blanks denote that figures are less than 0.005 or data are not available. a Include Taoist and Chinese folk-religion. b These figures are much smaller than the corresponding numbers reported by the religious organizations in Japan, but they are closer to the surveyed data (Ash, 1997, p. 160). c Both North and South Korea are also religiously linked by Chondogyo – a Korean folk-religion that is not listed in this table. d Only include Protestant. e As of 1985. f Only include Roman Catholic. g Only include Taoist and Confucian.

Source: Calculated by the author based on Encyclopedia Britannica (1986, 1996).

## Table 6.3 Sensitivity analyses for gravity model on international trade, 1985

| Coefficient | Reg. (1) | Reg. (1A) | Reg. (2) | Reg. (2A) | Reg. (3) | Reg. (3A) |
|---|---|---|---|---|---|---|
| Constant | -19.746 | -19.530 | -17.282 | -18.952 | -21.865 | -19.943 |
| | (1.557[a]) | (1.503[a]) | (1.666[a]) | (1.580[a]) | (1.681[a]) | (1.616[a]) |
| $\ln(GDP_iGDP_j)$ | 1.171 | 1.145 | 1.162 | 1.143 | 1.184 | 1.150 |
| | (0.032[a]) | (0.032[a]) | (0.032[a]) | (0.032[a]) | (0.033[a]) | (0.032[a]) |
| $\ln(GDPPC_iGDPPC_j)$ | 0.696 | 0.795 | 0.722 | 0.805 | 0.644 | 0.730 |
| | (0.059[a]) | (0.056[a]) | (0.059[a]) | (0.056[a]) | (0.061[a]) | (0.059[a]) |
| $\ln(DISTANCE_{ij})$ | -1.128 | -1.266 | -1.440 | -1.343 | -0.871 | -1.143 |
| | (0.129[a]) | (0.123[a]) | (0.147[a]) | (0.136[a]) | (0.149[a]) | (0.139[a]) |
| $LANGAUGE_{ij}$ | | | -9.048 | -2.409 | | |
| | | | (2.096[a]) | (1.515) | | |
| $RELIGION_{ij}$ | | | 0.192 | 0.318 | 0.024 | 0.188 |
| | | | (0.410) | (0.405) | (0.414) | (0.405) |
| BAHASA | | | | | 2.645 | 2.058 |
| | | | | | (0.866[a]) | (0.763[a]) |
| CHINESE | | | | | 0.466 | 0.130 |
| | | | | | (0.387) | (0.372) |
| ENGLISH | | | | | 0.345 | 0.623 |
| | | | | | (0.210) | (0.193[a]) |
| KHMER | | | | | 3.701 | -0.920 |
| | | | | | (2.032[c]) | (1.735) |
| THAI | | | | | 2.770 | 2.770 |
| | | | | | (2.998) | (2.998) |
| R square | 0.565 | 0.565 | 0.570 | 0.565 | 0.570 | 0.570 |
| F-statistic | 696.19 | 755.28 | 425.92 | 454.07 | 236.56 | 256.70 |
| Number of observations | 1612 | 1750 | 1612 | 1750 | 1612 | 1750 |

*Notes:* All regressions are estimated by ordinary least squares (OLS). Reg. (x) (x=1, 2 and 3) denotes regression including trade flows involving Hong Kong; Reg. (xA) denotes regression excluding trade flows involving Hong Kong. Dependent variable is the natural log of bilateral trade (sum of exports and imports) in 1984 (since many East Asian economies suffered from bad recessions in 1985). Figures within parentheses are standard errors. [a] and [c] denote significance at the 1% and 10% levels, respectively.

significant changes in transportation and communication technologies would have to be accounted for if a longer one is used. In addition, conditions affecting international trade are likely to have differed during and after the Cold War; thus, it is useful to compare estimates from both periods. Estimates for additional years would also be helpful to better analyze each period, but this is complicated by data constraints. We thus analyze data for 1985 and 1995 to compare Cold War era and the post-Cold War era, respectively. Since many East Asian economies suffered from bad recessions in 1985, data on trade from 1985 are replaced with those from 1984.

Data sources for the abovementioned economic variables are as follows. The data on TRADE are available from the NBER-UN Trade Data for 1962-2000 (available at http://cid.econ.undavis.edu/data/undata/undata.htm). As emphasized in Feenstra et al. (2005), it is generally better to use data from the importing country because it is usually much easier to measure imports than exports. In this case, country A's exports to country B is based on country B's import data, not country A's export data. Alternative data available from the IMF are not used for several reasons. First, the large amount of the 'entrepot trade' in Hong Kong and Singapore is not accounted for in the IMF's statistics. Second, data discrepancies between exporting and importing economies exist, particularly in China, Hong Kong, Indonesia and Singapore. For example, discrepancies in bilateral trade statistics as reported by China and its trading partners exist, particularly with industrial countries. Trade with these countries is classified by China as trade with Hong Kong Special Administrative Region (HKSAR) if it passes through HKSAR ports. However, the NBER-UN data have not solved all the problems included in the original trade data. Estimates of many problematic trade flows (including Indonesia and Singapore) are provided, but estimates of Hong Kong's trade have only been revised from 1988 onwards. The only practical way to provide an adequate explanation in this regard is to conduct a sensitivity analysis for the gravity model estimates in 1985.[1] The sensitivity analysis, which will be conducted later, compares estimates excluding trade flows involving Hong Kong (an unusual economy with a large amount of entrepot trade with China) and alternative estimates excluding these trade flows.

The PPP-adjusted GDP and GDPPC data are based on the Penn World Table (PWT) version 6.1 (available at http://pwt.econ.upenn.edu/php_site/pwt_index.php).[2] Although the PWT includes 168 economies, data on Brunei (1985 and 1995), North Korea (1985 and 1995), Lao PDR (1985 and 1995), Myanmar (1985 and 1995) and Vietnam (1985) are unavailable. My estimates of the unreported PPP-adjusted data of the East Asian countries are based on each country's nominal GDP per capita (in which the 1985 and 1995 data are available from World Bank, 1986, 1996) and the PPP conversion factors of an economically similar or geographically neighboring country. For example, China's PPP conversion factor is applied to North Korea, Singapore's to Brunei, and Cambodia's to both Lao PDR and Myanmar. Vietnam's PPP-adjusted GDP per capita in 1985, which is not reported in the above source, is estimated based on its PPP conversion factor in 1995. Moreover, since the 1985's GDP per capita data (in exchange rates) are unavailable in Cambodia, Laos and Vietnam, the figures estimated by Zhao (2002) are used. The data on the DISTANCE variable are measured by the author based on Rand McNally (1994).

---

[1] This idea is largely based on the suggestion by an anonymous referee.

[2] A country's GDP in 1985 or 1995 can be easily obtained by multiplying its GDP per capita (GDPPC) by its population (the latter is available from United Nations, 1986, 1996).

In this context, the analysis then turns to how linguistic and religious variables may affect international trade. The emphasis on the role of cultural linkage in international economic activities may be traced back to biological analyses showing that cooperation among animals is influenced by genetic similarity (Wilson, 1980). Trade and economic cooperation may also be affected by cultural similarities, as it is easier and more efficient for people with the same cultural identity (language, religion, or any other cultural element) to trust and communicate each other than for those with different cultural identities. Linguistic differences have clearly influenced international trade and marketing to some extent. Although it is not the only tool for building trusting relationships, doors usually open more quickly when knocked on by someone who speaks a familiar language. Compared to language, religion can provide more insights into the characteristics of inter-personal behavior. More importantly, religion can have a deep impact not only on attitudes towards economic matters but also on values that influence them. Specifically, religious attitudes and values help to determine what one thinks is right or appropriate, what is important, what is desirable, and so on.

Sixteen economies (Brunei, Cambodia, China, Hong Kong, Indonesia, Japan, Laos, North Korea, South Korea, Malaysia, Myanmar, Philippines, Singapore, Taiwan, Thailand and Vietnam) are included in this research. Because some key data are unavailable, I exclude Cambodia and Taiwan from 1985, as well as Macau from both 1985 and 1995. For each East Asian economy in the sample, 162 and 196 trade partners (economies) are included in the estimates for 1985 and 1995, respectively. As a result, the maximum number of observations is 2268 (14×162) for 1985 and 3136 (16×196) for 1995. The data on LANGUAGE and RELIGION are calculated by the author based on Equation 6.3 and Encyclopedia Britannica (1986, 1996).[3]

The above sample includes economies in vastly different political and cultural conditions. The attractive feature of this broad sample is that it results in large variation in the explanatory variables. This illustrates how it is impossible to make general inferences about the implications of a set of social, economic and cultural variables from the experiences of one or a few countries. However, one drawback of this kind of diverse sample is that it creates difficulties in measuring variables in a consistent and accurate way across countries and over time. For example, one reason that China, Japan and Korea may have relatively low transaction costs is because they share a common Buddhist/Confucian/Taoist past which left them with similar cultural legacies. The other empirical issue is the sorting out of the direction of causation. In a long-term framework, one could argue that changes in culture (especially language and religion) are influenced by international exchanges such as trade. However, causation of this nature is very weak in shorter time periods.

Using the gravity model and the reconstructed data described above, the determinants of foreign trade in East Asia can be estimated. The Pearson correlation coefficients of all explanatory variables are less than 0.50 (detailed information is not reported here). The variance of inflation factor (VIF) for each explanatory variable is further examined by utilizing SPSS statistics software. Since all VIF scores of the explanatory variables (which range from 1.021 to 1.556) are within the accepted threshold values, the regression outcomes are unlikely to be affected by potential multicollinearity problems. In addition, the heteroscedasticity tests performed for all regression equations show that the regressions are free from heteroscedasticity.

---

[3] The data on the bilateral linguistic and religious similarity indexes are available from the author upon request.

Since the data on Hong Kong's trade include large amount of entrepot trade that is unrelated to the standard gravity model variables and the NBER-UN Trade Data for 1962-2000 adjust Hong Kong's data only from 1988 onwards (Feenstra et al., 2005), a sensitivity analysis should be conducted for the model regressions in 1985. Table 6.3 compares estimates excluding trade flows involving Hong Kong (represented by three regressions as 1, 2 and 3) and alternative estimates including trade flows involving Hong Kong (represented by three regression as 1A, 2A and 3A). The estimated results show that the "Hong Kong factor" does affect the statistical consistency of the regressions, especially when linguistic and religious variables are included in the gravity model. For example, when Hong Kong is included, the coefficients on the dummy variables ENGLISH and KHMER are 0.623 (statistically significant at 1% level) and –0.920 (statistically insignificant), respectively. However, when Hong Kong is excluded, the coefficients become 0.345 (statistically insignificant) and 3.701 (statistically significant at the 10% level), respectively. Given Hong Kong's critical influences on the estimated results and its problematic trade data, the analysis for 1985 will be based on the regressions excluding Hong Kong.

In Tables 6.3 and 6.4, the regressions without linguistic and religious variables, those with the linguistic and religious similarity indexes and those with a combination of linguistic dummies and religious similarity index are denoted by Reg. (1), Reg. (2) and Reg. (3), respectively. All regressions, which are estimated by ordinary least squares (OLS), yield differing statistical evidence for the determinants of trade in East Asia, reflecting differences in the linguistic and religious influences on trade. For example, for the year 1995, when linguistic and religious variables are not considered, the estimated coefficients on the natural logs of distance and the product of per capita GDPs are –0.813 and 0.908, respectively [Reg. (1), Table 6.4]. However, after the linguistic and religious variables are added to the regressions, the coefficients on these variables become –0.648 and 0.868 in Reg. (2) and –0.219 and 0.764 in Reg. (3), respectively. In addition, Tables 6.3 and 6.4 show that the linguistic and religious influences on the determinants of trade are more statistically significant in 1995 than in 1985. When LANGAUGE variables is replaced with five dummy variables (BAHASA, CHINESE, ENGLISH, KHMER and THAI), the results show that two languages (Bahasa and Khmer) have positive and significant effects on trade in 1985 [Reg. (3), Table 6.3] and that four languages (Bahasa, Chinese, English and Khmer) have positive and significant effects on trade in 1995 [Reg. (3), Table 6.4]. By contrast, Thai is found to be statistically insignificant in both years.

The determinants of international trade seem controversial in the existing studies. For example, according to the Heckscher-Ohlin theorem, countries with dissimilar levels of per capita income will trade more than countries with similar levels (Heckscher, 1919; Ohlin, 1933). However, a number of empirical results indicate that if the distribution of national incomes across countries becomes more equal over time, the volume of trade should increase.

For example, Linder (1961) predicts that countries with similar levels of per capita income will tend to have similar preferences with somewhat differentiated marketable goods, and thus will trade more with each other. Moreover, Helpman (1987) and Krugman (1995) predict that the product of per capita GDP of two countries will have a positive effect on trade between two countries. With regard to the East Asian case, it is found that the coefficients on the product of per capita GDP are positive and statistically significant in all equations in 1985 and 1995.[4]

**Table 6.4. Gravity model regressions on international trade, 1995**

| Coefficient | Reg. (1) | Reg. (2) | Reg. (3) |
|---|---|---|---|
| Constant | -28.083 (1.207$^a$) | -29.303 (1.225$^a$) | -32.193 (1.280$^a$) |
| ln(GDP$_i$GDP$_j$) | 1.228 (0.026$^a$) | 1.236 (0.027$^a$) | 1.251 (0.027$^a$) |
| ln(GDPPC$_i$GDPPC$_j$) | 0.908 (0.046$^a$) | 0.868 (0.047$^a$) | 0.764 (0.050$^a$) |
| ln(DISTANCE$_{ij}$) | -0.813 (0.097$^a$) | -0.648 (0.103$^a$) | -0.219 (0.113$^b$) |
| LANGAUGE$_{ij}$ | | 2.860 (0.862$^a$) | |
| RELIGION$_{ij}$ | | 1.242 (0.330$^a$) | 0.715 (0.334$^b$) |
| BAHASA | | | 1.938 (0.757$^a$) |
| CHINESE | | | 1.901 (0.258$^a$) |
| ENGLISH | | | 0.571 (0.153$^a$) |
| KHMER | | | 6.125 (1.125$^a$) |
| THAI | | | -1.117 (1.110) |
| R square | 0.629 | 0.633 | 0.637 |
| F-statistic | 1380.43 | 841.41 | 496.85 |
| Number of observations | 2447 | 2446 | 2446 |

*Notes*: All regressions are estimated by ordinary least squares (OLS). Dependent variable is the natural log of bilateral trade (sum of exports and imports) in 1995. Figures within parentheses are standard errors. $^a$ and $^b$ denote significance at the 1% and 5% levels, respectively.

Previous studies have shown a negative and statistically significant relationship between distance and trade (e.g., Linnemann, 1966; Brada and Mendez, 1983; Bikker, 1987; Oguledo and MacPhee, 1994; Mansfield and Bronson, 1997).[5] As stated earlier, however, no observable tendency has been found for the effect of geographical proximity to fall over time. In contrast to the results of previous studies (e.g., Boisso and Ferrantino, 1997; Frankel et al., 1997a, 1997b; Rauch, 1999), the results presented in Tables 6.3 and 6.4 suggests that

---

[4] When I used GDP and GDP per capita in US dollar using market exchange rates and re-run the regressions, negative coefficients are found for 1995. The referee pointed out that failure to use the PPP-adjusted estimates of GDP and GDP per capita induces a measurement error, which can bias estimates of gravity equations.

[5] Specifically, Linnemann (1966) estimates the coefficient as –0.77, Brada and Mendez (1983) and Oguledo and MacPhee (1994) as 0.76, Bikker (1987) as –0.90 to –1.1, and Mansfield and Bronson (1997) as –0.51 to –0.69 (for 1950-1990).

geographical influence on trade was reduced during 1985 and 1995. For example, the estimated coefficient on ln(DISTANCE) in Reg. (3) changed from –0.871 in 1985 to –0.219 in 1995. One of the major driving forces contributing to this tendency might be technological advance in transportation and communications. Intuitively, wide application of E-commerce and the declining of distance-related transactions costs have increasingly contributed to the growth of international trade in East Asia.

While transactions are conducted via electronic devices, they may be transported using digital mechanisms, such as the download of a product from the Internet. It is the latter that provides the enabling mechanisms to foster the growth of electronic commerce. The actual and projected growth rates and uses of the Internet indicate that electronic commerce is no passing fad, but rather a fundamental change in the way in which businesses interact with one another and their consumers. The followings present the most obvious potential benefits from engaging in electronic commerce:[6]

a)   Internet and web-based electronic commerce can reach a more graphically dispersed customers base;
b)   procurement processing costs can be lowered;
c)   cost of purchasing can be lowered;
d)   reductions in inventories;
e)   lower cycle times;
f)   better customer service; and
g)   lower sales and, marketing costs.

It has been hypothesized that international relations among countries with similar ideology (but not culture) were emphasized in the Cold-War era (Huntington, 1996). Is this hypothesis consistent with the linguistic and religious influences on international trade in East Asia? As shown in Table 6.3, the estimated coefficient on LANGUAGE is negative and that on RELIGION is statistically insignificant in 1985, suggesting that neither linguistic nor religious similarity has positive influence on foreign trade. However, both of these estimated coefficients became positive and statistically significant in 1995 (Table 6.4), providing evidence to support that linguistic and religious factors have played positive roles in international trade during the post-Cold War era. With regard to the linguistic and religious influences in the post-Cold War era (represented by the year 1995), language plays a more important role than religion. Specifically, the estimated coefficients (i.e., 2.860 for LANGUAGE and 1.242 for RELIGION) in Reg. (2) of Table 6.4 suggest that the size of trade between the economies that are linguistically and religiously the same (i.e, LANGUAGE = RELIGION = 1) could have been risen by about 16.46 [exp(2.860)-1=16.46] and 2.46 [exp(1.242)-1=2.46] times compared with that between the economies that are linguistically and religiously different from each other (i.e., LANGUAGE = RELIGION = 0), respectively.[7] The stronger effect of linguistic influence on trade might be attributable to the East Asian Diaspora (the case of Chinese Diaspora is briefly discussed at the end of this section), as ethnicity is more represented by linguistic than by religious identities.

---

[6] Based on Greenstein and Feinman (2000, pp. 2-3).

[7] Note that the values of LANGUAGE and RELIGION are always larger than 0 but less than 1 in East Asia.

Since the 1980s, especially since the early 1990s when the Cold War came to an end, economic activities in homogeneous cultural environments have become more important than in heterogeneous cultural environments. Trade within the European Community constituted less than 50 percent of the community's total trade before the 1980s; by the 1990s this had grown to more than 60 percent. Similar shifts toward intraregional trade also occurred in intra-Latin American trade in the 1990s, with trade between Brazil and Argentina tripling and Colombia-Venezuela trade quadrupling between 1990 and 1993. In 1994 Brazil replaced the United States as Argentina's principal trading partner. Trade among the ASEAN countries, China, Hong Kong, South Korea and Taiwan increased from less than 10 percent to over 30 percent of their total trade from the 1950s to the 1990s.[8] How can one explain the rapid expansion of the intraregional trade in East Asia?

After dividing the bilateral trade into two groups – trade with East Asian economies (i.e., intra-East Asian or intra-regional trade) and trade with non-East Asian economies (i.e., inter-regional trade) – two sets of estimated results can be derived from each of Equations 6.1 and 6.2. As shown in Table 6.5, the geographical factor (expressed by the natural log of distance between trade partners) shows a decreasing influence on inter-regional trade. The estimated coefficients on distance (–1.806 for 1985 and –0.117 for 1995, both of which are statistically significant at the 1% level) suggest that a one percent increase in distance reduce the amount of trade with the non-East Asian economies by 1.806 and 0.117 percent for 1985 and 1995, respectively. However, for intra-East Asian trade, the estimated coefficients on distance are positive and statistically significant (0.842 for 1985 and 0.409 for 1995), suggesting that the geographical influence on intra-East Asian trade follows a different pattern from that on inter-regional trade.

For 1985, the coefficients on LANGUAGE and RELIGION, both of which are either negative or statistically insignificant in Table 6.3, become positive and statistically significant when the dependent variable is replaced with inter-regional and intra-regional trade, respectively (Table 6.5). More intriguing is the changing magnitude for the estimated coefficients on the linguistic and religious variables over time. For example, the estimated results in Table 6.5 show a decreasing tendency for linguistic influence on East Asia's inter-regional trade from 1985 to the 1995, as well as for religious influence on intra-East Asian trade for the same period. In addition, the linguistic influence on inter-regional trade are more significant than that on intra-regional trade. By contrast, the religious influence on East Asia's intra-regional trade is more significant than that on its inter-regional trade. The estimated results also indicate that (i) religion is more important in the determinants of intra-regional trade than language, and (ii) language is more important in the determinants of inter-regional trade than religion. The reason for the above findings is two-folds. On the one hand, trade within East Asia can be conducted by people speaking in each other's language as lingua franca. As a result, this could reduce the statistical significance of linguistic influence on trade within East Asia. On the other hand, religion should be more crucial for the neighboring economies that have already close interactions than the remote, inter-continental economies with much fewer frequent contacts.

---

[8] IMF (various issues).

**Table 6.5. Gravity model regressions on intra-regional and inter-regional trade (language as continuous variable)**

| Explanatory variable | Intra-regional trade | | Inter-regional trade | |
|---|---|---|---|---|
| | 1985 | 1995 | 1985 | 1995 |
| Constant | -43.961 | -35.433 | -12.572 | -33.563 |
| | (4.752$^a$) | (2.937$^a$) | (2.220$^a$) | (1.824$^a$) |
| ln(GDP$_i$GDP$_j$) | 1.076 | 1.071 | 1.149 | 1.260 |
| | (0.1129$^a$) | (0.081$^a$) | (0.033$^a$) | (0.028$^a$) |
| ln(GDPPC$_i$GDPPC$_j$) | 1.313 | 1.032 | 0.654 | 0.794 |
| | (0.218$^a$) | (0.144$^a$) | (0.061$^a$) | (0.049$^a$) |
| ln(DISTANCE$_{ij}$) | 0.842 | 0.409 | -1.806 | -0.117 |
| | (0.407$^b$) | (0.251$^c$) | (0.217$^a$) | (0.178) |
| LANGAUGE$_{ij}$ | 0.043 | 1.269 | 113.376 | 7.240 |
| | (2.893) | (1.239) | (68.839$^c$) | (1.434$^a$) |
| RELIGION$_{ij}$ | 4.475 | 2.897 | -0.163 | 0.411 |
| | (1.544$^a$) | (0.873$^a$) | (0.419) | (0.360) |
| R square | 0.504 | 0.578 | 0.570 | 0.624 |
| F-statistic | 27.99 | 68.56 | 387.08 | 725.91 |
| Number of observations | 143 | 255 | 1468 | 2190 |

*Notes*: All regressions are estimated by ordinary least squares (OLS). Dependent variable is the natural log of bilateral trade (sum of exports and imports) in 1984 (for 1985's regressions) and 1995 (for 1995's regressions). Hong Kong is excluded from regressions in 1985. Figures within parentheses are standard errors. $^a$, $^b$ and $^c$ denote significance at the at 1%, 5% and 10% levels, respectively.

**Table 6.6. Gravity model regressions on intra-regional and inter-regional trade (language as dummies)**

| Explanatory variable | Intra-regional trade | | Inter-regional trade | |
|---|---|---|---|---|
| | 1985 | 1995 | 1985 | 1995 |
| Constant | -46.816 | -39.547 | -12.519 | -33.077 |
| | (4.716$^a$) | (3.079$^a$) | (2.232$^a$) | (1.833$^a$) |
| ln(GDP$_i$GDP$_j$) | 1.147 | 1.107 | 1.148 | 1.260 |
| | (0.126$^a$) | (0.079$^a$) | (0.034$^a$) | (0.029$^a$) |
| ln(GDPPC$_i$GDPPC$_j$) | 1.313 | 1.093 | 0.642 | 0.742 |
| | (0.219$^a$) | (0.169$^a$) | (0.063$^a$) | (0.053$^a$) |
| ln(DISTANCE$_{ij}$) | 1.069 | 0.601 | -1.795 | -0.112 |
| | (0.288$^a$) | (0.210$^a$) | (0.217$^a$) | (0.178) |
| RELIGION$_{ij}$ | 2.697 | 2.332 | -0.206 | 0.454 |
| | (1.659) | (0.901$^b$) | (0.419) | (0.360) |
| BAHASA | 1.893 | 1.478 | Excl. | Excl. |
| | (1.036$^c$) | (0.753$^b$) | | |
| CHINESE | 0.056 | 1.755 | 0.529 | 1.012 |
| | (0.694) | (0.483$^a$) | (0.641) | (0.383$^a$) |
| ENGLISH | 1.734 | -0.419 | 0.258 | 0.679 |
| | (0.710$^b$) | (0.527) | (0.218) | (0.159$^a$) |
| KHMER | 6.806 | 5.922 | Excl. | Excl. |
| | (2.277$^a$) | (1.191$^a$) | | |
| THAI | -3.406 | -1.211 | Excl. | Excl. |
| | (4.114) | (1.137) | | |
| R square | 0.565 | 0.641 | 0.569 | 0.625 |
| F-statistic | 19.34 | 48.71 | 322.19 | 605.96 |
| Number of observations | 143 | 255 | 1468 | 2190 |

*Notes*: All regressions are estimated by ordinary least squares (OLS). Dependent variable is the natural log of bilateral trade (sum of exports and imports) in 1984 (for 1985's regressions) and 1995 (for 1995's regressions). Hong Kong is excluded from regressions in 1985. Figures within parentheses are standard errors. 'Excl.' denotes the left-hand variable is deleted from the analysis since it has missing correlation. $^a$, $^b$ and $^c$ denote significance at the at 1%, 5% and 10% levels, respectively.

Furthermore, from 1985 to 1995 the five individual languages (Bahasa, Chinese, English, Khmer and Thai) play different roles on trade in East Asia (see Table 6.6). For inter-regional trade, Chinese and English, the only two languages with no missing correlation in the regressions, are statistically insignificant in 1985. However, they become statistically significant in 1995. For intra-regional trade, Bahasa has a decreasing role from 1985 to 1995; the coefficients on English and Khmer are statistically significant in 1985 but statistically insignificant in 1995. For both years, the coefficient on Thai is not statistically significant. By contrast, the Chinese language plays a dramatically increasing role from 1985 (with a statistically insignificant coefficient of 0.056) to 1995 (with a statistically significant coefficient of 1.755).

Why does Chinese play a more important role in international trade than the other languages? I suspect that the stronger effect of linguistic influence on trade might be attributable to Chinese Diaspora. Rauch and Trindade (2002), for example, find that ethnic Chinese networks have a quantitatively important impact on bilateral trade through the mechanisms of market information and matching and referral services, in addition to their effect through community enforcement of sanctions that deter opportunistic behavior. Their estimated results show that for trade between countries with ethnic Chinese population shares at the levels prevailing in Southeast Asia, the smallest estimated average increase in bilateral trade in differentiated products attributable to ethnic Chinese networks is nearly 60 percent.

## 6.6. SUMMARY

Cultural influences on international trade are a complicated process. On the one hand, 'cultural dissimilarity' always generates the cost of intercultural transactions; on the other hand, it also results in 'economic complementarity', an important factor that has direct influences on trade. Although economists have attempted to quantitatively examine the effect of culture on international trade, few studies have dealt with the positive and negative correlations between the various cultural factors and trade.

We have clarified various conditions under which trade may be either encouraged or retarded. The adoption of a common standard between different cultural groups of people are not likely to be emphasized given that there exist markedly differing attitudes as well as different cultural values. As a result, the larger the number of cultural groups involved in a multicultural society, ceteris paribus, the higher the managerial risks and costs resulting from it. However, in addition to the cost of intercultural transactions, 'cultural dissimilarity' may also generate more or less 'economic complementarities' that will have direct influences on trade.

Although there has been a growing concern about the role of culture in international economic analyses, few quantitative studies have been conducted. Using a modified gravity model on trade and the data of the East Asian economies, this study finds that the East Asian trade patterns have changed significantly between the Cold War era and the post-Cold War era. These changes are related to declines in transportation costs as well as other distance-related transactions costs. The estimated coefficients on the linguistic and religious variables are either negative or statistically insignificant in the Cold War era. In contrast, they become positive and statistically significant in the post-Cold War era. With regard to the ling and religious influences during the post-Cold War era, religion is found to have larger effects on intra-regional trade than language and language is found to have larger effects on inter-regional trade than religion. From 1985 to 1995 there is also an indication that (i) English tended to become more important for inter-regional trade, (ii) Bahasa, English and Khmer tended to become less important for intra-regional trade, and (iii) Chinese played an increasing role in both intra- and inter-regional trade.

There is a long line of thought suggesting that the adoption of a common standard between different cultural groups of people cannot be fully realized if markedly different attitudes and values exist among cultural groups. As a result, the larger the number of cultural groups involved in a multicultural society, ceteris paribus, the higher the managerial risks and costs resulting from this diversity. On the other hand, cultural dissimilarity can also have positive effects on economic activities and result in 'economic complementarity', an important factor directly influencing trade. As a result, the relationship between international trade and linguistic/religious similarity may be non-linear (Guo, 2006, pp. 114-15). However, we did not find a non-linear correlation between religious similarity and foreign trade. Is East Asia the only exception in a world where such relationships are generally non-linear? Or are these estimated results biased by the fact that many East Asian economies were still in the initial stages of economic development during the period studied? Given that East Asia is one of the most diverse areas in the world – politically, socially and economically – more detailed econometric analysis should be conducted to address this question.

The treatment of linguistic and religious factors as continuous variables has improved on past studies, which analyzed language only with dummy variables and ignored religion. However, it should be noted that the data on linguistic and religious groups are not as accurate as those on the economic and geographical indicators used in this case study. Because of the difficulties encountered when quantifying linguistic and religious variables, only two years (1985 and 1995) were chosen to represent the Cold War era and the post-Cold War era, respectively. Obviously, more years of cross-sectional data are needed in order to provide more convincing comparisons between these two periods. This is especially true in East Asia, where many economies have experienced dramatic ideological and institutional transformations during the late 20th century. In future research, estimation of linguistic and religious influences on international trade should try to use more accurate linguistic and religious variables covering a longer period of time.

# Chapter 7

# CROSS-CULTURAL CONFLICT MANAGEMENT

Yea! Whoso, shaking off the yoke of flesh
Lives lord, not servant, of his lusts; set free
From pride, from passion, from the sin of 'Self'
Toucheth tranquility! O Pritha's Son!
That is the state of Brahma! There rests no dread
When that last step is reached! Live where he will,
Die when he may, such passeth from all planning,
To blest Nirvana, with the Gods, attaining.

(Bhagavad-Gita, ii)

## 7.1. GLOBALIZATION IN THE 21ST CENTURY

Economic globalization, as an increasingly dominant force since the last decades, is shaping the new era of interactions among various civilizations throughout the world. It is increasing the contacts between people across various boundaries – geographical, political and cultural. Today, the interactions among people with different national and cultural identities are deeper than ever before. The most obvious evidence can be found from at least the following aspects:

- Foreign direct investment (FDI) topped US$500 billion in the late 1990s, more than seven times the level in real terms in the 1970s.
- The daily turnover in foreign exchange markets increased from around US$10-20 billion in the 1970s to US$1.5 trillion in 1998.
- International bank lending grew from US$265 billion in 1975 to over US$6 trillion in 1999.
- People travel more around the world, with tourism more than doubling between 1980 and 1996, from 260 million to 590 million travelers a year.
- International migration, despite the tight restrictions, continues to grow, with the workers' remittance reaching US$58 billion in 1996.[1]

---

[1] Data source: UNDP (1999, p. 25) and www.undp.org/hdro/report.html.

There is no doubt about the increasing awareness of the importance of international and intercultural transactions in our daily life. When people say that 'the world is becoming smaller every day', they are referring not only to the increased speed of and ease of transportation and communications but also to the increased use of international and intercultural market to buy and sell goods. The overall heightened presence of foreign goods, foreign producers and even foreign-owned assets causes many to question the impact and desirability of all international and intercultural economic transactions. An increasing number of companies are now relying on production chains that straddle many politically and culturally distinctive areas. Raw materials and components may come from different linguistic or religious areas and be assembled in another, while marketing and distribution take place in still other venues. Consumers' decisions in, for example, New York or Tokyo may become information that has an almost immediate impact on the products that are being made—and the styles that influence them—all over the world.

Technology has been the most fundamental element in promoting intercultural influences. In pre-modern times the spread of ideas and technology could take centuries. Intercontinent journeys, which now only need a few hours via air, would have taken several months before the 20th century. Technological advances in communication have made it possible to know in an instant what is happening in a household or factory or on a stock market half a world away. The growing importance of services and information in the world economy means that an increasing proportion of economic value is weightless—that is, it can be transmitted over fiber-optic cable rather than transported in a container ship. At the same time improvements in transportation networks and technology are reducing the costs of shipping goods by water, ground and air and improvements in information technology have made it easier to raise productivity, as well as to increase intercultural specialization of labor. More important are the improvements in information technology (IT) that have made it easier to manage the new interconnections worldwide. Among them is the Internet, the fast-growing tool of communication. The Internet has provided a new means of commerce, with clear speed and cost advantages. Economic interculturalization has increasingly benefited from the declining costs of transportation and communication (see Table 7.1).

In general, cultural differences underlie many conflicts, both international and domestic. The conflicts in the Middle East, the Congo, Nigeria, Northern Ireland and Sri Lanka, to name but a few, all are framed in cultural terms, as ethnic or religious. By way of contrast to these examples of internal strife and dissent, there is another landscape in the heart of Western Europe where one may find a special Alpine country: in Switzerland different language groups live peacefully in cantons allocated to speakers of Swiss German, French, Italian and Rhaeto-Romanic. Intercultural conflict is usually attributed to cultural dissimilarity, since the latter implies a degree of difficulty that the disparate groups concerned have in communicating or cooperating with one another. Precisely, each culture possesses a common system of signifying and normative values, some shared basis (such as common history, language, race or ethnicity, religion) through which people identify themselves as members of a single group, and the will or decision to be primarily self-identified as a member of a given community. Ultimately, this may to some extent be traceable to a biological basis, since, in human societies, ascriptive ties are said to dampen coalition building and to inhibit compromise across groups (that cross-cutting cleavages promote), thus increasing chances for social conflict (Bollen and Jackman, 1985).

**Table 7.1. Declining costs of transportation and communication**

| Year | Average ocean freight and port charges per ton (US$) | Telephone call (3 minutes, New York/London) (US$) | Computers (index, 1990=100) |
|------|------|------|------|
| 1920 | 95 | - | - |
| 1930 | 60 | 245 | - |
| 1940 | 63 | 189 | - |
| 1950 | 34 | 53 | - |
| 1960 | 27 | 46 | 12500 |
| 1970 | 27 | 32 | 1947 |
| 1980 | 24 | 5 | 362 |
| 1990 | 29 | 3 | 100 |
| 2000[a] | - | <1 | 50[b] |

[a]: Calculated by the author. [b]: Based on the data estimated by Kanamori and Motohashi (2007) for Japan and Korea.
*Source*: IMF (1997a), except those that are noted otherwise.

However, it is too arbitrary to say that cultural dissimilarity will inevitably result in intercultural conflicts. Where diverse groups have learned to live with each other and purse their differences within a stable political system cultural difference is likely to have a very small effect on intercultural conflict. This leads at once to the presumption that the so-called industrial democracies will be less sensitive to the measures of cultural diversity than a developing country in which cultural diversity leads to barriers to intranational contacts or, more strongly, to violence. Furthermore, as Shanker (1996) argues, since the cultural raw material for any civilization allows for various options, different patterns will emerge as people combine modern rationality with cultural heritage, economic progress with national identity. Through this process peoples and countries will come to share experience, to walk parallel rather than converging paths.

To conlcude, it is reasonable to believe that culture plays differing roles in the formation of intercultural conflicts. On the one hand, cultural dissimilarity brings about political distrust or instability. On the other hand, it generates 'differentiation of production' or complementarity in economic terms, which in turn induces cooperation among distinctive groups of people. From the perspective of economics, 'differentiation of production' implies 'comparative advantages', while the latter influences to some extent the potential benefit of trade and cooperation between the cultures concerned.[2] As a result cultural dissimilarity is not only a determining source for intercultural conflicts, but also the source for intercultural dependence and intercultural cooperation.

---

[2] The term 'cultural monopolization of trade' is used here to denote that, since there are usually some culturally unique – both traditional and modern – commodities in each culture, intercultural exporters of these products can, at least in theory, realize a monopolized profit for each of their own. As a result, one culture's gross benefit of exporting its products to the other culture grows with greater degree of intercultural dissimilarity.

# 7.2. How Cross-Cultural Conflicts Occur

Throughout history, race, ethnicity, language and religion have divided states into separate political entities as much as physical terrain, political fiat, or conquest. The result is the man-made and sometimes arbitrary or even imposed boundaries (see Box 7.1). A host of factors, including, *inter alia*, immigration, increased diplomatic and cultural contacts, the diffusion of science and technology, the mass media, and international travel and trade, are transforming the contemporary international political and economic relations dramatically. As a result interactions between different cultures are becoming more and more important in our changing world. However conflicts and misunderstanding may also result from the increasing interactions between the cultures.

---

### Box 7.1 Making Good International Boundaries

Throughout history, race, ethnicity, language and religion have divided states into separate political entities as much as physical terrain, political fiat, or conquest. The result is the man-made and sometimes arbitrary or even imposed boundaries. Till now, there are over 300 international land boundaries, stretching over 250,000 km, which separate over 200 independent states and dependencies, areas of special sovereignty, and other miscellaneous entities of the world. At the same time, maritime states have claimed limits and have so far established over 130 maritime boundaries and joint development zones to allocate ocean resources and to provide for national security at sea.

There are various methods for boundary description. In practice, more than one of them may be employed for different parts of a boundary. Specifically, international boundaries can be defined: (1) by turning points or angles, (2) by courses and distances, (3) by natural features (such as mountains, rivers, lakes, seas or other water bodies), and (4) by spaces or zones. In most cases it is difficult to say what constitutes a good international boundary. Usually cases of discord of a serious nature have been caused by slight and unintentional ambiguities in the description of boundaries in formal documents. These flaws may be due to unfamiliarity with the peculiarities of the geographical features, human or natural, along which the boundary extends, or to lack of knowledge of the pitfalls in boundary description. In brief, while inappropriate boundary demarcation usually leads to territorial disputes, the following common errors in boundary description are of particular noteworthy:

- Use of topographical terms and place names
- Description based on inaccurate or inadequate maps or field knowledge
- Description based on vague geometrical features
- Description based on intricate human features
- Inconsistent definitions and contradictory statements

*Source*: Guo (2007b, pp. 3-7).

Because of the ethnic, linguistic and religious differences throughout the world, the intercultural relations have been differently formed, in patterns of either détente or confrontations. Thus, the need to understand differences in basic values, norms, and beliefs in how the peoples of the world approach resolving these conflicts is greater than ever before.

Early theoretical works such as Choucri and North (1975 and 1989) contend that internal demands on resources push states toward outward expansion, increasing the possibility for conflicts to arise through hostile lateral pressure. Resource poor regions will create environments that are highly competitive, where the creation of institutions to manage conflict will be lacking and/or ineffective. Resource rich regions, on the other hand, will be faced with fewer potential conflict situations overall, which will enhance the prospects for the creation of institutions to manage conflicts that do arise (Hensel et al., 2004). Gleditsch (2001, p. 253) provides a nice summary for these Malthusian type arguments. Population growth and high resource consumption per capita (demand-induced scarcity) lead to deteriorated environmental conditions (supply-induced scarcity), which increase resource scarcity further and create harsher resource competition. This process, when combined with inequality with respect to resource access (structural scarcity), increases the chances for violence. As a result, we have:

## Hypothesis 1. Conflicts Grow with Respect to Resource Scarcity and Population Growth

Resource scarcity and environmental damage involves real threats to public health, agricultural and industrial production, as well as national security. Clearly, as population increases the demand for the resources increases as well. The lack of alternatives for the resources increases the dependency of both sides of the border. Critchley and Terriff (1993, pp. 332-3) argue that resources directly result in conflict when (i) they are becoming increasingly scarce in a region, (ii) they are essential for human survival, and (iii) the resource can be physically seized or controlled. They assert that direct conflict over renewable resources will be rare, but competition over scarce resources will have a strong indirect effect on the propensity for conflict. Limited availability of resources places stress on society, which makes the society less stable and more conflict-prone.

Like Critchley and Terriff (1993), Homer-Dixon (1999) believes that the probability of conflict rises due to disruption of legitimate institutions and social relations, among others. As a result, we have

## Hypothesis 2. Conflicts Occur More Frequently in Areas with Less Developed Political and Legal Systems

The difficulties in cross-border management of natural and environmental resources has been one of the major obstacles for developing and transition nations differing in economic, political and cultural systems to implement sustainable development strategies (Guo, 2005). In certain circumstances, conflicts may arise because national interests differ and nations develop diverging policies and plans which are not compatible (Kirmani, 1990; Frey, 1993; Wolf, 1998; and Savenije and van der Zaag, 2000). As a result, we have

## Hypothesis 3. Conflicts Occur More Frequently in Areas with Different Political Systems and Development Strategies

Such factors as economic stagnation and income inequality may serve as very critical roles in political instability in some nations (see, for example, Londregan and Poole, 1989). There is a long line of thought suggesting that inequality of wealth and income motivates the poor to engage in crime, riots, and other disruptive activities (see, for example, Hibbs, 1973; Venieris and Gupta, 1986; Gupta, 1990; and Alesina and Perotti, 1996). As a result, we have

## Hypothesis 4. Conflicts Occur Less Frequently in Areas with Higher Average Income Levels and in Areas with Lower Income Inequalities

There has been a concern that border conflict is usually attributed to cultural dissimilarity (Huntington, 1993). Ultimately, this may to some extent be traceable to a biological basis, since in most circumstances cooperation among animals is importantly influenced by genetic similarity (Wilson, 1980). In human societies, ascriptive ties are said to dampen coalition building and to inhibit compromise across groups (that cross-cutting cleavages promote), thus increasing chances for social conflict (Bollen and Jackman, 1985). Consequently, we have

## Hypothesis 5. Conflicts Tend to be Less Serious between Culturally Homogeneous Areas than Between Culturally Heterogeneous Areas

There has been also a concern that people with some cultural identities generally prefer confrontational strategies to handle conflict situations, whereas people in the others generally prefer more passive strategies, such as avoiding conflicts (Chua and Gudykunst, 1987; Leung, 1987; and Ting-Toomey, 1988). As a result, we have

## Hypothesis 6. Conflicts Tend to be Less Tensional Between Cultures that Prefer Passive Strategies than between Those that Prefer Confrontational Strategies

There are various problems that are common to the studies of conflict management across cultures. First, culture embraces a wide range of elements including ethnicity, language, religion and so on. Second, the specific context matters a lot to each conflict incident, which means that each conflict process has unique characteristics. While some of the problems can be handled with methodological tools that are pretty standard, others are more difficult to address.

## 7.3 CROSS-CULTURAL CONFLICT RESOLUTION

International laws and treaties provide the normative framework and procedures by which to coordinate behaviors, to control conflicts, and to facilitate cooperation. Several doctrines can be applied to regulate cross-cultural conflict management. The Doctrine of Absolute Integrity stipulates that one side may not alter the natural state of natural and environmental resources passing through its territory in any manner that will affect the resources in the other side(s). The Doctrine of Limited Territorial Sovereignty has been the most widely accepted in various international treaties. The Doctrine of the Communality of International Resources assumes a communality or cross-border communalism of interest between countries concerned, and treats the total stock of resources as shared by these countries. The Doctrine of Correlative Rights emphasizes the most efficient exploitation and utilization of joint resources, rather than on ownership rights.

Some principles drawn from the above doctrines have been accepted as legal norms which are binding on the management of cross-cultural conflicts in many parts of the world. Specifically, they can be classified into three aspects, as the following:

(i) Prohibition of management practices likely to cause injury to other sides. This obligation includes the duty of preventive and cooperative actions. It conforms the general legal obligation to use one's property in a manner that will not cause injury to others. According to Dellapenna (1999, p. 1314), restricted sovereignty goes by the name of "equitable utilization" of the shared resources. The 1988 Report to the International Law Commission suggests that appreciable harm resulting from water pollution is a violation of the principle. The World Bank statement for projects in international waterways requires the assessment of potential significant harm before approving projects on international waterways (Solanes, 1992; Caponera, 1995; and McCarrey, 1996).

(ii) Principle of equitable utilization of shared resources. The principle of equitable use requires the interests of all countries concerned to be taken into account when exploiting and allocating their transboundary, shared resources. The principle has been applied by international courts and also by national courts of various federal countries. It is also endorsed by many writers (see, for example, Dellapenna, 1999, pp. 1314–5; and McCarrey, 1996), as well as by the Helsinki Rules and the UN's 1997 Convention. The International Court of Justice's (ICJ) opinion referred twice to the rule of equitable utilization (Green Cross, 2000, p. 52).

(iii) Duty of prior consultation and cooperation in good faith. There are three mechanisms to implement international consultation and cooperation: the first mechanism is to transform protocols into contracts and set up the authority to bring contracts into effect; the second is to cultivate the habits that everyone complies with the protocols; the third is that even though there is no trusts between people and there is no more powerful authority to implement the protocols, the protocols can still be stood by. There is hope that international protocols relating to environmental problems can come true through the last two mechanisms, especially the second one (Dasgupta, 1996).

## 7.4. A TACTICAL GUIDE TO GLOBAL LEADERS

In the remainder of this chapter, four approaches will be suggested to the resolution of cross-cultural conflicts. They are: (i) round table negotiation, (ii) third-party mediation, (iii) shelving disputes strategy, and (iv) neutral, buffer and demilitarized zones. In practice it is suggested two or more approaches be jointly employed in the resolution of each single case of cross-cultural conflicts.

### 7.4.1. Round Table Negotiation

The term 'Round Table' has come into being for a long time. In the legend of King Arthur, the Round Table was a mystical table in Camelot around which King Arthur and his knights sat to discuss matters crucial to the security of the realm. It was allegedly fashioned at the behest of Arthur to prevent quarrels among the knights over precedence. Generally, there is no 'head of the table' at a round table, and so no one person is at a privileged position. Thus the several knights were all peers and there was no 'leader' as there were at so many other medieval tables.[3]

The Round Table Negotiation has been a common method used by various stakeholders to peacefully settle international conflicts throughout the world. Most of what we know about the formation, operation and attributed outcomes of the Round Table Negotiation fit well with widely held understandings in the conflict resolution field. For certain purposes, 'conflict' can be defined as a situation wherein two or more engaged and interacting parties have a substantial and relevant difference in goals or interests that cannot be achieved simultaneously. A negotiation process is put into place wherein people who disagreed strongly and had fought with one another came to some agreements that permitted them to live together and the social system in which they lived to continue to operate without warfare or schism. The eruption of violent conflict does not only affect internal stability but also that of other countries of the region leading to border controls, and the displacement of people and refugees resulting from wars.

The Round Table itself covers an entire series of meetings and formal and informal negotiation processes that occurred over a considerable period of time. The purpose of the Round Table Negotiation is to:

- Familiarize all the stakeholders participating in the territorial dispute
- Identify issues related to, as well as the differences among, all the countries involved in the dispute
- Propose guidance for the formulation of strategies and policies that could influence action at the international level
- Form partnerships for follow-up

Chesler (2000, pp. 151–76) organizes six key issues or questions that are endemic to most discussions of conflict and conflict resolution, as the following:

---

[3] Cited from www.thefreedictionary.com/Round+Table.

1) What kind of issues can be negotiated? The vital issue in the analysis of territorial conflicts must be the nature and extent of the parties' different goals or interests. Are they truly incompatible? Are there issues where compromises or negotiations can occur, or is warfare and victory/defeat the appropriate model? Is this a zero-sum or a win-win situation?

2) When are negotiations (most) useful as a strategy? The vital issue in the analysis of territorial conflicts is the degree to which the parties are truly interdependent, unavoidably engaged, and interactive with one another. It is clear that the parties to the Round Table had been and were engaged and interacting with one another in a variety of ways and would continue to do so. Once that was clear, negotiations depended on each party's willingness, and their ability to convince the other, that they would reject (or withhold) system destruction or violence and coercion, and thus could legitimatize one another's existence, their mutual interdependence, and their desire to work together. That opened up the possibility of a 'deal' or compromise solution.

3) What is required for negotiations to work well? Once it is clear that parties are prepared to negotiate, successful negotiations require the presence of a variety of factors or conditions. The external societal context of conflict situations is a critical factor affecting the very possibility or existence of negotiations. Besides, a number of internal conditions also have to be met for negotiations to be successful. Chief among them are "process issues," such as power parity, the ability of each party to work effectively with its own constituency, as well as to develop effective communication with opponents and with allies, and representatives' interpersonal skills.

4) What are useful third party or 'intervenor' roles? A third party should be an individual or a collective that is external to a dispute between two or more people and that tried to help them reach agreement. Third party or 'intervenor' roles may be formal or informal, advisory and facilitative or directive and coercive, and partial or impartial. Neutrality is a hallmark of formal mediation rhetoric, but in practice it is usually redefined as a sense of fairness that gains the trust of varied parties. (We will discuss the "third-party mediation" as a single method in the next section.)

5) How do parties in conflict come to trust one another enough to negotiate? The development of some sort of trust in one's opponents, or (former) enemies, is essential for the negotiation process. But trust has various meanings, and interpersonal attraction or friendship is the least important ingredient in conflict resolution settings. More important is the ability to count on (trust) one's adversary to behave in a reliable and predictable way, hopefully but not necessarily in a way consistent with their public pronouncements, and to be committed to implement an agreement.

6) Can, and how can, negotiations lead to systemic change? The goal of negotiation is in part to transform a process of contested and resisted (and potentially violent) unplanned change into a process of more collaborative (and relatively peaceful) planned change. Therefore, the right direction of any negotiation or change process is in the action implementation that follows, not in the negotiating talk (or even its written agreements).

## 7.4.2. Third-Party Mediation

In addition to the face-to-face negotiations between parties concerned, the Third-Party Mediation may also play a critical role in resolving territorial disputes. In most cases the Third-Party Mediation might provide communication and the technical means for verifying complex boundary negotiations. Successful cases for using the Third-Party Mediation include the Indus Treaty between the Indian and Pakistani governments in 1960 (which was mediated by the World Bank) and the resolution of the dispute between Argentina and Chile over the Beagle Channel in 1981 (which was mediated by the Vatican, whose moral authority has had supreme influence over the large Catholic populations in South America).

Working out their troubles on their own or shake hands and get along may work occasionally, but most of the time the conflict will only be sent underground to resurface later in more destructive ways. A better approach is to allow both sides in conflicts to meet with a third party, or mediator, to assist them in their own resolution of the conflict. All things being equal, an outside mediator has a greater chance of succeeding. An insider may be part of the problem, may be perceived as favoring one of the stakeholders, and the stakeholders may be hesitant to share confidential information with an insider.

A substantial portion of the literature on conflict resolution addresses the utility of third-party intervention. In Rubin et al.'s terms, "a third party is an individual or a collective that is external to a dispute between two or more people and that tried to help them reach agreement" (1994, p. 197). Third party roles may be formal or informal, advisory and facilitative or directive and coercive, and partial or impartial. Neutrality is a hallmark of formal mediation rhetoric, but in practice it is usually redefined as a sense of fairness that gains the trust of varied parties (Forester and Stitzel, 1989; and Moore, 1996).

The conflict management process is more apt to succeed if stakeholders have respect for the mediator's integrity, impartiality, and ability. Respect for the mediator is important, so stakeholders will be on their best behavior, an important element in successful negotiation. All parties should be informed of exceptions to the confidentiality rule ahead of time. Any sharing of information based on the exceptions needs to be done on a need-to-know basis to minimize giving out information that could hurt one or both of the parties. Insiders may be less hesitant to speak out when assured of confidentiality. A much more sensitive situation involves the role of the mediator when stakeholders are not able to come to a negotiated resolution. In some instances mediation works best when the third party is able to change roles, and in the event that mediation fails, become an arbiter.

Mediation helps stakeholders discuss issues, repair past injuries, and develop the tools needed to face disagreements effectively. Mediators may help participants glimpse at their blind spots, broaden their perspectives, and even muddle through the problem-solving process. Yet, successful mediators remember that the challenges are owned by the stakeholders and do not attempt to short-circuit the process by solving challenges for them. In most circumstances mediators facilitate the conflict-resolution process by the following aspects (Billikopf, 2005):

- Understanding each participant's perspective through a pre-caucus
- Increasing and evaluating participant interest in solving the challenge through mediation

- Setting ground rules for improved communication
- Coaching participants through the joint session
- Equalizing power (e.g., between persons in different organizational levels)
- Helping participants plan for future interaction.

The application of the Third-Party Mediation in conflict resolution was remarkable in most circumstances. Mediation by a third party would be a way of catalyzing political negotiations at the highest levels. Perhaps a useful model for conducting such negotiations would be to consider 'proximity' talks hosted by a nonofficial third party—similar to the role provided by the United States during the Dayton negotiations on Bosnia (DOS, 1995). In the resolution of the Beagle Channel conflict between Argentina and Chile, the mediator was the Vatican, whose supreme moral authority and influence over the large Catholic populations in each country made it a mediating body that the parties could not ignore. Despite its vast power and resources, the U.S. government had very little leverage with either country. The United States took the Beagle Channel conflict seriously and attempted to play an active role in resolving the conflict. Chile and Argentina, for their part, never seriously considered requesting U.S. mediation. Indeed, the United States might not have satisfied Chile's principal requirement that the mediator have sufficient leverage to constrain any Argentine inclination to balk at the results or initiate hostilities.

International arbitration and mediation are not automatically good things. Relations between Argentina and Chile from the 1970s to the 1990s show how varied the outcomes may be. The 1977 British arbitration nearly brought the two countries to war; the papal arbitration in the early 1980s set the basis for the Beagle Channel settlement; and the Laguna del Desierto dispute was settled in the 1990s thanks to an ICJ decision. The role of the ICJ at The Hague in the dispute between Honduras and El Salvador illustrates other Janus-faced characteristics of such procedures. As Orozco (2001) has shown, both governments accepted the court's judgment, but that judgment raised the salience and the stakes of the bilateral dispute, injuring other aspects of bilateral relations for years while the definitive delimitation on the ground was still pending.

Only after all the parties concerned invite international actors to join, can the mediations become effective and successful. The peace settlement that followed the 1995 Ecuador–Peru war could not have been achieved without the active engagement of the governments of Argentina, Brazil, Chile, and the United States; the modest but essential financial, military, and technical resources provided by these governments, especially the United States; and the skill and dedication of U.S. ambassador (Domínguez et al., 2003, p. 35). When invited to mediate, international actors should be mindful of moral hazard problems. Countries that launch attacks should not be rewarded. The rewards for peace-making, such as shared financing for economic development at the border, should be received by the country that has been attacked.

The three islands at the Beagle Channel's eastern end, Lennox Picton, and Nueva Islands, had been the subject of territorial dispute between Argentina and Chile since the 1840s. The dispute almost led to war between the two nations in 1978. In 1979 the two countries agreed to allow the Vatican to mediate the dispute through the good offices of Antonio Cardinal Samoré, Pope's special envoy. On 12 December 1980, the Pope presented his proposal for resolving the conflict. Under the papal proposal, Chile would retain all of the islands, but

Argentina would be entitled to maintain certain limited facilities there and would receive important navigation rights. The Pope's ruling resulted in the ratification of a treaty to settle the dispute in Rome.

The dispute officially ended on 2 May 1985, when the treaty went into effect between the two countries. The key element to this proposal was the creation of a vast ocean area known as the 'Sea of Peace'. In this area, extending to the east and southeast from the disputed chain of islands, Chile would be limited to a narrow territorial sea, in which it would be obliged to afford Argentina equal participation in resource exploitation, scientific investigation, and environmental management. Beyond the Chilean territorial waters would be a much broader band of ocean subject to Argentine jurisdiction, but also subject to the same sharing provisions that applied in Chilean waters. The resolution of the Beagle Channel conflict has had at least two implications. First, it acts to defuse the situation by bringing the parties to an agreement that stopped the immediate military crisis. In the next phase, the mediator can craft a process that allows all parties concerned to grapple with increasingly difficult issues. The process was remarkable because it is flexible enough to accommodate the changing political environments for all parties concerned.

### 7.4.3. Shelving Disputes Strategy

The Shelving Disputes Strategy is the most logical solution to conflict management, because it allows all the parties concerned to postpone the final decision on how to eventually resolve the conflict. Instead, it provides opportunity and time for the participants concerned to find solutions at a later stage. The rationale for the Shelving Disputes Strategy is based on an understanding that some or all participants will have to pay additional costs if they want to find an immediate solution to a territorial dispute.

The main purpose of the Shelving Disputes Strategy is to shift attention from the dispute to more essential concerns which the countries involved could try to tackle together, and which do not necessarily depend on a resolution of the sovereignty dispute. Regular meetings or workshops can be held, with the participation of officials and expert groups from the countries involved in the dispute. The idea has been to build confidence, initiate cooperative projects, lay the foundation for joint management of cross-border resources, and ensure environmental protection. Sovereignty issues have been banned from the agenda at all meetings. Even though the Shelving Disputes Strategy is a fuzzy one and sometimes even not considered a practical approach to conflict resolution, it can be applied in most of the existing territorial disputes.

Perhaps the best way for the peaceful resolution of the dispute over the South China Sea would be to shelve the dispute and go for a combination of bilateral and multilateral solutions, based on the ideas for joint development or management. As the most powerful state in the region with rapid economic growth and a keen awareness of its need for access to resources, China holds the key to resolving the South China Sea conflict. There is much to win by peaceful means and much to lose by resorting to power. Fears exist that China will use its strength to increase its military presence in the southern part of the South China Sea. Another compelling reason is that the dispute will otherwise be intractable. Five states keep features in the occupied Spratlys. If any features are given status as islands with a right to EEZs, then this will make military aggression pay. This may also internationalize the conflict, since neither Japan nor the United States are likely to allow the South China Sea, with its vital sea-lanes, to be controlled by one single state (Tønnesson, 1999). The conflict over the South China Sea would be more easy to manage, and to eventually resolve, if the states around the South China Sea could agree to shelve the sovereignty disputes, and concentrate on more essential, shared concerns.[4]

A successful example of shelving disputes for transboundary collaboration is the biological protection during armed conflict in the Virungas, where montane forests in three adjacent protected areas in Rwanda, Uganda, and the Democratic Republic of Congo (DRC) are home to the endangered mountain gorilla. The gorilla population ranges freely across the borders of the three countries. In the 1980s, during which time the forests were seeing much fighting at various stages of the complex conflict, protected-area authorities started collaborating on gorilla conservation and tourism development on an ad hoc basis. The International Gorilla Conservation Program (IGCP) was created in 1991, as conditions began to deteriorate. The IGCP's works aim to strengthen the capacity to conserve the forests and gorillas in the face of ongoing threats, and to promote a framework for cross-border collaboration. More recently, when the DRC government forces were fighting against troops in the east backed by Rwanda and Uganda, its wildlife authority, was unable to support its staff in the Virungas in the east. The IGCP stepped in to provide this support, and helped to facilitate collaboration among the staff of the three protected areas. Remarkably, this collaboration continued, despite the worsening political situation (Lanjouw et al., 2001; and Kalpers, 2001).

The transboundary collaboration may include control of illegal hunters moving across borders, control of fires and diseases in border areas, monitoring of cross-border wildlife movements, and joint effort on conflict resolutions. Under the IGCP, only the military forces were allowed to carry arms in the Virungas. At such times, unarmed park guards underwent training and conducted joint patrols with the military. In turn, the military received training from the park authorities on the ecological importance of the forest; health, behavior, and social structure of gorillas; and park regulations. This collaboration ensured that the military presence was not disruptive to the park and also sensitized an important interest group. The high conservation and economic value of the gorillas, the enormous dedication of the government protected-area staff, and the presence of the IGCP are the key factors that have ensured conservation of the gorilla population during this long-lasting and complex conflict (Shanbaugh et al., 2003, p. 73).

## 7.4.4. Neutral, Buffer and Demilitarized Zones

In the WordNet Dictionary, 'neutral' is defined as "one who does not side with any party in a war or dispute."[5] Before discussing the functions of "Neutral Zone", let us first look at Switzerland—a special Alpine country in the heart of West Europe. As a neutral state, Switzerland combines almost all aspects of the heterogeneous European societies and plays

---

[4] Under the 'Shelving Disputes' principle an agreement has been reached to launch joint research projects on biodiversity and sea-level rise monitoring, and to exchange marine scientific research information among the states surrounding the South China Sea.

[5] Source: www.webster-dictionary.org/definition/neutral.

an important role as the headquarters of numerous international fora and serves to promote the cause of moderation between different parts of the West Europe. Due to its neutralism, Switzerland dodged two world wars in the 20th century.

The boundaries between Iraq, Saudi Arabia and Kuwait, like many other boundaries in the Near East, reflect the historic difficulty of boundary drawing in the desert. In addition to the geographical problems, there are substantial impediments to delimitation of a boundary on the ground, based on the way of life of the Nomad and Islamic tradition. In 1922, a British High Commissioner, exasperated at the disputes between Ibn Saud and the Amir of Kuwait, took a red pencil and drew the boundaries between them. He also decided the area of two 'neutral zones' along the borders between Saudi Arabia, Kuwait, and Iraq. While both were about 5,000 sq. km of desert, they were called 'neutral' because the Bedouin would be able to pass back and forth to graze their flocks (Yergin, 1992).

The present boundary between Iraq and Saudi Arabia is the first international boundary that has ever been defined in this area. The Iraq–Saudi Arabia boundary is about 686 km in length and is delimited. The additional "Neutral Zone," which begins at the Kuwait boundary at the junction of the Wadi al Awja with the Wadi al Batin at lat. 29°06′05″N and long. 46°33′19″E, is about 192 km long in the northern segment and about 201 km in length between the "Neutral Zone" and Saudi Arabia in the south. This desert boundary is essentially artificial and, historically, the first defined delimitation in the land between Mesopotamia and the Arabian Peninsula.

Kuwait's desert plain slopes gradually from the west, where it reaches 300 m above sea level, to the Gulf's shores. A number of discontinuities occur on the form of low depressions, sand dunes and escarpments. The Kuwait mainland, having no mountains or rivers or other natural features, was for a long time a transit area for nomadic tribes and caravans. Such freedom of movement made delineation of borders rather difficult and resulted in some border problems. The whole matter was amicably resolved following the creation of the Neutral Zone between the State of Kuwait and the Kingdom of Saudi Arabia on 7 July 1965. The northern part of the partitioned zone is administered by Kuwait, whilst the southern part is the administrative responsibility of Saudi Arabia. Both countries share the crude oil extracted from the partitioned zone equally.

Saudi Arabia shares the 'Neutral Zone' and its oil revenues equally with Kuwait. The long-running saga of negotiations between Arabian Oil Company (AOC) of Japan and Saudi Arabia came to an end in 2000 when the kingdom refused to extend the AOC's offshore concession, replacing the firm as operator with Saudi Aramco. The breakdown of negotiations led to expiration of the AOC's concession on 27 February 2000. However, the AOC's concession for Kuwait's half-interest in the Neutral Zone's offshore area was not affected. The Saudis had demanded increased access to Japan's energy markets and an increase in Japanese investment in Saudi Arabia. The AOC was replaced by Aramco's subsidiary, Aramco for Gulf Operations (AGO). The AGO was established specifically to take over AOC's concession. The new company inherited all the offshore fields and installations in the Saudi half of the zone and will employ the AOC's 1,300 Saudi personnel. The takeover by the AGO was surprisingly smooth, and crude oil production and exports were not interrupted. Operations have been carried out under a temporary 50–50 agreement between the AGO (Saudi Arabia) and the AOC (Kuwait) until a formal agreement between the two companies is reached (Alhajji, 2000).

There have been a number of disputes among the tribes of Iraq, Kuwait and Saudi Arabia since the delimitation of the boundary in 1922. In recent decades, however, the administrative controls by the respective governments have reduced tribal conflict. In December 1969, Kuwait and Saudi Arabia signed an agreement dividing the Neutral Zone (now called the Divided Zone) and demarcating a new international boundary. The Saudi–Kuwaiti neutral zone was administratively partitioned in 1971, with each state continuing to share the petroleum resources of the former zone equally. This treaty also established the Kuwait–Saudi Arabia Neutral Zone, an area of about 5,180 sq. km adjoining Kuwait's southern border. Whatever potential for disputes exists between Iraq and Saudi Arabia does not relate to the boundary itself. Saudi Arabia and Kuwait have demarcated their water boundaries. The Neutral Zone was also the center of attention, when Iran began exploring in the area's waters that are disputed with Kuwait and Saudi Arabia. However, within their Neutral Zone, there are no active disputes regarding the specific alignment of the boundary itself. Grazing and watering practice traditionally conducted by tribes crossing the boundary remain undisturbed.

The term "buffer zone" refers to "a neutral area between hostile or belligerent forces that serves to prevent conflict" (American Heritage Dictionary of English Language, 2003). In some intractable conflicts, buffer zones have been the conceptual basis for managing interactions among disputants. This concept that the relative proximity of disputants affects levels of anxiety and the potential for violence guides the development of buffer zones intended to de-escalate or avoid military conflict. That is, the time it takes to mount a military offensive is a function of the distance between the attacker and the victim.

Different from the aforementioned approaches that are either to seek a cessation of hostilities or to facilitate cooperative behavior as a means to end a conflict, buffer zones are often used simply to reduce tensions where a conflict is largely intractable. Where militarized conflicts occur inevitably, buffer zones can be established and monitored by third parties. By widening the involvement of actors and providing extra assurances that the opponents are upholding their share of obligations, such monitoring may help legitimize, institutionalize, and reinforce the agreed-upon arrangements and facilitate cooperation toward resolving the larger dispute. There are three general reasons for establishing buffer zones: (i) to provide sanctuary, (ii) to provide a neutral area that allows for supervision where contending claims exist (in order to, potentially, facilitate cooperation), and (iii) to simply reduce tensions through separation of disputants (Smith, 2003).

Violations of the buffer-zone agreements, or endangering the peacekeepers by resuming hostilities, would likely result in international condemnation and pressure. These measures dissuade would-be aggressors, while holding the door open for potential negotiations toward resolving the larger conflict. During times of war, sanctuaries are often developed to provide refuge to non-combatants or to protect areas that may have environmental or social significance, where disputants agree that hostilities should not spread. For instance, during the Middle East hostilities of 1948, the International Committee of the Red Cross fostered an agreement for establishing demilitarized zones within the city. This provided a buffer zone between combatants and non-combatants that helped protect certain areas and sectors of society (Bailey, 1980).

Cyprus is situated in the eastern Mediterranean south of Turkey. The separation of Greek and Turkish Cyprus was defined by the 'Attila Line' with a buffer zone on either side. To keep the Turkish and Greek Cypriots apart, the UN has set up a buffer zone along the Green Line (boundary). The UN buffer zone is divided into three sections. In the west the buffer zone lies around the TRNC controlled village of Kokkina. The main part goes from the north coast to through Nicosia until it reaches the western tripoint with the ESBA. The last section runs from the eastern tripoint with the ESBA to the east coast. Parts of the buffer zone remain inaccessible. The UN Buffer Zone in Cyprus is a 300 km separation barrier along the 1974 Green Line (or ceasefire line) between the self-proclaimed Turkish Republic of Northern Cyprus and the internationally recognized Republic of Cyprus.

The barrier itself consists of concrete walls, barbed wire fencing, watch-towers, anti-tank ditches, and minefields. Tensions nearby the barrier rose several times in the past, with the latest being in 1996, when in a demonstration at the Dherynia region, a Greek Cypriot was beaten to death by Turkish Cypriots while trying to cross the Green line, and the next day another was shot and killed trying to climb up on a Turkish flag-pole. After a near 30-year ban on crossings, the Turkish Cypriot de facto government significantly eased travel restrictions across the barrier in April 2003, by opening four crossing points (two into the UK sovereign base of Dhekelia). Since Cyprus joined the European Union (de facto only the southern part joined), travel restrictions have been abolished for all EU citizens.[6]

Though having the same or similar functions in most cases, demilitarized zone (DMZ) is slightly different from the buffer zone. A DMZ is an area, separated by a border between two or more groups, where military forces or operations or installations are prohibited, usually by treaty or other agreement. Often a DMZ lies upon a line of control (which is defined as a line which demarcates the boundary between two militaries or political entities) and forms a de-facto international border.

If two military forces are face to face, the time needed for one to attack the other is negligible. Both sides must, therefore, remain in a constant state of alert, which discourages cooperative behavior that may be misinterpreted as a sign of weakness and exploited by the other side. In contrast, the larger the physical area between disputants, the greater the warning time each actor has of an impending military confrontation. Increasing the area between disputants, then, can help facilitate more cooperative behavior, reducing tensions and encouraging less-provocative postures by providing a 'buffer' in the event that conciliatory gestures are exploited (Smith, 2003). Moreover, it is reasonably to believe that the greater the distance between opposing armed forces, the less likely that they will come into physical contacts and that miscommunication will lead to violence.

The DMZ option is the last comprehensive solution for cross-border disputes. It would require, as essential preconditions, the prevention of any potential reoccurrence of armed conflict. The creation of DMZs should be accompanied by the complete withdrawal of all military presence. Such a withdrawal would be accompanied by the removal of all military hardware from the disputed area, and a prohibition on aerial patrolling and reconnaissance by either side. The agreement should also include a commitment on both sides to refrain from reoccupying vacated positions. Another confidence building measure could be the use of hotlines between force commanders as well as senior personnel at military headquarters.

A military disengagement agreement should incorporate many of the clauses of an agreement specifically aimed at de-escalating hostilities, including confidence-building measures such as prior notification of over-flights and flag meetings between all sides concerned. Such an accord would, however, move from conflict management to conflict resolution since it would demonstrate the willingness of both parties to find a more

---

[6] Based on www.ppu.org.uk/war/countries/mideast/cyprus.html#background.

comprehensive solution to the dispute. It could also serve as a continuum from cease-fire to demilitarization should the political will exist. Relocating troops to minimize the chance of conflict implies (1) gradual reductions of forces in forward positions and (2) an incremental dismantlement of forward pickets and observation posts. Forces would then be redeployed and repositioned in agreed areas (Ahmed and Sahni, 1998).

## 7.5. SUMMARY

The world is changing so rapidly that any rational forecast of future events is simply not feasible. According to Huntington (1993), 'cultural communities are replacing Cold War blocs'. Specifically, during the post-Cold War era countries with similar cultures are coming together; countries with different cultures are coming apart. He argues that world politics is entering a new phase, in which the great divisions among humankind and the dominating source of international conflict will be cultural. Civilizations – the highest cultural groupings of people – are differentiated from each other by religion, history, language and tradition. These divisions are deep and increasing in importance. Sometimes, the fault lines of civilizations are the battle lines of the future. In this emerging era of cultural conflict the United States must, he argues, forge alliances with similar cultures and spread its values wherever possible. With alien civilizations the West must be accommodating if possible, but confrontational if necessary.

Pearson (1955, pp. 83-4) warns that humans are moving into 'an age when different civilizations will have to learn to live side by side in peaceful interchange, leaning from each other, studying each other's history and ideas and arts and culture, mutually enriching each other's lives. The alternative, in this overcrowded little world, is misunderstanding, tension, clash, and catastrophe'. Finally, and for those who are interested in a further study of intercultural relations, a neutral methodology should be applied in the investigations of the characteristics and mechanisms of intercultural conflicts and cooperation. Any attempts to illustrate correlation between the peculiarity of a specific culture and the extent of intercultural conflict will be unwise and potentially risky. It would provoke the possibility of reductionism, elitism, and ethnocentrism. We hope such studies will not be themselves a part of conflict making.

# APPENDIX 1. ETHNIC, LINGUISTIC AND RELIGIOUS CHARACTERISTICS OF THE WORLD

| Country | Major ethnic groups | Major linguistic groups | Major religious groups |
|---|---|---|---|
| Afghanistan | Pashtun, Tajik, Hazara, Uzbek, Aimak, Turkmen, Baloch | Afghan Persian (Dari), Pashtu, Uzbek, Turkmen, Balochi, Pashai | Sunni Muslim, Shi'a Muslim |
| Albania | Albanian, Greek, Vlach, Roma (Gypsy), Serb, Macedonian, Bulgarian | Albanian, Greek, Vlach, Romani, Slavic dialects | Muslim, Albanian Orthodox, Roman Catholic |
| Algeria | Arab-Berber, European | Arabic, French, Berber dialects | Sunni Muslim (state religion), Christian, Jewish |
| American Samoa | Native Pacific islander, Asian, white, mixed | Samoan, English, Tongan, other Pacific islander | Christian Congregationalist, Roman Catholic, Protestant |
| Andorra | Spanish, Andorran, Portuguese, French | Catalan, French, Castilian, Portuguese | Roman Catholic |
| Angola | Ovimbundu, Kimbundu, Bakongo, mixed European and African | Portuguese, Bantu and other African languages | Indigenous beliefs, Roman Catholic, Protestant |

| Country | Ethnic Groups | Languages | Religions |
|---|---|---|---|
| Anguilla | Black, mixed, mulatto, white | English | Anglican, Methodist, other Protestant, Roman Catholic, other Christian |
| Antigua and Barbuda | Black, British, Portuguese, Lebanese, Syrian | English, local dialects | Christian (predominantly Anglican with other Protestant, and some Roman Catholic) |
| Argentina | White (mostly Spanish and Italian), mixed white and Amerindian ancestry, Amerindian | Spanish, English, Italian, German, French | Roman Catholic, Protestant, Jewish |
| Armenia | Armenian, Yezidi (Kurd), Russian | Armenian, Yezidi, Russian | Armenian Apostolic, other Christian, Yezidi (monotheist with elements of nature worship) |
| Aruba | Mixed white/Caribbean Amerindian | Dutch, Papiamento (a Spanish, Portuguese, Dutch, English dialect), English, Spanish | Roman Catholic, Protestant, Hindu, Muslim, Confucian, Jewish |
| Australia | Caucasian, Asian, aboriginal | English, Chinese, Italian | Catholic, Anglican, other Christian, Buddhist, Muslim |
| Austria | Austrians, Croatians, Slovenes, Serbs, and Bosniaks, Turks, German | German, Slovene, Croatian, Hungarian | Roman Catholic, Protestant, Muslim |
| Azerbaijan | Azeri, Dagestani, Russian, Armenian | Azerbaijani (Azeri), Russian, Armenian | Muslim, Russian Orthodox, Armenian Orthodox |
| Bahamas, The | Black, white, Asian and Hispanic | English, Creole | Baptist, Anglican, Roman Catholic, Pentecostal, Church of God, Methodist, other Christian |
| Bahrain | Bahraini, non-Bahraini | Arabic, English, Farsi, Urdu | Muslim (Shi'a and Sunni), Christian |
| Bangladesh | Bengali, tribal groups, non-Bengali Muslims | Bangla (Bengali), English | Muslim, Hindu |
| Barbados | Black, white, Asian and mixed | English | Anglican, Pentecostal, Methodist, other Protestant, Roman Catholic |
| Belarus | Belarusian, Russian, Polish, Ukrainian | Belarusian, Russian | Eastern Orthodox, Roman Catholic, Protestant, Jewish, and Muslim |

| Country | Ethnic groups | Languages | Religions |
|---|---|---|---|
| Belgium | Fleming, Walloon, mixed | Dutch, French, German | Roman Catholic, Protestant |
| Belize | Mestizo, Creole, Maya, Garifuna | English, Spanish, Mayan, Garifuna (Carib), Creole | Roman Catholic, Protestant |
| Benin | Fon, Adja, Yoruba, Bariba, etc, Europeans | French, Fon and Yoruba (in south), tribal languages | Indigenous beliefs, Christian, Muslim |
| Bermuda | Black, white, mixed, other races | English, Portuguese | Anglican, Roman Catholic, African Methodist Episcopal, other Protestant |
| Bhutan | Bhote, ethnic Nepalese, indigenous or migrant tribes | Dzongkha, Tibetan dialects, Nepalese dialects | Lamaistic Buddhist, Hinduism |
| Bolivia | Quechua, mixed white and Amerindian ancestry, Aymara, white | Spanish, Quechua, Aymara | Roman Catholic, Protestant (Evangelical Methodist) |
| Bosnia and Herzegovina | Bosniak, Serb, Croat | Bosnian, Croatian, Serbian | Muslim, Orthodox, Roman Catholic |
| Botswana | Tswana (or Setswana), Kalanga, Basarwa, Kgalagadi | Setswana, Kalanga, Sekgalagadi, English | Christian, Badimo |
| Brazil | White, mulatto, black, Japanese, Arab, and Amerindian | Portuguese, Spanish, English, French | Roman Catholic, Protestant, Spiritualist, Bantu/voodoo |
| British Virgin Islands | Black, white, Indian, Asian and mixed | English | Protestant, Roman Catholic |
| Brunei | Malay, Chinese, indigenous | Bahasa-Malay, English, Chinese | Muslim, Buddhist, Christian, indigenous beliefs |
| Bulgaria | Bulgarian, Turk, Roma, Macedonian, Armenian, Tatar, and Circassian | Bulgarian, Turkish, Roma | Bulgarian Orthodox, Muslim, other Christian |
| Burkina Faso | Mossi over, Gurunsi, Senufo, Lobi, Bobo, Mande, Fulani | French, native African languages | Muslim, indigenous beliefs, Roman Catholic |
| Burma (Myanmar) | Burmese, minority ethnic languages | Buddhist, Christian, Muslim, animist | Burman, Shan, Karen, Rakhine, Chinese, Indian, Mon |
| Burundi | Hutu (Bantu), Tutsi (Hamitic), Twa (Pygmy), Europeans, South Asians | Kirundi, French, Swahili (along Lake Tanganyika and in the Bujumbura area) | Roman Catholic, indigenous beliefs, Muslim, Protestant |

| Country | Ethnic groups | Languages | Religions |
|---|---|---|---|
| Cambodia | Khmer, Vietnamese, Chinese, other | Khmer, French, English | Theravada Buddhist |
| Cameroon | Cameroon Highlanders, Equatorial/Northwestern Bantu, Kirdi, Fulani, Eastern Nigritic | major African language groups, English, French | indigenous beliefs, Christian, Muslim |
| Canada | British Isles origin, French origin, other European, Amerindian, Asian, African, and Arab | English, French | Roman Catholic, Protestant, other Christian, Muslim |
| Cape Verde | Creole (mulatto), African, European | Portuguese, Crioulo (a blend of Portuguese and West African words) | Roman Catholic (infused with indigenous beliefs); Protestant (mostly Church of the Nazarene) |
| Cayman Islands | Mixed, white, black, expatriates of various ethnic groups | English | United Church, Anglican, Baptist, Church of God, other Protestant, Roman Catholic |
| Central African Republic | Baya, Banda, Mandjia, Sara, Mboum, M'Baka, Yakoma | French, Sangho (lingua franca), tribal languages | indigenous beliefs, Protestant, Roman Catholic, Muslim |
| Chad | Arabs, Gorane, Zaghawa, Kanembou, Ouaddai, Baguirmi, Hadjerai, Fulbe, Kotoko, Hausa, Boulala, and Maba (in north and center); Sara, Moundang, Moussei, Massa (in south) | French, Arabic, Sara (in south), over other languages and dialects | Muslim, Christian, animist |
| Chile | White and white-Amerindian, Amerindian | Spanish | Roman Catholic, Protestant, Jewish |
| China | Han Chinese, Zhuang, Uygur, Hui, Yi, Tibetan, Miao, Manchu, Mongol, Buyi, Korean | Mandarin, Cantonese, Wu, Minnan (Taiwanese), Xiang, Gan, Hakka dialects | Chinese-folk religion, Buddhist, Christian, Muslim |
| Christmas Island | Chinese, European, Malay | English, Chinese, Bahasa-Malay | Buddhist, Muslim, Christian |
| Cocos (Keeling) Islands | Europeans, Cocos Malays | Bahasa-Malay (Cocos dialect), English | Sunni Muslim |
| Colombia | Mestizo, white, mulatto, black, mixed black-Amerindian, Amerindian | Spanish | Roman Catholic |

| Country | Ethnic groups | Languages | Religions |
|---|---|---|---|
| Comoros | Antalote, Cafre, Makoa, Oimatsaha, Sakalava | Arabic, French, Shikomoro (a blend of Swahili and Arabic) | Sunni Muslim, Roman Catholic |
| Congo, Democratic Republic of the | Mongo, Luba, Kongo (all Bantu), Mangbetu-Azande (Hamitic) | French, Lingala (lingua franca), Kingwana (dialect of Kiswahili or Swahili), Kikongo, Tshiluba | Roman Catholic, Protestant, Kimbanguist, Muslim |
| Congo, Republic of the | Kongo, Sangha, M'Bochi, Teke, Europeans | French, Lingala and Monokutuba (lingua franca), Kikongo | Christian, animist, Muslim |
| Cook Islands | Cook Island Maori (Polynesian), part Cook Island Maori | English, Maori | Cook Islands Christian Church, Roman Catholic, Seventh-Day Adventists, Church of Latter Day Saints, other Protestant |
| Costa Rica | White (including mestizo), black, Amerindian, Chinese | Spanish, English | Roman Catholic, Evangelical, Jehovah's Witnesses, other Protestant |
| Cote d'Ivoire | Akan, Voltaiques or Gur, Northern Mandes, Krous, Southern Mandes | French, native dialects with Dioula the most widely spoken | Muslim, indigenous, Christian |
| Croatia | Croat, Serb, Bosniak, Hungarian, Slovene, Czech, Roma | Croatian, Serbian, Italian, Hungarian, Czech, Slovak, and German | Roman Catholic, Orthodox, other Christian, Muslim |
| Cuba | Mulatto, white, black, Chinese | Spanish | Roman Catholic, Protestants, Jehovah's Witnesses, Jews, and Santeria |
| Cyprus | Greek, Turkish | Greek, Turkish, English | Greek Orthodox, Muslim, Maronite, Armenian Apostolic |
| Czech Republic | Czech, Moravian, Slovak | Czech | Roman Catholic, Protestant |
| Denmark | Scandinavian, Inuit, Faroese, German, Turkish, Iranian, Somali | Danish, Faroese, Greenlandic (an Inuit dialect), German | Evangelical Lutheran, other Protestant and Roman Catholic, Muslim |
| Djibouti | Somali, Afar, French, Arab, Ethiopian, and Italian | French, Arabic, Somali, Afar | Muslim, Christian |

| Country | Ethnic groups | Languages | Religion |
|---|---|---|---|
| Dominica | Black, mixed black and European, European, Syrian, Carib Amerindian | English, French patois | Roman Catholic, Protestant |
| Dominican Republic | Mixed, white, black | Spanish | Roman Catholic |
| East Timor | Austronesian (Malayo-Polynesian), Papuan, small Chinese minority | Tetum, Portuguese, Indonesian, English | Roman Catholic, Muslim, Protestant, Hindu, Buddhist, Animist |
| Ecuador | Mestizo (mixed Amerindian and white), Amerindian, Spanish, black | Spanish, Amerindian languages (especially Quechua) | Roman Catholic |
| Egypt | Egyptian, Berber, Nubian, Bedouin, and Beja, Greek, Armenian, other Europeans | Arabic, English and French | Muslim (mostly Sunni), Coptic, other Christian |
| El Salvador | Mestizo, white, Amerindian | Spanish, Nahua (among some Amerindians) | Roman Catholic, other |
| Equatorial Guinea | Bioko (primarily Bubi, some Fernandinos), Rio Muni (primarily Fang), Spanish | Spanish, French, pidgin English, Fang, Bubi, Ibo | Christian (predominantly Roman Catholic), pagan practices |
| Eritrea | Ethnic Tigrinya, Tigre and Kunama, Afar, Saho (Red Sea coast dwellers) | Afar, Arabic, Tigre and Kunama, Tigrinya, other Cushitic languages | Muslim, Coptic Christian, Roman Catholic, Protestant |
| Estonia | Estonian, Russian, Ukrainian, Belarusian, Finn | Estonian, Russian | Evangelical Lutheran, Orthodox, other Christian |
| Ethiopia | Oromo, Amhara and Tigre, Sidamo, Shankella, Somali, Afar, Gurage | Amharic, Tigrinya, Oromigna, Guaragigna, Somali, Arabic, English | Muslim, Ethiopian Orthodox, animist |
| Fiji | Fijian (predominantly Melanesian with a Polynesian admixture), Indian, European, other Pacific Islanders, Chinese | English, Fijian, Hindustani | Christian, Hindu, Muslim |
| Finland | Finn, Swede, Russian, Estonian, Roma, Sami | Finnish, Swedish, Sami and Russian | Lutheran National Church, Greek Orthodox in Finland, other Christian |
| France | Celtic and Latin with Teutonic, Slavic, | French, Provencal, Breton, | Roman Catholic, Muslim, Protestant, |

| | | | |
|---|---|---|---|
| | North African, Indochinese, Basque minorities | Alsatian, Corsican, Catalan, Basque, Flemish | Jewish |
| French Guiana | Black or mulatto, white, East Indian, Chinese, Amerindian | French | Roman Catholic |
| French Polynesia | Polynesian, Chinese, local French, metropolitan French | French, Polynesian, Asian languages | Protestant, Roman Catholic |
| Gabon | Bantu tribes (including Fang, Bapounou, Nzebi, Obamba), other Africans and Europeans | French, Fang, Myene, Nzebi, Bapounou/Eschira, Bandjabi | Christian, animist, Muslim |
| Gambia, The | Mandinka, Fula, Wolof, Jola, Serahuli, non-African | English, Mandinka, Wolof, Fula, other indigenous vernaculars | Muslim, Christian, indigenous beliefs |
| Gaza Strip | Palestinian Arab, Jewish | Arabic, Hebrew (spoken by many Palestinians), English | Muslim (predominantly Sunni), Christian, Jewish |
| Georgia | Georgian, Azeri, Armenian, Russian | Georgian, Russian, Armenian, Azeri | Orthodox Christian, Muslim, Armenian-Gregorian, Catholic |
| Germany | German, Turkish, Greek, Italian, Polish, Russian, Serbo-Croatian, Spanish | German | Protestant, Roman Catholic, Muslim |
| Ghana | Akan, Moshi-Dagomba, Ewe, Ga, Gurma, Yoruba, European | English, Akan, Moshi-Dagomba, Ewe, Ga | Christian, Muslim, indigenous beliefs |
| Gibraltar | Spanish, Italian, English, Maltese, Portuguese, German, North Africans | English, Spanish, Italian, Portuguese | Roman Catholic, Church of England, other Christian, Muslim, Jewish, Hindu |
| Greece | Greek, other | Greek, English, French | Greek Orthodox, Muslim |
| Greenland | Greenlander (Inuit and Greenland-born whites), Danish | Greenlandic (East Inuit), Danish, English | Evangelical Lutheran |
| Grenada | Black, mixed black and European, European and East Indian, and trace of Arawak/Carib Amerindian | English, French patois | Roman Catholic, Anglican, other Protestant |
| Guadeloupe | Black or mulatto, white, East Indian, Lebanese, Chinese | French, Creole patois | Roman Catholic, Hindu and pagan African, Protestant |

| Country | Ethnic groups | Languages | Religions |
|---|---|---|---|
| Guam | Chamorro, Filipino, other Pacific islander, white, other Asian | English, Chamorro, Philippine languages, other Pacific island languages, Asian languages | Roman Catholic |
| Guatemala | Mestizo and European, K'iche, Kaqchikel, Mam, Q'eqchi, other Mayan, non-Mayan | Spanish, Amerindian languages | Roman Catholic, Protestant, indigenous Mayan beliefs |
| Guernsey | UK and Norman-French descent with small percentages from other European countries | English, French, Norman-French dialect | Anglican, Roman Catholic, Presbyterian, Baptist, Congregational, Methodist |
| Guinea | Peuhl, Malinke, Soussou, smaller ethnic groups | French | Muslim, Christian, indigenous beliefs |
| Guinea-Bissau | Balanta, Fula, Manjaca, Mandinga, Papel, European and mulatto | Portuguese, Crioulo, African languages | Indigenous beliefs, Muslim, Christian |
| Guyana | East Indian, black, Amerindian, white, Chinese, mixed | English, Amerindian dialects, Creole, Hindi, Urdu | Christian, Hindu, Muslim |
| Haiti | Black, mulatto, white | French, Creole | Roman Catholic, Baptist, Pentecostal, Adventist |
| Honduras | Mestizo (mixed Amerindian and European), Amerindian, black, white | Spanish, Amerindian dialects | Roman Catholic, Protestant |
| Hong Kong | Chinese, other | Chinese (Cantonese), English | Eclectic mixture of local religions, Christian |
| Hungary | Hungarian, Roma, other or unknown | Hungarian, other or unspecified | Roman Catholic, Calvinist, Lutheran, Greek Catholic, other Christian |
| Iceland | Mix of descendants of Norse and Celts, population of foreign origin | Icelandic, English, Nordic languages, German | Lutheran Church of Iceland, Roman Catholic, Free Church (Reykjavik / Hafnarfjorour), other Christian |
| India | Indo-Aryan, Dravidian, Mongoloid | English, Hindi, Bengali, Telugu, Marathi, Tamil, Urdu, Gujarati, Malayalam, Kannada, Oriya, Punjabi, | Hindu, Muslim, Christian, Sikh |

| Country | Languages | Religions |
|---|---|---|
| | Assamese, Kashmiri, Sindhi, and Sanskrit | |
| Indonesia | Javanese, Sundanese, Madurese, coastal Malays | Bahasa Indonesia, English, Dutch, local dialects (of which Javanese is most widely spoken) | Muslim, Protestant, Roman Catholic, Hindu, Buddhist |
| Iran | Persian, Azeri, Gilaki and Mazandarani, Kurd, Arab, Lur, Baloch, Turkmen | Persian and Persian dialects, Turkic and Turkic dialects, Kurdish, Luri, Balochi, Arabic, Turkish | Shi'a Muslim, Sunni Muslim, Zoroastrian, Jewish, Christian, and Baha'I |
| Iraq | Arab, Kurdish, Turkoman, Assyrian | Arabic, Kurdish, Assyrian, Armenian | Muslim (Shi'a, Sunni), Christian |
| Ireland | Celtic, English | English, Irish, Gaelic (or Gaeilge) | Roman Catholic, Church of Ireland, other Christian |
| Isle of Man | Manx (Norse-Celtic descent), Briton | English, Manx Gaelic | Anglican, Roman Catholic, Methodist, Baptist, Presbyterian, Society of Friends |
| Israel | Jewish, Arab | Hebrew, Arabic, English | Jewish, Muslim, Arab Christians, other Christian, Druze |
| Italy | Italian, small clusters of German, French, and Slovene-Italians in north, Albanian-Italians and Greek-Italians in south | Italian, German, French, Slovene | Roman Catholic; Protestant, Jewish, Muslim |
| Jamaica | Black, East Indian, white, Chinese, mixed | English, patois English | Protestant, Roman Catholic |
| Japan | Japanese, Korean, Chinese, Brazilian, Filipino | Japanese | Both Shinto and Buddhist, Christian |
| Jersey | Jersey, British, Irish, French, and other white, Portuguese/Madeiran | English, Portuguese | Anglican, Roman Catholic, Baptist, Congregational New Church, Methodist, Presbyterian |
| Jordan | Arab, Circassian, Armenian | Arabic, English | Sunni Muslim, Christian, Shi'a Muslim |
| Kazakhstan | Kazakh (Qazaq), Russian, Ukrainian, Uzbek, German, Tatar, Uygur | Kazakh (Qazaq, state language), Russian | Muslim, Russian Orthodox, Protestant |

| | | |
|---|---|---|
| Kenya | Kikuyu, Luhya, Luo, Kalenjin, Kamba, Kisii, Meru, Asian, European, Arab | Protestant, Roman Catholic, indigenous beliefs, Muslim |
| Kiribati | Micronesian | I-Kiribati, English |
| | | Roman Catholic, Protestant (Congregational), some Seventh-Day Adventist, Muslim, Baha'i, Latter-day Saints, Church of God |
| Korea, North | Korean, Chinese, ethnic Japanese | Korean |
| | | Buddhist, Confucianist, Christian, Chondogyo |
| Korea, South | Korean, Chinese | Korean, English |
| | | Christian, Buddhist, Confucianist, Chondogyo |
| Kuwait | Kuwaiti, other Arab, South Asian, Iranian | Arabic, English |
| | | Muslim (Sunni, Shi'a ), Christian, Hindu, Parsi |
| Kyrgyzstan | Kyrgyz, Uzbek, Russian, Dungan, Ukrainian, Uygur | Kyrgyz, Russian |
| | | Muslim, Russian Orthodox |
| Laos | Lao Loum (lowland), Lao Theung (upland), Lao Soung (highland), Vietnamese, Chinese | Lao, French, English, and various ethnic languages |
| | | Buddhist, animist, Christian |
| Latvia | Latvian, Russian, Belarusian, Ukrainian, Polish, Lithuanian | Latvian, Russian, Lithuanian |
| | | Lutheran, Roman Catholic, Russian Orthodox |
| Lebanon | Arab, Armenian, other | Arabic, French, English, Armenian |
| | | Muslim (Shi'a, Sunni, Druze, etc.), Catholic, Orthodox, Protestant |
| Lesotho | Sotho, Europeans, Asians | Sesotho (southern Sotho), English, Zulu, Xhosa |
| | | Christian, indigenous beliefs |
| Liberia | Kpelle, Bassa, Gio, Kru, Grebo, Mano, Krahn, Gola, Gbandi, Loma, Kissi, Vai, Dei, Bella, Mandingo, and Mende, Americo-Liberians, Congo People | English, some ethnic group languages |
| | | Indigenous beliefs, Christian, Muslim |
| Libya | Berber and Arab, Greeks, Maltese, Italians, Egyptians, Pakistanis, Turks, Indians, Tunisians | Arabic, Italian, English |
| | | Sunni Muslim |

| | | |
|---|---|---|
| Liechtenstein | Alemannic, Italian, Turkish | Roman Catholic, Protestant |
| Lithuania | Lithuanian, Polish, Russian | Lithuanian, Russian, Polish | Roman Catholic, Russian Orthodox, Protestant |
| Luxembourg | Celtic base (with French and German blend), Portuguese, Italian, Slavs, European | Luxembourgish (national language), German (administrative language), French (administrative language) | Roman Catholic, Protestants, Jews, and Muslims |
| Macau | Chinese, Macanese (mixed Portuguese and Asian ancestry) | Cantonese, Hokkien, Mandarin, other Chinese dialects | Buddhist, Roman Catholic |
| Macedonia | Macedonian, Albanian, Turkish, Roma, Serb | Macedonian, Albanian, Turkish, Roma, Serbian | Macedonian Orthodox, Muslim, other Christian |
| Madagascar | Malayo-Indonesian, Cotiers (mixed African, Malayo-Indonesian, and Arab ancestry), French, Indian, Creole, Comoran | French, Malagasy | Indigenous beliefs, Christian, Muslim |
| Malawi | Chewa, Nyanja, Tumbuka, Yao, Lomwe, Sena, Tonga, Ngoni, Ngonde, Asian, European | Chichewa, Chinyanja, Chiyao, Chitumbuka, Chisena, Chilomwe, Chitonga | Christian, Muslim |
| Malaysia | Malay, Chinese, Indigenous, Indian | Bahasa Melayu, English, Chinese, Tamil, Telugu, Malayalam, Panjabi, Thai | Muslim, Buddhist, Daoist, Hindu, Christian, Sikh, Shamanism |
| Maldives | South Indians, Sinhalese, Arabs | Maldivian Dhivehi (dialect of Sinhala, script derived from Arabic), English | Sunni Muslim |
| Mali | Mande, Peul, Voltaic, Songhai, Tuareg, Moor | French, Bambara, numerous African languages | Muslim, indigenous beliefs, Christian |
| Malta | Maltese (with elements of Italian and other Mediterranean stock) | Maltese, English | Roman Catholic |

| Country | Ethnic groups | Languages | Religions |
|---|---|---|---|
| Marshall Islands | Micronesian | Marshallese, other languages | Protestant, Assembly of God, Roman Catholic, Bukot nan Jesus, Mormon, other Christian |
| Martinique | African and African-white-Indian mixture, white, East Indian, Chinese | French, Creole patois | Roman Catholic, Protestant, Muslim, Hindu |
| Mauritania | Mixed Maur/black, Moor, black | Arabic, Pulaar, Soninke, French, Hassaniya, Wolof | Muslim |
| Mauritius | Indo-Mauritian, Creole, Sino-Mauritian, Franco-Mauritian | Creole, Bhojpuri, French, English | Hindu, Roman Catholic, other Christian, Muslim |
| Mayotte | NA | Mahorian (a Swahili dialect), French () | Muslim, Roman Catholic |
| Mexico | Mestizo (Amerindian-Spanish), Amerindian, white | Spanish, various Mayan, Nahuatl, and other indigenous languages | Roman Catholic, Protestant |
| Micronesia, Federated States of | Nine ethnic Micronesian and Polynesian groups | English, Trukese, Pohnpeian, Yapese, Kosrean, Ulithian, Woleaian, Nukuoro, Kapingamarangi | Roman Catholic, Protestant |
| Moldova | Moldovan/Romanian, Ukrainian, Russian, Gagauz, Bulgarian | Moldovan, Russian, Gagauz (a Turkish dialect) | Eastern Orthodox, Jewish, Baptist |
| Monaco | French, Monegasque, Italian | French, English, Italian, Monegasque | Roman Catholic |
| Mongolia | Mongol (mostly Khalkha), Turkic (mostly Kazakh), Chinese, Russian | Khalkha Mongol, Turkic, Russian () | Buddhist Lamaist, none, Shamanist and Christian, Muslim |
| Montenegro | Montenegrin, Serbian, Bosniak, Albanian, Muslims, Croats, Roma | Serbian (Ijekavian dialect) | Orthodox, Muslim, Roman Catholic |
| Montserrat | Black, white | English | Anglican, Methodist, Roman Catholic, Pentecostal, Seventh-Day Adventist, other Christian |
| Morocco | Arab-Berber, Jewish | Arabic, Berber dialects, | Muslim, Christian, Jewish |

French

| Country | Ethnic groups | Languages | Religions |
|---|---|---|---|
| Mozambique | Makhuwa, Tsonga, Lomwe, Sena, etc., Europeans, Euro-Africans, Indians | Emakhuwa, Xichangana, Portuguese, Elomwe, Cisena, Echuwabo, other Mozambican languages | Catholic, Muslim, Zionist Christian |
| Namibia | Ovambo and Kavangos tribes, Herero, Damara, Nama, Caprivian, Bushmen, Baster, and Tswana, white, mixed | English, Afrikaans, German, indigenous languages (Oshivambo, Herero, Nama) | Christian (Lutheran at least), indigenous beliefs |
| Nauru | Nauruan, other Pacific Islander, Chinese, European | Nauruan (distinct Pacific Island language), English | Christian (two-thirds Protestant, one-third Roman Catholic) |
| Nepal | Chhettri, Brahman-Hill, Magar, Tharu, Tamang, Newar, Muslim, Kami, Yadav | Nepali, Maithali, Bhojpuri, Tharu (Dagaura/Rana), Tamang, Newar, Magar, Awadhi | Hindu, Buddhist, Muslim, Kirant |
| Netherlands | Dutch, Turks, Moroccans, Antilleans, Surinamese, and Indonesians | Dutch, Frisian | Roman Catholic, Dutch Reformed, Calvinist, Muslim |
| Netherlands Antilles | Mixed black, Carib Amerindian, white, East Asian | Papiamento (Spanish-Portuguese-Dutch-English dialect), English, Dutch, Spanish, Creole | Roman Catholic, Pentecostal, Protestant, Seventh-Day Adventist, Methodist, Jehovah's Witnesses, Jewish |
| New Caledonia | Melanesian, European, Wallisian, Polynesian, Indonesian, Vietnamese | French, Melanesian-Polynesian dialects | Roman Catholic, Protestant |
| New Zealand | European, Maori, Asian, Pacific islander | English, Maori | Anglican, Roman Catholic, Presbyterian, Methodist, Pentecostal, Baptist |
| Nicaragua | Mestizo (mixed Amerindian and white), white, black, Amerindian | Spanish, Miskito | Roman Catholic, Evangelical, Moravian, Episcopal |
| Niger | Hausa, Djerma, Fula, Tuareg, Beri Beri (Kanouri), Arab, Toubou, and Gourmantche | French, Hausa, Djerma | Muslim, indigenous beliefs, Christian |
| Nigeria | Hausa and Fulani, Yoruba, Igbo (Ibo), | English, Hausa, Yoruba, Igbo | Muslim, Christian, indigenous beliefs |

|  | Ethnic groups | Languages | Religions |
|---|---|---|---|
|  | Ijaw, Kanuri, Ibibio, Tiv | (Ibo), Fulani |  |
| Niue | Niuen, Pacific islander, European, mixed, Asian | Niuean, a Polynesian language closely related to Tongan and Samoan; English | Ekalesia Niue (a Protestant church closely related to the London Missionary Society), Latter-Day Saints, Roman Catholic, Jehovah's Witnesses, Seventh-Day Adventist |
| Norfolk Island | Descendants of the Bounty mutineers, Australian, New Zealander, Polynesian | English, Norfolk a mixture of English and ancient Tahitian | Anglican, Roman Catholic, Uniting Church in Australia, Seventh-Day Adventist, Australian Christian, Jehovah's Witness |
| Northern Mariana Islands | Asian, Pacific islander, Caucasian, other, mixed | Philippine languages, Chinese, Chamorro, English, other Pacific island languages | Christian (Roman Catholic majority, traditional beliefs and taboos) |
| Norway | Norwegian, Sami | Bokmal Norwegian, Nynorsk Norwegian, Sami and Finnish | Church of Norway, Pentecostal, Roman Catholic, other Christian, Muslim |
| Oman | Arab, Baluchi, Indian, Pakistani, Sri Lankan, Bangladeshi, African | Arabic, English, Baluchi, Urdu, Indian dialects | Ibadhi Muslim, Sunni Muslim, Shi'a Muslim, Hindu |
| Pakistan | Punjabi, Sindhi, Pashtun (Pathan), Baloch, Muhajir | Punjabi, Sindhi, Siraiki, Pashtu, Urdu, Balochi, Hindko, Brahui, English, Burushaski | Muslim: Sunni, Shi'a, Christian, Hindu |
| Palau | Palauan, Filipino, Chinese, other Asian, white, Carolinian, other Micronesian | Palauan, Tobi, and Angaur, Filipino, English, Chinese, Carolinian, Japanese, other Asian | Roman Catholic, Protestant, Modekngei (indigenous to Palau), Seventh-Day Adventist, Jehovah's Witness, Latter-Day Saints |
| Panama | Mestizo (mixed Amerindian and white), Amerindian and mixed (West Indian), white, Amerindian | Spanish, English | Roman Catholic, Protestant |
| Papua New Guinea | Melanesian, Papuan, Negrito, Micronesian, Polynesian | Melanesian Pidgin (lingua franca), English, Motu (in Papua region) | Roman Catholic, Lutheran, Presbyterian/Methodist/London Missionary Society, Anglican, Evangelical Alliance, |

| Country | Ethnicity | Languages | Religion |
|---|---|---|---|
| Paraguay | Mestizo (mixed Spanish and Amerindian | Spanish, Guarani | Roman Catholic, Mennonite and other Protestant |
| Peru | Amerindian, mestizo (mixed Amerindian and white), white, black, Japanese, Chinese | Spanish, Quechua, Aymara, and a large number of minor Amazonian languages | Roman Catholic, Seventh Day Adventist, other Christian |
| Philippines | Tagalog, Cebuano, Ilocano, Bisaya/Binisaya, Hiligaynon Ilonggo, Bikol, Waray | Filipino, English, Tagalog, Cebuano, Ilocano, Hiligaynon or Ilonggo, Bicol, Waray, Pampango, and Pangasinan | Roman Catholic, Evangelical, Iglesia ni Kristo, Aglipayan, other Christian, Muslim |
| Pitcairn Islands | Descendants of the Bounty mutineers and their Tahitian wives | English, Pitcairnese (mixture of English and a Tahitian dialect) | Seventh-Day Adventist |
| Poland | Polish, German, Belarusian, Ukrainian | Polish, other and unspecified | Roman Catholic, Eastern Orthodox, Protestant |
| Portugal | Homogeneous Mediterranean stock; black African descents; East Europeans | Portuguese, Mirandese | Roman Catholic, Protestant |
| Puerto Rico | White (mostly Spanish origin), black, Amerindian, Asian | Spanish, English | Roman Catholic, Protestant and other |
| Qatar | Arab, Indian, Pakistani, Iranian | Arabic, English | Muslim |
| Reunion | French, African, Malagasy, Chinese, Pakistani, Indian | French, Creole widely used | Roman Catholic, Hindu, Muslim, Buddhist |
| Romania | Romanian, Hungarian, Roma, Ukrainian, German, Russian, Turkish | Romanian, Hungarian, German | Eastern Orthodox, Protestant, Roman Catholic, Muslim |
| Russia | Russian, Tatar, Ukrainian, Bashkir, Chuvash | Russian, many minority languages | Russian Orthodox, Muslim, other Christian |
| Rwanda | Hutu, Tutsi, Twa (Pygmoid) | Kinyarwanda, French, English, Kiswahili (Swahili) | Roman Catholic, Protestant, Adventist, Muslim, indigenous beliefs |
| Saint Helena | African descent, white, Chinese | English | Anglican (majority), Baptist, Seventh-Day Adventis, other Protestant, indigenous beliefs |

| Country | Ethnic groups | Language | Religion |
|---|---|---|---|
| | | | Adventist, Roman Catholic |
| Saint Kitts and Nevis | Predominantly black; some British, Portuguese, and Lebanese | English | Anglican, other Protestant, Roman Catholic |
| Saint Lucia | Black, mixed, East Indian, white | English, French patois | Roman Catholic, Seventh Day Adventist, Pentecostal, Anglican, Evangelica, other Christian, Rastafarian |
| Saint Pierre and Miquelon | Basques and Bretons (French fishermen | French | Roman Catholic |
| Saint Vincent and the Grenadines | Black, mixed, East Indian, Carib Amerindian | English, French patois | Anglican, Methodist, Roman Catholic, Hindu, Seventh-Day Adventist, other Protestant |
| Samoa | Samoan, Euronesians (European and Polynesian blood), Europeans | Samoan (Polynesian), English | Congregationalist, Roman Catholic, Methodist, Latter-Day Saints, Assembly of God, Seventh-Day Adventist, other Christian, Worship Center |
| San Marino | Sammarinese, Italian | Italian | Roman Catholic |
| Sao Tome and Principe | Mestico, angolares (descendants of Angolan slaves), forros (descendants of freed slaves), servicais (contract laborers from Angola, Mozambique, and Cape Verde), tongas (children of servicais born on the islands), Portuguese | Portuguese | Catholic, Evangelical, New Apostolic, Adventist |
| Saudi Arabia | Arab, Afro-Asian | Arabic | Muslim |
| Senegal | Wolof, Pular, Serer, Jola, Mandinka, Soninke, European and Lebanese | French, Wolof, Pulaar, Jola, Mandinka | Muslim, Roman Catholic, indigenous beliefs |
| Seychelles | Mixed French, African, Indian, Chinese, and Arab | Creole, English, other | Roman Catholic, Anglican, Seventh Day Adventist, other Christian, Hindu, Muslim |
| Sierra Leone | Temne, Mende, other African tribes, Creole (Krio) | English, Mende (in south), Temne (in north), Krio (English-based Creole) | Muslim, indigenous beliefs, Christian |

| Country | Ethnic groups | Languages | Religions |
|---|---|---|---|
| Singapore | Chinese, Malay, Indian | Mandarin, English, Malay, Hokkien, Cantonese, Tamil, other Chinese dialects | Buddhist, Muslim, Taoist, Hindu, Catholic, other Christian |
| Slovakia | Slovak, Hungarian, Roma, Ruthenian/Ukrainian | Slovak, Hungarian, Roma, Ukrainian | Roman Catholic, Protestant, Greek Catholic |
| Slovenia | Slovene, Serb, Croat, Bosniak | Slovenian, Serbo-Croatian | Catholic, Orthodox, other Christian, Muslim |
| Solomon Islands | Melanesian, Polynesian, Micronesian, other | Melanesian pidgin; English | Church of Melanesia, Roman Catholic, South Seas Evangelical, Seventh-Day Adventist, United Church, Christian Fellowship Church, other Christian |
| Somalia | Somali, Bantu and other non-Somali (including Arabs) | Somali, Arabic, Italian, English | Sunni Muslim |
| South Africa | Black African, white, colored, Indian/Asian | IsiZulu, IsiXhosa, Afrikaans, Sepedi, English, Setswana, Sesotho, Xitsonga | Zion Christian, Pentecostal/Charismatic, Catholic, Methodist, Dutch Reformed, Anglican, other Christian, Islam |
| Spain | Composite of Mediterranean and Nordic types | Castilian Spanish, Catalan, Galician, Basque | Roman Catholic, other |
| Sri Lanka | Sinhalese, Sri Lankan Moors, Indian Tamil, Sri Lankan Tamil | Sinhala, Tamil | Buddhist, Muslim, Hindu, Christian |
| Sudan | Black, Arab, Beja, foreigners | Arabic, Nubian, Ta Bedawie, dialects of Nilotic, Nilo-Hamitic, Sudanic languages, English | Sunni Muslim (in north), indigenous beliefs, Christian |
| Suriname | Hindustani, Creole (mixed white and black), Javanese, Maroons, Amerindian, Chinese, white | Dutch, English, Sranang Tongo (or Taki-Taki), Hindustani, Javanese | Hindu, Protestant, Roman Catholic, Muslim, indigenous beliefs |
| Swaziland | African, European | English, siSwati | Zionist (blend of Christianity and indigenous ancestral worship), Roman Catholic, Muslim, Anglican, Bahai, |

| Country | Ethnic groups | Languages | Religion |
|---|---|---|---|
| | | | Methodist, Mormon, Jewish |
| Sweden | Swedes with Finnish and Sami minorities; Finns, Yugoslavs, Danes, Norwegians, Greeks, Turks | Swedish, small Sami- and Finnish-speaking minorities | Lutheran, Roman Catholic, Orthodox, Baptist, Muslim, Jewish, Buddhist |
| Switzerland | German, French, Italian, Romansch, other | German, French, Italian, Serbo-Croatian, Albanian, Portuguese, Spanish, English, Romansch | Roman Catholic, Protestant, Orthodox, other Christian, Muslim |
| Syria | Arab, Kurds, Armenians | Arabic, Kurdish, Armenian, Aramaic, Circassian; French, English | Sunni Muslim, Alawite, Druze, and other Muslim sects, Christian (various sects), Jewish |
| Taiwan | Taiwanese (including Hakka), mainland Chinese, aborigine | Mandarin Chinese, Taiwanese (Minnan), Hakka dialects | Mixture of Buddhist, Confucian, and Taoist, Christian |
| Tajikistan | Tajik, Uzbek, Russian, Kyrgyz | Tajik, Russian | Sunni Muslim, Shi'a Muslim |
| Tanzania | Bantu (over tribes), Asian, European, and Arab | Kiswahili or Swahili, Kiunguja (Swahili in Zanzibar), English, Arabic (in Zanzibar) | Mainland: Christian, Muslim, indigenous beliefs; Zanzibar: Muslim |
| Thailand | Thai, Chinese, other | Thai, English, ethnic and regional dialects | Buddhist, Muslim, Christian |
| Togo | Ewe, Mina, Kabre, and other native African tribes, European, Syrian-Lebanese | French, Ewe and Mina (in south), Kabye (Kabiye) and Dagomba (in north) | Indigenous beliefs, Christian, Muslim |
| Tokelau | Polynesian | Tokelauan (a Polynesian language), English | Congregational Christian Church, Roman Catholic |
| Tonga | Polynesian, Europeans | Tongan, English | Christian |
| Trinidad and Tobago | Indian (South Asian), African, mixed | English, Hindi, French, Spanish, Chinese | Roman Catholic, Hindu, Anglican, Baptist, Pentecostal, other Christian, Muslim, Seventh Day Adventist |
| Tunisia | Arab, European, Jewish | Arabic, French | Muslim, Christian, Jewish |

| | | |
|---|---|---|
| Turkey | Turkish, Kurdish | Turkish, Kurdish, Dimli (or Zaza), Azeri, Kabardian | Muslim (mostly Sunni), Christians, Jews |
| Turkmenistan | Turkmen, Uzbek, Russian | Turkmen, Russian, Uzbek | Muslim, Eastern Orthodox |
| Turks and Caicos Islands | Black, mixed, European, or North American | English | Baptist, Anglican, Methodist, Church of God |
| Tuvalu | Polynesian, Micronesian | Tuvaluan, English, Samoan, Kiribati (on the island of Nui) | Church of Tuvalu (Congregationalist), Seventh-Day Adventist, Baha'i |
| Uganda | Baganda, Ankole, Basoga, Iteso, Bakiga, Langi, Rwanda, Bagisu, Acholi, Lugbara, Batoro, Bunyoro, Alur, Bagwere, Bakonjo, Jopodhola, Karamojong, and Rundi | English, Ganda or Luganda, other Niger-Congo languages, Nilo-Saharan languages, Swahili, Arabic | Roman Catholic, Protestant, Muslim, indigenous beliefs |
| Ukraine | Ukrainian, Russian, Belarusian, Moldovan, Crimean Tatar, Bulgarian, Hungarian, Romanian, Polish, Jewish | Ukrainian, Russian, Romanian, Polish, and Hungarian | Ukrainian Orthodox (Kiev Patri, Moscow Patri. ), Orthodox, Ukrainian Greek Catholic and Autocephalous Orthodox, Protestant, Jewish |
| United Arab Emirates | Emirati, other Arab and Iranian, South Asian, Westerners, East Asians | Arabic, Persian, English, Hindi, Urdu | Muslim (mostly Sunni), Christian, Hindu |
| United Kingdom | English, Scottish, Welsh, Northern Irish, black, Indian, Pakistani, mixed | English, Welsh (about in Wales), Scottish form of Gaelic | Christian (Anglican, Roman Catholic, Presbyterian, Methodist), Muslim, Hindu |
| United States | White, black, Asian, Amerindian and Alaska native, native Hawaiian and other Pacific islander | English, Spanish, other Indo-European, Asian and Pacific island | Protestant, Roman Catholic, Mormon, Jewish, Muslim |
| Uruguay | White, mestizo, black, Amerindian | Spanish, Portunol, or Brazilero (Portuguese-Spanish mix on the Brazilian frontier) | Roman Catholic, Protestant, Jewish |
| Uzbekistan | Uzbek, Russian, Tajik, Kazakh, Karakalpak, Tatar | Uzbek, Russian, Tajik | Muslim (mostly Sunnis), Eastern Orthodox |

| | | |
|---|---|---|
| Vanuatu | Ni-Vanuatu, other | local languages, pidgin (Bislama or Bichelama), English, French | Presbyterian, Anglican, Roman Catholic, Seventh-Day Adventist, other Christian, indigenous beliefs |
| Venezuela | Spanish, Italian, Portuguese, Arab, German, African, indigenous people | Spanish, numerous indigenous dialects | Roman Catholic, Protestant |
| Vietnam | Kinh (Viet), Tay, Thai, Muong, Khome, Hoa, Nun, Hmong | Vietnamese, English, French, Chinese, Khmer, Mon-Khmer, Malayo-Polynesian | Buddhist, Catholic, Hoa Hao, Cao Dai, Protestant, Muslim |
| Virgin Islands | Black, white, Asian, other | English, Spanish or Spanish Creole, French or French Creole | Baptist, Roman Catholic, Episcopalian |
| Wallis and Futuna | Polynesian | Wallisian (indigenous Polynesian language), Futunian, French | Roman Catholic |
| West Bank | Palestinian Arab and other, Jewish | Arabic, Hebrew, English | Muslim (predominantly Sunni), Jewish, Christian |
| Western Sahara | Arab, Berber | Hassaniya Arabic, Moroccan Arabic | Muslim |
| Yemen | Arab; Afro-Arab, South Asians, Europeans | Arabic | Muslim including Shafi'i (Sunni) and Zaydi (Shi'a), small numbers of Jewish, Christian, and Hindu |
| Zambia | African, European | English, Bemba, Kaonda, Lozi, Lunda, Luvale, Nyanja, Tonga | Christian, Muslim and Hindu, indigenous beliefs |
| Zimbabwe | Shona, Ndebele, other African, mixed and Asian, white | English, Shona, Sindebele (Ndebele), other minor tribal dialects | Mix of Christian and indigenous beliefs, Christian, indigenous beliefs, Muslim |

Source: CIA (2007), Britannica Book for the Year 2001 and Guo (2007a).

# APPENDIX 2. LINGUISTIC AND RELIGIOUS DIVERSITY INDEXES OF THE WORLD

| Economy | Language | | | Religion | | |
|---|---|---|---|---|---|---|
| | NUM | POP | DIVERSITY | NUM | POP | DIVEFRSITY |
| Afghanistan | 11 | 52.425 | 2.129 | 3 | 83.993 | 0.192 |
| Albania | 4 | 97.965 | 0.029 | 4 | 70.213 | 0.511 |
| Algeria | 3 | 59.675 | 0.557 | 3 | 99.559 | 0.005 |
| American Samoa | 5 | 49.593 | 1.251 | 3 | 57.377 | 0.597 |
| Andorra | 6 | 46.875 | 1.591 | 2 | 92.188 | 0.056 |
| Angola | 14 | 27.603 | 5.757 | 3 | 72.740 | 0.349 |
| Antigua and Barbuda | 2 | 95.313 | 0.033 | 4 | 41.538 | 1.249 |
| Argentina | 4 | 96.837 | 0.045 | 5 | 87.715 | 0.219 |
| Armenia | 3 | 93.369 | 0.076 | 2 | 64.456 | 0.279 |
| Aruba | 5 | 76.190 | 0.467 | 2 | 71.429 | 0.219 |
| Australia | 22 | 81.319 | 0.781 | 8 | 27.337 | 3.531 |
| Austria | 9 | 92.000 | 0.192 | 4 | 77.998 | 0.357 |
| Azerbaijan | 5 | 88.976 | 0.194 | 4 | 93.307 | 0.097 |
| Bahamas, The | 2 | 89.655 | 0.074 | 4 | 55.052 | 0.865 |
| Bahrain | 2 | 68.333 | 0.245 | 3 | 61.290 | 0.530 |
| Bangladesh | 10 | 95.219 | 0.116 | 3 | 88.304 | 0.137 |
| Barbados | 2 | 95.094 | 0.035 | 4 | 32.830 | 1.537 |
| Belarus | 5 | 65.637 | 0.739 | 3 | 50.676 | 0.719 |
| Belgium | 8 | 59.274 | 1.332 | 2 | 87.929 | 0.087 |
| Belize | 5 | 50.661 | 1.212 | 4 | 93.220 | 0.099 |
| Benin | 11 | 34.407 | 3.820 | 4 | 62.034 | 0.693 |
| Bermuda | 1 | 100.000 | 0.000 | 4 | 37.097 | 1.392 |
| Bhutan | 3 | 50.000 | 0.732 | 2 | 74.713 | 0.192 |
| Bolivia | 8 | 42.193 | 2.327 | 3 | 88.417 | 0.136 |
| Bosnia and Herzegovina | 2 | 99.042 | 0.007 | 4 | 40.064 | 1.295 |
| Botswana | 7 | 53.952 | 1.450 | 4 | 56.000 | 0.840 |
| Brazil | 6 | 97.545 | 0.045 | 3 | 72.323 | 0.355 |
| Brunei | 8 | 45.752 | 2.090 | 2 | 67.208 | 0.255 |
| Bulgaria | 6 | 80.863 | 0.409 | 3 | 50.420 | 0.724 |

| | | | | | | |
|---|---|---|---|---|---|---|
| Burkina Faso | 24 | 47.400 | 4.321 | 3 | 50.000 | 0.732 |
| Burundi | 5 | 75.492 | 0.484 | 3 | 65.124 | 0.467 |
| Cambodia | 5 | 88.632 | 0.201 | 3 | 94.995 | 0.057 |
| Cameroon | 26 | 14.858 | 15.023 | 4 | 34.963 | 1.464 |
| Canada | 28 | 60.808 | 2.691 | 11 | 45.196 | 2.722 |
| Cape Verde | 1 | 100.000 | 0.000 | 2 | 99.579 | 0.003 |
| Central African Republic | 11 | 44.709 | 2.765 | 4 | 31.250 | 1.594 |
| Chad | 14 | 27.014 | 5.863 | 5 | 53.986 | 1.097 |
| Chile | 4 | 89.687 | 0.154 | 3 | 76.749 | 0.291 |
| China | 49 | 65.783 | 2.787 | 7 | 51.915 | 1.549 |
| Colombia | 7 | 98.165 | 0.036 | 2 | 91.906 | 0.058 |
| Comoros | 8 | 71.337 | 0.815 | 2 | 99.322 | 0.005 |
| Congo, Dem. Rep. of the | 15 | 30.401 | 5.585 | 6 | 41.011 | 1.878 |
| Congo, Rep. of the | 12 | 30.992 | 4.556 | 4 | 40.927 | 1.268 |
| Costa Rica | 6 | 97.240 | 0.051 | 2 | 81.268 | 0.139 |
| Cote d'Ivoire | 7 | 25.768 | 3.240 | 6 | 41.458 | 1.855 |
| Croatia | 2 | 96.017 | 0.028 | 5 | 72.117 | 0.566 |
| Cuba | 1 | 100.000 | 0.000 | 2 | 60.500 | 0.315 |
| Cyprus | 3 | 74.118 | 0.329 | 3 | 73.256 | 0.342 |
| Czech Republic | 15 | 81.186 | 0.664 | 7 | 39.961 | 2.217 |
| Denmark | 10 | 94.456 | 0.136 | 2 | 87.121 | 0.093 |
| Djibouti | 4 | 50.746 | 0.979 | 2 | 97.267 | 0.019 |
| Dominica | 2 | 52.482 | 0.390 | 3 | 70.270 | 0.386 |
| Dominican Republic | 2 | 97.951 | 0.014 | 3 | 81.795 | 0.221 |
| Ecuador | 2 | 92.965 | 0.050 | 2 | 92.462 | 0.054 |
| Egypt | 3 | 98.349 | 0.018 | 3 | 89.003 | 0.128 |
| El Salvador | 1 | 100.000 | 0.000 | 3 | 78.269 | 0.270 |
| Equatorial Guinea | 3 | 84.091 | 0.191 | 2 | 93.182 | 0.048 |
| Eritrea | 9 | 49.025 | 2.065 | 2 | 69.359 | 0.237 |
| Estonia | 6 | 64.138 | 0.901 | 3 | 66.438 | 0.446 |
| Ethiopia | 8 | 31.012 | 3.198 | 5 | 34.156 | 1.886 |
| Faroe Islands | 1 | 100.000 | 0.000 | 2 | 79.545 | 0.152 |
| Fiji | 4 | 42.431 | 1.221 | 4 | 52.956 | 0.920 |
| Finland | 6 | 92.847 | 0.137 | 2 | 85.825 | 0.103 |
| France | 15 | 87.870 | 0.389 | 7 | 76.220 | 0.588 |
| French Guiana | 3 | 94.079 | 0.067 | 2 | 54.605 | 0.370 |
| French Polynesia | 4 | 46.309 | 1.105 | 3 | 50.220 | 0.728 |
| Gabon | 8 | 26.415 | 3.619 | 4 | 50.420 | 0.988 |
| Gambia, The | 11 | 34.054 | 3.861 | 2 | 95.200 | 0.034 |
| Gaza Strip | 2 | 99.514 | 0.003 | 2 | 98.735 | 0.009 |
| Georgia | 7 | 71.642 | 0.736 | 5 | 44.238 | 1.453 |
| Germany | 8 | 90.816 | 0.210 | 4 | 42.805 | 1.210 |
| Ghana | 8 | 37.599 | 2.660 | 6 | 29.337 | 2.547 |
| Gibraltar | 3 | 88.889 | 0.130 | 2 | 77.778 | 0.167 |
| Greece | 3 | 98.575 | 0.016 | 3 | 91.746 | 0.095 |

| Greenland | 2 | 87.500 | 0.091 | 2 | 98.214 | 0.012 |
|---|---|---|---|---|---|---|
| Grenada | 1 | 100.000 | 0.000 | 3 | 53.061 | 0.675 |
| Guadeloupe | 2 | 95.150 | 0.034 | 2 | 81.395 | 0.138 |
| Guam | 9 | 37.179 | 2.976 | 3 | 74.359 | 0.325 |
| Guatemala | 7 | 41.354 | 2.131 | 3 | 75.979 | 0.302 |
| Guernsey | 1 | 100.000 | 0.000 | 2 | 64.516 | 0.279 |
| Guinea | 12 | 35.661 | 3.947 | 4 | 86.775 | 0.201 |
| Guinea-Bissau | 10 | 29.881 | 4.026 | 3 | 65.254 | 0.465 |
| Guyana | 3 | 96.382 | 0.041 | 6 | 34.023 | 2.261 |
| Haiti | 2 | 83.565 | 0.121 | 3 | 68.533 | 0.413 |
| Honduras | 5 | 98.214 | 0.029 | 3 | 86.770 | 0.156 |
| Hong Kong | 12 | 59.279 | 1.751 | 4 | 73.806 | 0.438 |
| Hungary | 7 | 98.524 | 0.029 | 3 | 63.091 | 0.500 |
| Iceland | 2 | 95.941 | 0.029 | 2 | 90.406 | 0.069 |
| India | 72 | 10.704 | 44.554 | 10 | 80.257 | 0.576 |
| Indonesia | 10 | 39.431 | 3.034 | 6 | 87.211 | 0.258 |
| Iran | 20 | 45.259 | 4.155 | 3 | 93.420 | 0.075 |
| Iraq | 6 | 77.127 | 0.507 | 3 | 62.483 | 0.510 |
| Ireland | 3 | 74.120 | 0.329 | 2 | 91.758 | 0.059 |
| Isle of Man | 1 | 100.000 | 0.000 | 2 | 62.500 | 0.297 |
| Israel | 4 | 62.898 | 0.673 | 3 | 80.389 | 0.240 |
| Italy | 12 | 94.070 | 0.159 | 3 | 81.739 | 0.222 |
| Jamaica | 3 | 94.071 | 0.067 | 4 | 47.244 | 1.078 |
| Japan | 7 | 99.092 | 0.018 | 4 | 53.393 | 0.908 |
| Jersey | 2 | 93.407 | 0.047 | 3 | 61.628 | 0.524 |
| Jordan | 3 | 97.792 | 0.025 | 2 | 96.460 | 0.025 |
| Kazakstan | 11 | 45.954 | 2.655 | 4 | 47.009 | 1.085 |
| Kenya | 31 | 37.992 | 7.409 | 7 | 29.529 | 2.940 |
| Kiribati | 3 | 98.908 | 0.012 | 3 | 53.659 | 0.664 |
| Korea, North | 2 | 99.836 | 0.001 | 4 | 68.298 | 0.552 |
| Korea, South | 2 | 99.890 | 0.001 | 8 | 50.099 | 1.823 |
| Kuwait | 2 | 78.082 | 0.164 | 4 | 45.000 | 1.144 |
| Kyrgyzstan | 10 | 59.565 | 1.537 | 3 | 70.000 | 0.390 |
| Laos | 5 | 66.992 | 0.701 | 3 | 57.813 | 0.590 |
| Latvia | 7 | 55.061 | 1.398 | 4 | 62.864 | 0.673 |
| Lebanon | 4 | 74.948 | 0.415 | 8 | 33.938 | 2.950 |
| Lesotho | 3 | 70.954 | 0.376 | 5 | 39.000 | 1.669 |
| Liberia | 19 | 42.428 | 4.448 | 3 | 67.692 | 0.426 |
| Libya | 3 | 95.929 | 0.046 | 2 | 96.991 | 0.021 |
| Liechtenstein | 4 | 87.859 | 0.183 | 2 | 80.645 | 0.144 |
| Lithuania | 6 | 81.183 | 0.401 | 3 | 71.968 | 0.361 |
| Luxembourg | 12 | 67.381 | 1.249 | 2 | 95.238 | 0.034 |
| Macau | 6 | 85.308 | 0.301 | 3 | 60.808 | 0.538 |
| Macedonia | 7 | 66.532 | 0.918 | 3 | 53.769 | 0.662 |
| Madagascar | 3 | 89.974 | 0.116 | 4 | 52.028 | 0.945 |

| | | | | | | |
|---|---|---|---|---|---|---|
| Malawi | 6 | 55.556 | 1.217 | 6 | 23.771 | 2.919 |
| Malaysia | 14 | 33.053 | 4.852 | 6 | 52.920 | 1.325 |
| Maldives | 1 | 100.000 | 0.000 | 1 | 100.000 | 0.000 |
| Mali | 17 | 42.689 | 4.072 | 3 | 89.950 | 0.117 |
| Malta | 3 | 95.733 | 0.048 | 2 | 93.333 | 0.047 |
| Marshall Islands | 3 | 50.000 | 0.732 | 3 | 63.333 | 0.496 |
| Martinique | 2 | 96.742 | 0.023 | 2 | 87.500 | 0.091 |
| Mauritania | 8 | 76.953 | 0.615 | 2 | 99.585 | 0.003 |
| Mauritius | 13 | 61.734 | 1.668 | 4 | 50.877 | 0.976 |
| Mayotte | 5 | 42.105 | 1.539 | 2 | 96.875 | 0.022 |
| Mexico | 38 | 86.580 | 0.629 | 4 | 90.390 | 0.142 |
| Micronesia | 9 | 41.628 | 2.606 | 3 | 41.121 | 0.910 |
| Moldova | 6 | 62.069 | 0.973 | 3 | 55.505 | 0.630 |
| Monaco | 5 | 41.935 | 1.546 | 2 | 81.250 | 0.139 |
| Mongolia | 12 | 78.819 | 0.693 | 2 | 96.203 | 0.027 |
| Morocco | 3 | 65.026 | 0.468 | 2 | 99.816 | 0.001 |
| Mozambique | 26 | 27.793 | 9.513 | 5 | 47.771 | 1.318 |
| Myanmar (Burma) | 9 | 68.952 | 0.978 | 6 | 89.449 | 0.208 |
| Namibia | 12 | 46.816 | 2.749 | 5 | 51.445 | 1.185 |
| Nauru | 6 | 49.758 | 1.460 | 3 | 50.962 | 0.714 |
| Nepal | 22 | 50.327 | 3.643 | 4 | 86.468 | 0.206 |
| Netherlands, The | 5 | 91.845 | 0.140 | 6 | 40.013 | 1.929 |
| Netherlands Antilles | 3 | 85.981 | 0.167 | 2 | 73.832 | 0.199 |
| New Caledonia | 6 | 45.274 | 1.666 | 3 | 61.194 | 0.532 |
| New Zealand | 4 | 90.912 | 0.134 | 9 | 21.644 | 4.594 |
| Nicaragua | 4 | 94.848 | 0.074 | 3 | 76.674 | 0.292 |
| Niger | 10 | 46.019 | 2.466 | 3 | 87.007 | 0.153 |
| Nigeria | 16 | 25.060 | 6.987 | 7 | 42.995 | 2.032 |
| Northern Mariana | 11 | 47.502 | 2.521 | 2 | 79.630 | 0.152 |
| Norway | 5 | 96.549 | 0.057 | 2 | 88.209 | 0.085 |
| Oman | 2 | 76.652 | 0.176 | 5 | 73.451 | 0.533 |
| Pakistan | 10 | 43.107 | 2.706 | 5 | 75.004 | 0.495 |
| Palau | 6 | 50.000 | 1.449 | 4 | 41.176 | 1.260 |
| Panama | 9 | 77.276 | 0.648 | 3 | 80.147 | 0.244 |
| Papua New Guinea | 6 | 45.644 | 1.648 | 4 | 60.000 | 0.741 |
| Paraguay | 6 | 48.634 | 1.510 | 2 | 88.409 | 0.084 |
| Peru | 5 | 79.770 | 0.385 | 3 | 88.839 | 0.130 |
| Philippines | 44 | 29.540 | 13.387 | 6 | 82.919 | 0.358 |
| Poland | 4 | 97.628 | 0.033 | 3 | 90.696 | 0.108 |
| Portugal | 2 | 98.995 | 0.007 | 2 | 92.254 | 0.055 |
| Puerto Rico | 4 | 51.326 | 0.964 | 3 | 64.829 | 0.472 |
| Qatar | 2 | 59.677 | 0.322 | 2 | 95.009 | 0.035 |
| Reunion | 7 | 61.386 | 1.120 | 2 | 88.235 | 0.085 |
| Romania | 14 | 90.679 | 0.279 | 3 | 86.841 | 0.156 |
| Russia | 36 | 86.592 | 0.617 | 5 | 72.356 | 0.560 |

| | | | | | | |
|---|---|---|---|---|---|---|
| Rwanda | 2 | 93.591 | 0.045 | 4 | 64.987 | 0.625 |
| St. Kitts and Nevis | 1 | 100.000 | 0.000 | 3 | 38.462 | 0.966 |
| St. Lucia | 2 | 79.310 | 0.154 | 2 | 79.054 | 0.156 |
| St. Vincent and the Grenadines | 2 | 99.107 | 0.006 | 4 | 41.964 | 1.236 |
| Samoa | 3 | 52.071 | 0.693 | 5 | 26.036 | 2.288 |
| San Marino | 1 | 100.000 | 0.000 | 2 | 88.462 | 0.083 |
| Sao Tome and Principe | 3 | 86.131 | 0.165 | 2 | 89.781 | 0.073 |
| Saudi Arabia | 2 | 95.018 | 0.035 | 3 | 95.440 | 0.051 |
| Senegal | 10 | 45.795 | 2.484 | 3 | 92.021 | 0.092 |
| Seychelles | 6 | 40.113 | 1.924 | 2 | 88.462 | 0.083 |
| Sierra Leone | 13 | 45.764 | 3.019 | 3 | 60.000 | 0.552 |
| Singapore | 5 | 56.262 | 1.022 | 7 | 53.866 | 1.454 |
| Slovakia | 9 | 85.696 | 0.369 | 4 | 60.370 | 0.732 |
| Slovenia | 4 | 87.877 | 0.183 | 2 | 82.653 | 0.128 |
| Solomon Islands | 5 | 84.010 | 0.294 | 4 | 41.849 | 1.239 |
| Somalia | 2 | 98.253 | 0.012 | 2 | 99.853 | 0.001 |
| South Africa | 13 | 22.408 | 6.317 | 30 | 29.709 | 9.921 |
| Spain | 5 | 74.415 | 0.509 | 3 | 66.734 | 0.441 |
| Sri Lanka | 8 | 60.398 | 1.278 | 5 | 69.320 | 0.638 |
| Sudan, The | 11 | 49.371 | 2.367 | 4 | 72.998 | 0.454 |
| Suriname | 3 | 40.476 | 0.923 | 5 | 27.358 | 2.219 |
| Swaziland | 3 | 90.291 | 0.113 | 2 | 66.990 | 0.257 |
| Sweden | 13 | 89.541 | 0.308 | 2 | 86.456 | 0.098 |
| Switzerland | 5 | 63.624 | 0.796 | 3 | 46.067 | 0.809 |
| Syria | 3 | 90.007 | 0.116 | 5 | 73.968 | 0.520 |
| Taiwan | 13 | 66.713 | 1.349 | 13 | 47.734 | 2.821 |
| Tajikistan | 4 | 62.149 | 0.690 | 4 | 80.000 | 0.320 |
| Tanzania | 20 | 47.063 | 3.883 | 3 | 34.997 | 1.042 |
| Thailand | 10 | 52.566 | 1.981 | 4 | 94.802 | 0.075 |
| Togo | 35 | 19.802 | 16.311 | 5 | 58.774 | 0.942 |
| Tonga | 2 | 98.020 | 0.014 | 3 | 43.564 | 0.859 |
| Trinidad and Tobago | 4 | 93.495 | 0.094 | 6 | 29.389 | 2.544 |
| Tunisia | 6 | 69.881 | 0.715 | 2 | 99.458 | 0.004 |
| Turkey | 4 | 87.579 | 0.188 | 2 | 99.764 | 0.002 |
| Turkmenistan | 10 | 70.357 | 0.979 | 2 | 93.166 | 0.049 |
| Tuvalu | 2 | 92.632 | 0.052 | 2 | 85.437 | 0.106 |
| Uganda | 30 | 24.056 | 12.237 | 5 | 38.835 | 1.676 |
| Ukraine | 8 | 64.647 | 1.086 | 8 | 30.733 | 3.222 |
| United Arab Emirates | 2 | 58.140 | 0.337 | 3 | 80.156 | 0.244 |
| United Kingdom | 4 | 97.284 | 0.038 | 10 | 43.483 | 2.674 |
| United States | 50 | 86.176 | 0.717 | 15 | 50.503 | 2.821 |
| Uruguay | 2 | 95.611 | 0.031 | 2 | 78.616 | 0.160 |
| Uzbekistan | 13 | 71.284 | 1.089 | 3 | 87.997 | 0.141 |
| Vanuatu | 4 | 56.604 | 0.825 | 4 | 35.795 | 1.435 |

| | | | | | | |
|---|---|---|---|---|---|---|
| Venezuela | 5 | 96.882 | 0.051 | 3 | 87.445 | 0.148 |
| Vietnam | 23 | 86.811 | 0.512 | 5 | 66.667 | 0.710 |
| Virgin Islands (U.S.) | 4 | 80.612 | 0.308 | 3 | 44.330 | 0.843 |
| West Bank | 2 | 92.179 | 0.056 | 3 | 82.123 | 0.217 |
| Western Sahara | 1 | 100.000 | 0.000 | 1 | 100.000 | 0.000 |
| Yemen | 2 | 98.182 | 0.013 | 2 | 99.879 | 0.001 |
| Yugoslavia | 9 | 75.259 | 0.722 | 4 | 62.559 | 0.680 |
| Zambia | 31 | 20.218 | 14.482 | 4 | 33.262 | 1.522 |
| Zimbabwe | 6 | 49.282 | 1.481 | 5 | 40.543 | 1.604 |

Notes: NUM=number of linguistic (religious) groups; POP=ratio of population of the largest linguistic (religious) groups.

*Source*: calculation by the author based on Equation 5.1 and *Britannica Book for the Year 1996*.

# REFERENCES

Abramovitz, M. (1986): 'Catching up, Forging Ahead, and Falling Behind', *Journal of Economic History*, vol. 56 (June), 23-34.

Abu-Taleb, F.M. (1994): 'Environmental Management in Jordan: Problems and Recommendations', *Environmental Conservation*, vol. 21, 35-40.

ACCU (2005): 'Literacy Facts and Figures in the Asia-Pacific', Asia/Pacific Cultural Center for UNESCO (ACCU), Tokyo [online; cited June 2005]. Available from URL: http://www.accu.or.jp/litdbase/stats/

Acemoglu, D., and S. Johnson (2005), 'Unbundling Institutions', *Journal of Political Economy*, vol. 113(5), 949-95.

Adelman, I., and C.T. Morris (1967): *Society, Politics, and Economic Development*, Baltimore: Johns Hopkins University Press.

Ager, D. (2001): *Motivation in Language Planning and Language Policy*, Clevedon: Multilingual Matters Ltd.

Aghion, P., E. Caroli, and C. Garcia-Penalosa (1999): 'Inequality and Economic Growth: The Perspective of the New Growth Theories', *Journal of Economic Literature*, 37(4), 1615-60.

Ahluwalia, M.S. (1976): 'Inequality, Poverty and Development', *Journal of Development Economics*, vol. 3(December), 1803-15.

Ahmed, S. and V. Sahni (1998): *Freezing the Fighting: Military Disengagement on the Siachen Glacier*. Cooperative Monitoring Center, Sandia National Laboratories, Oak Ridge, TN, USA.

Alesina, A. and D. Rodrik. (1994): 'Distribution Politics and Economic Growth', *The Quarterly Journal of Economics*, vol. 109, 465-490.

Alesina, A. and E. Spolaore (1997): 'On the Number and Size of Nations', *The Quarterly Journal of Economics*, vol. 112 (Nov.), 1027-56.

Alesina, A. and E.A. Ferrara (2005): 'Ethnic Diversity and Economic Performance', *Journal of Economic Literature*, vol. 43(3), 762-800.

Alesina, A. and R. Perotti (1996): 'Income Distribution, Political Instability and Investment', *European Economic Review*, vol. 81, 1170-89.

Alesina, A., A. Devleeschauwer, R. Wacziarg and W. Easterly (2002): 'Fractionalization', unpublished draft, Stanford University, Stanford, CA.

Alesina, A., A. Devleeschauwer, W. Easterly, S. Kurlat and R. Wacziarg (2003): 'Fractionalization', *Journal of Economic Growth*, vol. 8(2), 155-94.

Alhajji, A.F. (2000): 'Disciplined Output Pays Off. World Oil', August, available at www.findarticles.com/p/articles/mi_m3159/is_8_221/ai_65378738.

*American Heritage Dictionary of the English Language*, 2000, 4th edn, updated in 2003, New York: Houghton Mifflin Company.

Anand, S., and S.M. Kanbur (1993a): 'The Kuznets Process and the Inequality: Development Relationship', *Journal of Development Economics*, vol. 40, 25-52.

Anand, S., and S.M. Kanbur (1993b): 'Inequality and Development: A Critique', *Journal of Development Economics*, vol. 41, 19-43.

Anunobi, F.O. (1994): *International Dimensions of African Political Economy: Trends, Challenges, and Realities*, Washington, DC: University Press of America.

Aono, T. (1979): *New Geography* (B) (in Japanese), Tokyo: Nigong Shiyoten.

Ash, R. (1997): *The Top 10 of Everything*, New York: DK Publishing.

Bacon, E. (1946): 'A Preliminary Attempt to Determine the Culture Areas of Asia', *Southwestern Journal of Anthropology*, vol. 2, 117-32.

Bagby, P. (1958): *Culture and History: Prolegomena to the Comparative Study of Civilizations*, London: Longmans, Green.

Bailey, S.D. (1980): 'Nonmilitary Areas in UN Practice', *American Journal of International Law*, vol. 74, No. 3(July), 499–524.

Baldwin, R.E. (1971): 'Determinants of the Commodity Structure of US Trade', *American Economic Review*, vol. 61 (Mar.), 126-46.

Banks, A.S. (1979): 'Cross-National Time-Series Data Archive', Center for Social Analysis, State University of New York at Binghamton, September.

Banks, A.S., and R.B. Textor (1963): *A Cross-Polity Survey*, Cambridge, MA: The MIT Press.

Barrett, D.B. (1982): *World Christian Encyclopedia: A Comparative Study of Churches and Religions in the Modern World 1900-2000*, Oxford: Oxford University Press.

Barrett, D.B., G.T. Kurian, and T.M. Johnson (2001): *World Christian Encyclopedia*, 2nd edn, Oxford, Oxford University Press.

Barro, R.J. (1991): 'Economic Growth in a Cross Section of Nations', *The Quarterly Journal of Economics*, vol. 106(May), 407-43.

Barro, R.J. (2000): 'Inequality and Growth in a Panel of Countries', *Journal of Economic Growth*, vol. 5, 5-32.

Barro, R.J. and R.M. McCleary (2003): 'Religion and Economic Growth across Countries', *American Sociopolitical Review*, vol. 68(5), 760-81.

Barro, R.J., and X. Sala-i-Martin (1995): *Economic Growth*, New York: McGraw-Hill.

Barudel, F. (1994): *History of Civilizations*, New York: Allen Lane-Penguin Press.

Bates, R.H., A. Greif, M. Levi, J.-L. Rosenthal, and B.R. Weingast (1998): *Analytic Narratives*, Princeton, N.J.: Princeton University Press.

Bateson, G. (1936) (1958): *Naven: A Survey of the Problems Suggested by a Composite Picture of the Culture of New Guinea Tribe Drawn From Three Points of View*, 2nd edn, Stanford: Stanford University Press.

Behari, B. (1992): *Mismanagement of Indian Economy*, New Delhi: South Asia Books.

Belkindas, M., M. Dinc, and O. Ivanova (1999): 'Statistical Systems Need Overhaul in Transition Economies', *Transition*, vol. 10(4), 22-4.

Benabou, R. (1996): 'Inequality and Growth', *NBER Macroeconomics Annual*, 11-73.

Bernhardt, R. (1990, ed.): *Encyclopedia of Public International Law*, vol. 12, Amsterdam: North Holland

Bhagwati, J.H. (1969, ed.): *International Trade: Selected Readings*, Baltimore: Penguin.

Bhagwati, J.N. (1981, ed.): *International Trade: Selected Readings*, Cambridge, MA: The MIT Press.

Bikker, J. (1987): 'An International Trade Flow Model with Substitution: An Extension of the Gravity Model', *Kyklos*, vol. 40, 315-37.

Billikopf, G.E. (2005): 'Conflict Management Skills', University of California, Berkeley, CA. Available at: www.cnr.berkeley.edu/ucce50/ag-labor/7labor/13.pdf.

Blanchard, O. (1997): *Macroeconomics*, Beijing: Tsinghua University Press and Prentice-Hall International, Inc.

Bluedorn, J.C. (2001): 'Can Democracy Help? Growth and Ethnic Divisions', *Economic Letters*, vol. 70, 121-6.

Bodley, J.H. (1994): 'Cultural Anthropology: Tribes, States, and the Global System', available at: www.wsu.edu:8001/vcwsu/commons/topics/culture/culture-definitions/bodley-text.html.

Boisso, D., and M. Ferrantino (1997): 'Economic Distance, Cultural Distance and Openness in International Trade: Empirical Puzzles', *Journal of Economic Integration*, vol. 12, 456-84.

Bollen, Kenneth, A. and Robert Jackman (1985): 'Economic and Noneconomic Determinants of Political Democracy in the 1960s', in Braungart (ed.), pp. 123-43.

Bond, M.H., K. Leung, and K.C. Wan (1982): 'How Does Cultural Collectivism Operate?' *Journal of Cross-Cultural Psychology*, vol. 13, 186-200.

Bowen, H.P., E.E. Leamer, and L. Sveikauskas (1987): 'Multicountry, Multifactor Tests of the Factor Abundance Theory', *American Economic Review*, vol. 77 (Dec.), 791-809.

Brada, J., and J. Mendez (1983): 'Regional Economic Integration and the Volume of Intra-Regional Trade: A Comparison of Developed and Developing Country Experience', *Kyklos*, vol. 36, 589-603.

Branson, W.H., and N. Monoyios (1977): 'Factor Inputs in US Trade', *Journal of International Economics*, vol. 20, 111-31.

Braudel, F. (1994): *History of Civilizations*, New York: Allen Lane-Penguin Press.

Braungart, R.G. (1985, ed.): *Research in Political Sociology*, Greenwich, Conn.: Jai.

Bräutigam, D. (1998): *Chinese Aid and African Development: Exporting Green Revolution*, London: Macmillan Press.

Britannica Book of the Year (various issues), Chicago: Encyclopedia Britannica, Inc.

Brown, N. (2005): 'Friedrich Ratzel, Clark Wissler, and Carl Sauer: Culture Area Research and Mapping', available at www.csiss.org/classics/content/15.

Buzan, B. (1991): 'New Patterns of Global Security in the Twenty-first Century', *International Affairs*, vol. 67, 441-9.

Byres, T.J. (1998, ed.): *The Indian Economy: Major Debates Since Independence*, Oxford: Oxford University Press.

Caponera, D. (1995): 'Shared Waters and International Law', In: G. Balk, W. Hildesley and M. Pratt (Eds.): *The Peaceful Management of Transboundary Resources* (pp. 121–6). Londond/Dordrecht: Graham and Trotman.

Carson, R.L. (1996): *Comparative Economic Systems: Market and State in Economic Systems*, 2nd Edn, New York: M.E. Sharpe.

Caselli, F. and W.J. Coleman II (2002): 'On the Theory of Ethnic Conflict', unpublished draft, Harvard University, MA.

Cass, D. (1965): 'Optimum Growth in a Aggregative Model of Capital Accumulation', *Review of Economics and Statistics*, vol. 32, 233-40.

Castle, F. and C.G. Carrasco (2007): 'Doing Business in Central and South Latin America', available at http://intercultural-training.blogspot.com, Wednesday, 3 October.

Cateora, P.R., and J.L. Graham (1998): *International Marketing*, 7th edn, Burr Ridge, IL: Richard d'Irwin.

Cecchini, P. (1988): *The European Challenge: 1992*, Aldershot, England: Wildwood House, 1988.

Chaves, M. and D.E. Cann (1992): 'Regulation, Pluralism, and Religious Market Structure', *Rationality and Society*, July, 272-90.

Chenery, H.B. and M. Syrquin (1975): *Pattern of Development, 1950-70*, New York: Oxford University Press.

Chesler, M. (2000): 'Conflict Resolution and the Polish Round Table: Negotiating Systemic Change?' In Negotiating Radical Change: Understanding and Extending the Lessons of the Polish Round Table Talks, A Project funded by The United States Institute for Peace (pp. 151–76). Ann Arbor, MI: University of Michigan. Available at: www.umich.edu/~iinet/PolishRoundTable/frame.html.

China Ethnic Statistical Yearbook, 1997, edited by the Minstry of Civil Affairs, Beijing: China Statitics Press.

Choucri, N. and R. C. North (1989): 'Lateral Pressure in International Relations: Concept and Theory', in M. I. Midlarsky (ed., 1989): *Handbook of War Studies*, Ann Arbor, MI: University of Michigan Press.

Choucri, N. and R.C. North (1975): *Nations in Conflict*, San Francisco, CA: W.H. Freeman and Company.

Chua, E.G. and W.B. Gudykunst (1987): 'Conflict Resolution Styles in Low- and High-Context Cultures', *Communication Research Reports*, vol. 4, 32-7.

CIA (2007): *World Factbook*, Washington DC: Central Intelligence Agency (CIA).

Cline, W. (1975): 'Distribution and Development: A Survey of the Literature', *Journal of Development Economics*, vol. 2, 31-56.

CMCC (2006): 'Masters of the Plains: Ancient Nomads of Russia and Canada' (Prairie vs. Steppe Nomads: Similar, or different?), Canadian Museum of Civilization Cooperation, available at www.civilization.ca/cmc/maitres/masters04e.html.

Combes, Pierre-Philippe, Miren Lafourcade, Thierry Mayer (2005): 'The Trade-Creating Effects of Business and Social Networks: Evidence from France', *Journal of International Economics*, vol. 66, no. 1, 1-29.

Condon, J.C. (1985): *Good Neighbors: Communicating with the Mexicans*, Yarmouth, ME: Intercultural Press.

Cooley, J.K. (1984): 'The War over Water', *Foreign Policy*, vol. 54, 3-26.

Copaken, S.N. (1996): 'The Perception of Water as Part of Territory in Israeli and Arab Ideologies between 1964 and 1993: Toward a Further Understanding of the Arab-Jewish Conflict', Working paper No.8, University of Haifa, Haifa, Israel, May.

Critchley, W.H. and T. Terriff (1993): 'Environment and Security', in Shultz et al. (eds), pp. 312-48.

Cullen, R. (1993): 'Human Rights Quandary', *Foreign Affairs*, vol. 71 (Winter), 79-88.

Dacin, M.T., Goldstein, J., and Scott, W. R. (2002): 'Institutional Theory and Institutional Change: Introduction to the Special Research Forum', *Academy of Management Journal*, vol. 45(1), 45-57.

Dahl, R., and E. Tufle (1973): *Size and Democracy*, Stanford, CA: Stanford University Press.

Dasgupta, P. (1996): 'The Economics of Environment', *Environment and Development Economics*, vol. 1(4), 387–428.

Deardorff, A. (1998): 'Determinants of Bilateral Trade: Does Gravity Work in a Classical World?' in Frankel (ed.), pp. 213-43.

Deininger, K. and L. Squire (1998): 'New Ways of Looking at Old Issues: Inequality and Growth', *Journal of Development Economics*, vol. 57, 259–87

Dellapenna, J.W. (1999): 'Adapting the Law of Water Management to Global Climate Change and Other Hydropolitical Stress', Journal of the American Water Resources Association, vol. 35, 1301–26.

Desai, P. (1997, ed.): *Going Global: Transition from Plan to Market in the World Economy*, Cambridge, MA: The MIT Press.

Domínguez, J.I., D. Mares, M. Orozco, D.S. Palmer, F.R. Aravena, and A. Serbin (2003): 'Boundary Disputes in Latin America', Peaceworks No. 50 (September), United States Institute of Peace, Washington, DC.

Diehl, P.F. and N.P. Gleditsch (2001, eds): *Environmental Conflict*, Boulder, CO: Westview.

Djankov, S, O. Hart, C. McLiesh, and A. Shleifer (2006), 'Debt Enforcement around the World', *NBER Working Paper* 12807, Cambridge, MA: National Bureau of Economic Research.

Dodsworth, J., and D. Mihaljek (1997): 'Hong Kong, China: Growth, Structural Change, and Economic Stability During the Transition', *International Monetary Fund Occasional Paper* No. 152, Washington, DC: IMF.

DOS (1995): 'Summary of the Dayton Peace Agreement on Bosnia-Herzegovina', Washington, DC: U.S. Department of State, 30 November.

Driver, H. (1962): *The Contribution of A. L. Kroeber to Culture Area Theory and Practice, Indians University Publications in Anthropology and Linguistics*, No. 18, Baltimore, MD: Waverly Press.

Duetsch, K.W. (1953): *Nationalism and Social Communication: An Inquiry into the Foundations of Nationality*, New York: Technology Press of the MIT.

Dunning, J.H. (1998): 'Location and the Multinational Enterprise: A neglected factor?' *Journal of International Business Studies*, vol. 19(1), 45-66.

Easterly, W. and R. Levine (1997): 'Africa's Growth Tragedy: Policies and Ethnic Division', *Quarterly Journal of Economics*, vol. 112, 1203-50.

Eckstein, H. (1966): *Division and Cohesion in Democracy: A Study of Norway*, Princeton, NJ: Princeton University Press.

*Economist, The* (1994): 'The New World Order: Back to the Future', January, pp. 21-3.

*Economist, The* (2001): 'The Origins of Racism—Them,' 1 December, p. 61.

*Economist, The*, June 15, 2002; 27 November 1993, p. 33; 17 July 1993, p. 61.

Eichengreen, B., and D. Irwin (1995): 'Trade Blocs, Currency Blocs and the Reorientation of Trade in the 1930s', *Journal of International Economics*, vol. 38(2), 89-106.

Eichengreen, B., F. Frieden, and J. von Hagen (1995, eds): *Monetary and Fiscal Policy in an Integrated Europe*, New York: Springer-Verlag.

Eichera, T.S., C. Garcia-Penalosab (2001): 'Inequality and Growth: the Dual Role of Human Capital in Development', *Journal of Development Economics*, vol. 66, 173–97

Elashmawi, F. (2001): *Competing Globally – Mastering Multicultural Management and Negotiations*, Burlington, MA: Butterworth-Heinemann/Elsevier.

Ellis, H.S., and L.M. Metzler (1950, eds): *Readings in the Theory of International Trade*, Homewood, Ill.: Irwin.

Elmandjra, M. (1994): 'Cultural Diversity: Key to Survival in the Future', paper presented to the First Mexican Congress on Future Studies, Mexico City, September.

Esman, M.J. (1990): 'Economic Performance and Ethnic Conflict', in Montville and Binnendijk (eds), pp. 41-76.

Esteban, J.-M. and D. Ray (1994): 'On the Measurement of Polarization', *Econometrica*, vol. 62(4), 819-51.

Fanelli, J.M. and G. McMahon (2006): 'Introduction to the Regional Syntheses and Country Case Studies', in J.M. Fanelli and G. McMahon (eds., 2006): *Understanding Market Reforms, Volume 2 (Motivation, Implementation and Sustainability)*, London and New York: Palgrave Macmillan, pp. 1-67.

Farrand, L. (1904): *Basis of American History, 1500-1900*, New York: Ungar.

Fearon, J.D. (2003): 'Ethnic and Cultural Diversity by Country', *Journal of Economic Growth*, vol. 8(2), 195-222.

Fearon, J.D. and D.D. Laitin (2003): 'Ethnicity Insurgency and Civil War', *American Political Science Review*, vol. 97(1), 75-90.

Fields, G.S. (1991): 'Growth and Income Distribution', in Psachropoulos (ed.), pp. 41-5.

Fisher, G. (1980): *International Negotiation: A Cross-Cultural Perspective*, Chicago: Intercultural Press.

Forbes, K. (1997): 'A Reassessment of the Relationship Between Inequality and Growth', Unpublished paper, MIT.

Forester, J. and D. Stitzel (1989): 'Beyond Neutrality: The Possibilities of Activist Mediation in Public Sector Conflicts', *Negotiation Journal*, vol. 5(3), 251–263.

Foroutan, F., and L. Pritchett (1993): 'Intra-Sub-Saharan African Trade: Is It Too Little?' *Journal of African Economics*, vol. 2 (May), 74-105.

Fox, J. (1997): 'The Salience of Religious Issues in Ethnic Conflicts: A Large-N Study', *Nationalism and Ethnic Politics*, vol. 3(3), 807-21.

Frankel, J.A. (1998, ed.): *The Regionalization of the World Economy*, Chicago: University of Chicago Press.

Frankel, J.A., and D. Romer (1996): 'Trade and Growth', *NBER Working Paper* No. 5476, Cambridge, MA: National Bureau of Economic Research.

Frankel, J.A., and S.-J. Wei (1995): 'European Integration and the Regionalization of World Trade and Currencies: The Economics and the Politics', in Eichengreen, Frieden, and von Hagen (eds), pp. 89-123.

Frankel, J.A., D. Romer, and T. Cyrus (1995): 'Trade and Growth in East Asian Countries: Cause and Effect?' *Pacific Basin Working Paper Series* No. 95-03, San Francisco: Federal Reserve Bank of San Francisco.

Frankel, J.A., E. Stein, and S.-J. Wei (1997a): *Regional Trading Blocs in the World Economic System*, Washington, DC: Institute for International Economics.

Frankel, J.A., E. Stein, and S.-J. Wei (1997b): 'Trading Blocs and the Americas: The Natural, the Unnatural, and the Super-natural', *Journal of Development Economics*, vol. 47(1), 61-95.

Frey, F. (1993): 'The Political Context of Conflicts and Cooperation over International River Basins', *Water International*, vol. 18, 544-68.

Friedman, D. (1977): 'A Theory of the Size and Shape of Nations', *Journal of Political Economy*, vol. 85(1): 59-77.

Gabrielides, C., W.G. Stephan, O. Ybarra, V.M.S. Pearson, and L. Villareal (1997): 'Cultural Variables and Preferred Styles of Conflict Resolution: Mexico and the United States', *Journal of Cross-Cultural Psychology*, vol. 28, 661-7.

Galtung, J. (1992): 'The Emerging Conflict Formations', in Tehranian and Tehranian (eds), pp. 20-39

Gastil, R.D. (1987): *Freedom in the World*, Westport, CT: Greenwood Press.

Gilpin, R. (1993): *The Cycle of Great Powers: Has It Finally Been Broken?* Princeton, NJ: Princeton University, May.

Gleditsch, N.P. (2001): 'Armed Conflict and The Environment', in Diehl and Gleditsch (eds), pp. 240-69.

Gomes-Casseres, B. (1991): 'Firm Ownership Preferences and Host Government Restrictions. An Integral Approach', *Journal of International Business Studies*, vol. 21(1), 22.

Gottmann, J. (1973): *The Significance of Territory*, Charlottesville: University of Virginia Press.

Gould, D.M., and B.J. Ruffin (1993): 'What Determines Economic Growth?' *Economic Review*, 2nd Quarter, 25-40.

Goulet, D. (1980; 1995): *Development Ethics: A Guide to Theory and Practice*, New York: Apex Press.

Graham, J.L. (1983): 'Brazilian, Japanese, and American Business Negotiations', *Journal of International Business Studies*, vol. 14, 47-61.

Graham, J.L. (1985): 'The Influence of Culture on Business Negotiations', *Journal of International Business Studies*, vol. 16, 81-96.

Graham, J.L., and J.D. Andrews (1987): 'A Holistic Analyses of Japanese and American Business Negotiations', *Journal of Business Communications*, vol. 24, 63-77.

Green Cross (2000): *National Sovereignty and International Water Courses*, Hague: Green Cross International.

Greenaway, D., and C.R. Milner (1986): *The Economics of Intra-Industry Trade*, Oxford: Basil Blackwell.

Greenstein, M., and T.M. Feinman (2000): *Electronic Commerce: Security, Risk Management*, Beijing: McGraw-Hill and China Machine Press.

Greertz, C. (1963): 'The Integrative Revolution: Primordial Sentiments and Civil Politics in the New States', in Greertz (ed.), pp. 21-56.

Greertz, C. (1963, ed.): *Old Societies and New States*, Chicago: Free Press of Glencoe

Gregory, P.R., and R.C. Stuart (1998): *Comparative Economic Systems*, 6th edn, New York: Houghton Mifflin College.

Griliches, Z. (1979): 'Issues in Assessing the Contributions of Research and Development to Productivity Growth', *Bell Journal of Economics*, vol. 10 (Spring), 92-116

Grossman, G., and E. Helpman (1989): 'Product Development and International Trade', *Journal of Political Economy*, vol. 97 (Dec.), 1261-83.

Grossman, G., and E. Helpman (1991): *Innovation and Growth in the World Economy*, Cambridge, MA: The MIT Press.

Grossman, G.M. and E. Helpman (1994): 'Endogenous Innovation in the Theory of Growth', *Journal of Economic Perspectives*, vol. 8, 23-44.

Grubel, H.G., and P.J. Lloyd (1975): *Intra-Industry Trade: The Theory and Measurement of International Trade in Differentiated Products*, London: Macmillan Press.

Grunfeld, L. (1997): 'Jordan River Dispute', ICE Case Studies, No. 6, available at www.american.edu/projects/mandala/TED/ice/JORDAN.HTM.

*Guangxu Da Qing Huidian Shili*, vols. 775 and 776, Beijing: National Library of China.

Gudykunst, W.B. (1994): *Bridging Differences: Effective Intergroup Communications*, Thousand Oaks, CA: Sage Publications.

Guiso, L., P. Sapienza, and L. Zingales (2004): 'Cultural Biases in Economic Exchange', *NBER Working Paper Series* 11005. Cambridge: National Bureau of Economic Research. December.

Guo, R. (1993): *Economic Analysis of Border-Regions: Theory and Practice of China*, (in Chinese), Beijing: China Ocean Press.

Guo, R. (1996): *Border-Regional Economics*, Berlin: Springer.

Guo, R. (2003): 'Review of Culture and Economy', *Journal of Evolutionary Economics* (Springer), vol. 13(3), 155-7.

Guo, R. (2004): 'How Culture Influences Foreign Trade—Evidence from the US and China', *The Journal of Socio-Economics*, vol. 33(6), 785-812.

Guo, R. (2006): *Cultural Influences on Economic Analysis—Theory and Empirical Evidence*, New York: Palgrave-Macmillan.

Guo, R. (2007a): 'Linguistic and Religious Influences on Foreign Trade: Evidence from East Asia', *Asian Economic Journal*, vol. 21(1), 101-21.

Guo, R. (2007b): *Territorial Disputes and Resource Management – A Global Handbook*, New York: Nova Science.

Guo, R. (2009a): *Intercultural Economic Analysis – Theory and Method*, New York: Springer.

Guo, R. (2009b): *The Land and Maritime Boundary Disputes of Asia*, New York: Nova Science.

Gupta, A. and J. Ferguson (1997): *Culture, Power, Place: Explorations in Critical Anthropology*, Durham, NC: Duke University Press.

Gupta, D. (1990): *The Economics of Political Violence*, New York: Praeger.

Haberler, G. (1964): 'Comparative Advantage, Agricultural Production and International Trade', *The International Journal of Agrarian Affairs*, May, 130-49.

Hagen, E.E. (1986): *The Economics of Development*, Homewood, Ill.: Irwin.

Hannan, M.T. and G.R. Carroll (1981): 'Dynamics of Formal Political Structure: An Event-History Analysis', *American Sociological Review*, vol. 46 (February), 567-98.

Hardt, J.P., and R.F. Kaufman (1995, eds): *East-Central European Economies in Transition*, New York: M.E. Sharpe.

Harris, P.R., R.T. Moran, and S. Moran (2004): *Managing Cultural Differences: Global Leadership Strategies for the 21st Century*, Amsterdam: Butterworth-Heinemann.

Harrison, L.E. (1993): *Who Prospers? How Cultural Values Shape Economic and Political Success*, New York: Basic Books.

Harrison, L.E. (2000): *Underdevelopment Is a State of Mind*, 2nd edition, New York: Madison Books.

Harrison, L.E. (2006): *The Central Liberal Truth: How Politics Can Change a Culture and Save It as Itself*, New York: Oxford University Press.

Harrison, L.E., S.P. Huntington (2001; ed.): *Culture Matters: How Values Shape Human Progress*, New York: Basic Books.

Hartz, L. (1964): *The Founding of New Societies: Studies in the History of the United States, Latin America, South Africa, Canada, and Australia*, New York: Harcourt, Brace and World.

Haug, M.R. (1967): 'Social and Cultural Pluralism as a Concept in Social System Analysis', *American Journal of Sociology*, vol. 73 (Nov.), 294-304.

Havrylyshyn, O., and L. Pritchett (1991): 'European Trade Patterns after the Transition', *Policy, Research and External Affairs Working Paper Series* No. 74, Washington, DC: World Bank.

Heckscher, E.F. (1919): 'The Effect of Foreign Trade on the Distribution of Income', Ekonomisk Tidskirift, 497-512. Reprinted in Ellis and Metzler (eds), pp. 272-300.

Helpman, E. (1987): 'Imperfect Competition and International Trade: Evidence from Fourteen Industrial Countries', *Journal of the Japanese and International Economies*, vol. 1 (Mar.), 62-81.

Henisz, W.J. (2000): 'The Institutional Environment for Multinational Investment', *Journal of Law, Economics and Organization*, vol. 16(2), 334– 364.

Hensel, P.R. (2001): 'Contentious Issues and World Politics: The Management of Territorial Claims in the Americas, 1816–1992', *International Studies Quarterly* vol. 45, no. 1 (March), 81-109.

Hensel, P.R., S.M. Mitchell, T.E. Sowers II (2004): 'Conflict Management of Riparian Disputes: A Regional Comparison of Dispute Resolution', paper presented at the 2004 International Studies Association Meeting, Montreal, Quebec.

Hibbs, D. (1973): *Mass Political Violence: A Cross-Sectional Analysis*, New York: Wiley.

Hill, H. (1989, ed.): *Unity and Diversity: Regional Economic Development in Indonesia Since 1970*, Singapore: Oxford University Press.

Hill, H. and A. Weidemann (1989): 'Regional Development in Indonesia: Patterns and Issues', in Hill (ed.), pp. 1-7.

Hoebel, A. (1960): *Man, Culture and Society*, New York: Oxford University Press.

Hofstede, G. (1980; 2003): *Culture's Consequences: Comparing Values, Behaviors, Institutions, and Organizations Across Nations*, Newbury Park, CA: Sage Publications.

Holesovsky, V. (1977): *Economic Systems: Analysis and Comparison*, New York: McGraw-Hill.

Holms, W. (1903): 'Classification and Arrangement of the Exhibits of an Anthropological Museum', Washington DC: Government Printing Office.

Homer-Dixon, T.F. (1999): *Environment, Scarcity, and Violence*. Princeton, N.J.: Princeton University Press.

Hong, L. and S.E. Page (1998): 'Diversity and Optimality', Santa Fe Institute, Working Paper 98-08-077.

Horowitz, D.L. (1971): 'Three Dimensions of Ethnic Politics', *World Politics*, vol. 23 (January), 232-44.

Horowitz, D.L. (1985): *Ethnic Groups in Conflict*, Berkeley, CA: University of California Press.

Hoskisson, R.E., Eden, L., Lau, C.M., and Wright, M. (2000): 'Strategy in Emerging Markets', *Academy of Management Journal*, vol. 43(3), 249– 268.

Hu, H., and S. Zhang (1982): *World Population Geography*, Shanghai: East China Normal University Press.

Huntington, S.P. (1993): 'The Clash of Civilizations?' *Foreign Affairs*, vol. 71 (Summer), 2-32.

Huntington, S.P. (1996): *The Clash of Civilization and the Remaking of World Order*, New York: Simon & Schuster.

Hwang, E.-G. (1993): *The Korean Economies: A Comparison of North and South*, Oxford: Clarendon Press.

Inglehart, R. and W.E. Baker (2000): 'Modernization, Cultural Change, and the Persistence of Traditional Values', *American Sociological Review*, vol. 65(February), 19-51.

International Encyclopedia of the Social Sciences, 1972, vol. 3, ed. by David L. Sills, New York: The Macmillan Company and The Free Press; and London: Collier-Macmillan Publishers.

International Monetary Fund (1997a): *World Economic Outlook*, May, Washington DC: the IMF.

International Monetary Fund (1997b): *International Financial Statistics Yearbook*, Washington DC: the IMF.

International Monetary Fund (various issues): *Direction of Trade Statistics*, Washington DC: the IMF.

Isard, W. (1949): 'Gravity, Potential, and Spatial Interaction Models', reprinted in Smith (ed., 1990), pp. 1-23.

Israel-PLO (1995): 'Agreement on Establishing the Palestinian Self-Rule in Most of the West Bank', signed by the Government of Israel and the Palestinian Liberation Organization (PLO), Washington DC, 28 September.

Jenkins, S. (1995): 'Accounting for Inequality Trends: Decomposition Analysis for the UK, 1971-86', *Economica*, vol. 62, 29-63.

Jha, S. (1996): 'The Kuznets Curve: A Reassessment', *World Development*, vol. 24, 773-80.

Jin, H., Y. Qian and B. Weiingast (2001): 'Regional Decentralization and Fiscal Incentives: Federalism, Chinese Style', mimeo, Stanford University, Stanford, CA.

Johnson, H.G. (1968, eds): *Readings in International Economics*, Homewood, Ill.: Irwin.

Jurajda, S. and D. Munich (2006): 'Selective Schools Select Alphabetically', *Beyond Transition*, vol. 17(3), p. 22.

Kalpers, J. (2001): 'Volcanoes under Siege: Impact of a Decade of Armed Conflict in the Virungas', Washington DC: Biodiversity Support Program, World Wildlife Fund (WWF).

Kaminski, B. (1996, ed.): *Economic Transition in Russia and the New States of Eurasia* (The International Politics of Eurasia, vol. 8), New York: M.E. Sharpe.

Kanamori, T. and K. Motohashi (2007): 'Information Technology and Economic Growth: Comparison between Japan and Korea', RIETI Discussion Paper Series 07-E-009, Tokyo: Research Institute of Economy, Trade and Industry (RIETI).

Kapila, U. (1999): *Indian Economy Since Independence*, New Delhi: South Asia Books.

Kassiola, J.J. (1990): *The Death of Industrial Civilization: The Limits to Economic Growth and the Repoliticization of Advanced Industrial Society*, New York: State University of New York Press.

Keesing, D.B. (1966): 'Labor Skills and Comparative Advantage', *American Economic Review*, vol. 56 (May), 249-58.

Kendall, H.M. (1976): *Introduction to Cultural Geography*, London: Arnold.

Kenen, P. (1965): 'Nature, Capital and Trade', *Journal of Political Economy*, vol. 73 (Oct.), 437-60.

Kim, Y. and W. Gudykunst (eds): *Theories in Intercultural Communication*, Newbury Park, CA: Sage.

Kirmani, S. (1990): 'Water, Peace and Conflict Management: The Experience of the Indus and the Mekong River Basins', *Water International*, vol. 15(1), 200-5.

Knight, C., S. Kagan, and S. Martinez-Romero (1982): 'Culture and Development of Conflict Resolution Style', *Journal of Cross-Cultural Psychology*, vol. 13, 43-59.

Kockel, U. (2002, ed.): *Culture and Economy: Contemporary Perspectives*, Aldershot, Hampshire: Ashgate.

Kohler, H. (1996): *Economic Systems and Human Welfare: A Global Survey*, Cincinnati, Ohio: South-Western College Publishing Co.

Koopmans, T.C. (1965): 'On the Concept of Optimal Economic Growth', in *The Econometric Approach to Development Planning*, Amsterdam: North-Holland.

Kravis, I.B. (1956a): 'Wages and Foreign Trade', *Review of Economics and Statistics*, vol. 38(Feb.), 14-30.

Kravis, I.B. (1956b): 'Availability and Other Influences on the Commodity Composition of Trade', *Journal of Political Economy*, vol. 73 (Apr.), 143-55.

Kroeber, A.L. (1939): *Cultural and Natural Areas of Native North America*, Berkeley, CA: University of California Press.

Kroeber, A.L. (1947): 'Culture Groupings in Asia', *Southwestern Journal of Anthropology*, vol. 3, 322-30.

Krugman, P.R. (1980): 'Scale Economies, Product Differentiation, and the Pattern of Trade', *American Economic Review*, vol. 70 (December), 950-9.

Krugman, P.R. (1995): 'Growing World Trade: Causes and Consequences', *Brookings Papers on Economic Activity*, no. 1, 327-62.

Kuznets, S. (1955): 'Economic Growth and Income Inequality', *American Economic Review*, vol. 45 (March), 1-8.

La Porta, R, F. Lopez de Silanes, A. Shleifer, and R.W. Vishni (1999): 'The Quality of Government', *Journal of Law, Economics and Organization*, vol. 15(1), 222-79.

La Porta, R, F. Lopez de Silanes, and A. Shleifer (2008), 'The Economic Consequences of Legal Origins', *Journal of Economic Literature*, vol. 46(2), 285-332.

Lancaster, K. (1980): 'Intra-Industry Trade Under Perfect Monopolistic Competition', *Journal of International Economics*, vol. 23, 151-75.

Landes, D.S. (1999): *The Wealth and Poverty of Nations: Why Some Are so Rich and Some So Poor*, New York: Norton.

Lanjouw, A., A. Kayitare, H. Rainer, E. Rutagarama, M. Sivha, S. Asuma, and J. Kalpers (2001): 'Beyond Boundaries: Transboundary Natural Resource Management for Mountain Gorillas in the Virunga–Bwindi Region', Washington DC: Biodiversity Support Program, World Wildlife Fund (WWF).

Lavigne, M. (1999): *The Economics of Transition: From Socialist Economy to Market Economy*, 2nd edn, London: Macmillan Press.

Leamer, E.E. (1980): 'The Leontef Paradox Reconsidered', *Journal of Political Economy*, vol. 88 (June), 495-503.

Leamer, E.E. (1984): *Sources for International Comparative Advantage*, Cambridge, MA: The MIT Press.

Leamer, E.E. (1993): 'Factor–Supply Differences as a Source of Comparative Advantage', *American Economic Review*, vol. 83 (May), 436-44.

Lee, R., and J. Wills (1997, eds): *Geographies of Economies*, London: Arnold.

Lee, S.-W. (2002): 'Preventive Diplomacy and UN Peacekeeping in Conflict Regions: Lessons from the Rwanda Genocide', *Korea Review of International Studies*, vol. 5(1), 71-91.

Lemco, J. (1991): *Political Stability in Federal Governments*, New York: Praeger.

Leontief, W. (1954): 'Domestic Production and Foreign Trade: The American Capital Position Re-examined', *Economia Internationale*, Feb., 2-32. (Reprinted in Caves and Johnson (eds), pp. 503-27; and in Bhagwati (ed.), pp. 93-139.)

Leontief, W. (1956): 'Factor Proportions and the Structure of American Trade; Further Theoretical and Empirical Analysis', *Review of Economics and Statistics*, vol. 38(Nov.), 386-407.

Leung, K. (1987): 'Some Determinants of Reactions to Procedural Models for Conflict Resolution: A Cross-National Study', *Journal of Personality and Social Psychology*, vol. 53, 898-908.

Levine, D.N. (1972): "Cultural Integration," in Sillis, D.L. (1972, ed.): International Encyclopedia of the Social Sciences, vol. 3, New York: The Macmillan Company & The Free Press, pp. 372-80.

Lewis, P. (1998, ed.): *Africa: Dilemmas of Development*, Boulder, CO: Westview Press.

Lewis, R.D. (2003): *The Cultural Imperative*, Yarmounth, ME: Intercultural Press.

Li, H. and H. Zou (1998): 'Income Inequality Is Not Harmful for Growth: Theory and Evidence', *Review of Development Economics*, vol. 2, 318-34.

Lian, B., and J.R. Oneal (1997): 'Cultural Diversity and Economic Development: A Cross-National Study of 98 Countries, 1960-1985', *Economic Development and Cultural Change*, 46(1), 61-77.

Lijphart, A. (1977): *Democracies in Plural Societies: A Comparative Exploration*, New Haven, Conn.: Yale University Press.

Lijphart, A. (1990): 'The Power-Sharing Approach', in Montville and Binnendijk (ed.), pp. 13-34.

Lin, J.Y. (2001): 'Development Strategy, Viability, and Economic Convergence', The Inaugural D. Gale Johnson Lecture, University of Chicago, 14 May.

Lind, M. (1990): 'American as an Ordinary Country', *American Enterprise*, vol. 1, 19-23.

Lind, W.S. (1992): 'North-South Relation: Returning to a World of Cultures in Conflict', *Current World Leaders*, vol. 35, 1075-80.

Lind, W.S. (1994): 'Defending Western Culture', *Foreign Policy*, vol. 84, 40-50.

Linder, S.B. (1961): *An Essay on Trade and Transformation*, New York: John Wiley and sons.

Linnemann, H. (1966): *An Econometric Study of International Trade Theory*, Amsterdam: North-Holland.

Liu, S., Q. Li, and T. Hsueh (eds.), *Studies on China's Regional Economic Development*, Beijing: China Statistics Publishing House.

Londregan, J.B., and K.T. Poole (1989): 'Coups d'Etat and the Military Business Cycle', working paper No. 36-88-89, Carnegie Mellon University, March.

Lucas, R.E., Jr. (1988): 'On the Mechanics of Development Planning', *Journal of Monetary Economics*, vol. 22, 3-42.

Luqmani, M., Z.A. Quraeshi, and L. Deline (1980): 'Marketing in Islamic Countries', *MSU Business Topics*, Summer.

Maddison, A. (1992): 'A Long-Run Perspectives on Saving', *Scandinavian Journal of Economics*, June, 181-203.

Maddison, A. (1995): *Explaining the Economic Performance of Nations: Essays in Time and Space*, Camberley, Surrey: Edward Elgar.

Maddison, A. (1996): *A Retrospect for the 200 Years of the World Economy, 1820—1992*, Paris: OECD Development Center.

Maddison, A. (2001): *The World Economy: a Millennial Perspective*, Paris: OECD Development Center.

Maddison, A. (2003): *The World Economy: Historical Statistics*, Paris: OECD Development Center.

Mandelbaum, D. (1949, ed.): *Edward Spair, Selected Writings in Language, Culture and Personality*, Berkeley, CA: University of California Press.

Mansfield, E., and H. Milner (1997, eds): *The Political Economy of Regionalism*, New York: Columbia University Press.

Mansfield, E., and R. Bronson (1997): 'The Political Economy of Major-Power Trade Flows', in Mansfield and Milner (eds), pp. 213-56.

Markusen, J. (1986): 'Explaining the Volume of Trade: An Eclectic Approach', *American Economic Review*, vol. 76 (Dec.), 1002-11.

Maslichenko, S. (2004): 'Institutional Determinants of Economic Development', University of Oxford, Oxford, mimeo.

Mauro, P. (1995): 'Corruption and Growth', *Quarterly Journal of Economics*, vol. 110, 681-712.

McCarrey, S.C. (1996): 'An Assessment of the Work of the International Law Commission', *Natural Resources Journal*, vol. 36, 659–71.

McMahon, G. and L. Squire (2003; eds.): *Explaining Growth: A Global Research Project*, London and New York: Plagrave-Macmillan.

McNeil, W.H. (1963): *The Rise of the West: A History of the Human Community*, Chicago: University of Chicago Press.

Meadows, D.H. (1972): *Limits to Growth: A Report of the Club of Rome's Project on the Predicament of Mankind*, Rome: the Club of Rome.

Melko, M. (1969): *The Nature of Civilizations*, Boston: Porter Sargent.

Mencius (or Mengzi) (c. 300 BC): *Mencius* (Teng Wen Gong II), Beijing: Foreign Languages Press, 1999 (an English-Chinese edition).

Merton, R.C and Z. Bodie (2004): 'The Design of Financial Systems: Toward a Synthesis of Function and Structure', NBER Working Paper No. 10620, Cambridge, MA.

Messick, R.E. (2005), 'Judicial Reform and Economic Development: A Survey of the Issues', *The World Bank Observer*, vol. 14(1), 117-36.

Mishra, G.P. (ed.): *Regional Structure of Development and Growth in India*, New Delhi: Ashish Publishing House, 1985.

Molinar, J. (1991): 'Counting the Number of Parties: An Alternative Index', *American Political Science Review*, vol. 85, 1383-91.

Montalvo, J.G. and M. Reynal-Querol (2002): 'Why Ethnic Fractionalization? Polarization, Ethnic Conflict and Growth', unpublished, Universitat Pompeu Fabra.

Montalvo, J.G. and M. Reynal-Querol (2003): 'Ethnic Polarization, Potential Conflict, and Civil Wars', University of Pompeu Fabra, Economic Working Papers No. 770, available at http://ideas.repec.org/p/upf/upfgen/770.html.

Montalvo, J.G. and M. Reynal-Querol (2005): 'Ethnic Diversity and Economic Development', *Journal of Development Economics*, vol. 76, 293-323.

Montville, J.V., and H. Binnendijk (1990, eds): *Conflict and Peacemaking in Multiethnic Societies*, Lexington, MA: Lexington Books.

Mookherjee, D., and A.F. Shorrocks (1982): 'A Decomposition of the Trend in UK Income Inequality', *The Economic Journal*, vol. 92, 886-902.

Moore, C. (1996): *The Mediation Process: Practical Strategies for Managing Conflict*. San Francisco, CA: Jossey-Bass.

Mudambi, R., and Navarra, R. (2002): 'Institutions and International Business: A Theoretical Overview', *International Business Review*, vol. 11(6), 635-46.

Murrell, P. (ed.) (2001): *Assessing the Value of Law in Transition Economies*, Ann Arbor: University of Michigan Press.

Naff, W. E. (1986): 'Reflections on the Question of 'East and West' from the Point of Japan', *Comparative Civilizations Review*, vol. 14, 224-36.

Nair, K.R.G. (1985): 'Inter-State Income Differentials in India, 1970–71 to 1979–80', in Mishra (ed.), pp. 133-68.

Naroll, R.S. (1950): 'A Draft Map of the Culture Areas of Asia', *Southwestern Journal of Anthropology*, vol. 6, 183-7.

Nelson, R., and E.S. Phelps (1966): 'Investment in Humans, Technological Diffusion, and Economic Growth', *American Economic Review*, vol. 56, 69-75.

Neurath, P. (1994): *From Malthus to the Club of Rome and Back: Problems of Limits to Growth, Population Control, and Migrations* (Columbia University Seminars), New York: M.E. Sharpe.

Noland, M. (2005): 'Affinity and International Trade', Institute for International Economics, Washington DC, Working Paper Series No. WP 05-3, June.

Nordlinger, E.A. (1972): *Conflict Regulation in Divided Societies*, Cambridge, MA: Harvard University Center for International Affairs.

North, D.C. (1981): *Structure and Change in Economic History*, New York: Norton.

North, D.C. (1990): *Institutions, Institutional Change and Economic Performance*, Cambridge: Cambridge University Press.

North, D.C. (1991) 'Institutions', *The Journal of Economic Perspectives*, vol. 5 (1), 97-112.

North, D.C., and R.P. Thomas (1973): *The Rise of the Western World*, Cambridge: Cambridge University Press.

ODN (2006): 'Understanding Reforms in Oceania', in J.M. Fanelli and G. McMahon (eds., 2006): Understanding Market Reforms, Volume 2 (Motivation, Implementation and Sustainability), London and New York: Palgrave Macmillan.

Ofosu-Amaah, G. (1990): 'Niger River Regime', in Bernhardt (ed.), pp. 246-8.

Oguledo, V., and C. MacPhee (1994): 'Gravity Models: A Reformulation and an Application to Discriminatory Trade Arrangement', *Applied Economics*, vol. 26, 107-20.

Ohlin, B. (1933): *Interregional and International Trade*, Cambridge, MA: Harvard University Press.

Oi, J. (1992): 'Fiscal Reform and the Economic Foundations of Local State Corporatism in China', *World Politics*, vol. 45 (Oct.), 99-129.

Oliver, C. (1997): 'Sustainable Competitive Advantage: Combining Institutional and Resource-based Views', *Strategic Management Journal*, vol. 18, 697-713.

OMVS (1988): 'The Senegal River Basin Development Authority', *UN Natural Resources Water Series* (UN Conference on River and Lake Basin Development, Addis, Ababa, 10-15 October), No. 2, 276-94.

Orozco, M. (2001): 'Boundary Disputes in Central America: Past Trends and Present Developments', *Pensamiento propio*, vol. 14 (July–December), 99–134.

Ottaviano, G. and G. Peri (2004): 'The Economic Value of Cultural Diversity: Evidence from US Cities', *NBER Working Paper* No. 10904 (November), National Bureau of Economic Research, Cambridge, MA, USA.

Oxley, J.E. (1999): 'Institutional Environment and the Mechanisms of Governance: The impact of intellectual property protection on the structure of inter-firm alliances', *Journal of Economic Behavior and Organization*, 38(3), 283– 310.

Pack, H. (1994): 'Endogenous Growth Theory: Intellectual Appeal and Empirical Shortcomings', *Journal of Economic Perspectives*, vol. 8, 55-72.

Pan, G. (2006): 'Synergy of East and West for greater creativity' (paper in both Chinese and in English), The Tan Kah Kee Young People's Invention Award Committee, Singapore, 25 September.

Patai, R. (1951): 'Nomadism: Middle Eastern and Central Asian', *Southwestern Journal of Anthropology*, vol. 7, 401-14.

Paukert, F. (1973): 'Income Distribution at Different Levels of Development: A Survey of Evidence', *International Labor Review*, August-September, 32-46.

Pearson, L. (1955): *Democracy in World Politics*, Princeton, NJ: Princeton University Press.

Pearson, V.M.S., and W.G. Stephan (1999): 'Preferences for Styles of Negotiation: A Comparison of Brazil and the US', *International Journal of Intercultural Relations*, vol. 22, 67-83.

Peng, M. W. (2000): *Business Strategies in Transition Economies*, Thousand Oaks, CA: Sage.

Perotti, R. (1993): 'Political Equilibrium, Income Distribution and Growth', *Review of Economic Studies,* vol. 60, 755-76.

Perotti, R. (1996): 'Growth, Income Distribution, and Democracy: What the Data Say', *Journal of Economic Growth*, vol. 1, 149-87.

Persson, T. and G. Tabellini (1994): 'Is Inequality Harmful for Growth? Theory and Evidence', *American Economic Review,* vol. 84, 600-21.

Pinker, S. (1994): *The Language Instinct*, London: Penguin Books.

Posner, D.N. (2004): 'Measuring Ethnic Fractionalization in Africa', *American Journal of Political Science*, vol. 48(4), 849-63.

Pöyhönen, P. (1963): 'A Tentative Model for the Volume of Trade Between Countries', *Weltwirtschaftliches Archiv*, vol. 90 (1), 93-9.

Przeworski, A., M.E. Alvarez, J.A. Cheibub, and F. Limongi (2000): *Democracy and Development,* Cambridge: Cambridge University Press.

Psachropoulos, G. (1991, ed.): *Essays on Poverty, Equity, and Growth*, Oxford: Pergamon.

Puchala, D.J. (1994): The History of the Future of International Relations', *Ethics and International Affairs*, vol. 8, 177-202.

Quigley, C. (1979): *The Evolution of Civilizations: An Introduction to Historical Analysis*, 2nd edn, Indianapolis: Liberty Press.

Rae, D.W. (1967): *The Political Consequences of Electoral Laws*, New Haven, Conn.: Yale University Press.

Ramamurti, R. (2000): 'Risks and Rewards in the Globalization of Telecommunications in Emerging Economies', *Journal of World Business*, vol. 35(2), 149-170.

Ramdas, A.L. (2005): 'Kashmir, Nuclear Weapons and Peace', Institute of Energy and Environment Research, Takoma Park, Maryland, USA, 22 March (available at: www.ieer.org/latest/ramukashmir.html).

Rangeley, R., B. Thiam, R. Andersen, C. Lyle (1994): 'International River Basins in Sub-Saharan Africa', *World Bank Technical Paper*, No. 250, Washington DC: the World Bank.

Rapoport, C. (1989): 'Understanding How Japan Works', *Fortune*, vol. 120(13), 17-19.

Rauch, J.E. (1999): 'Networks versus Markets in International Trade', *Journal of International Economics*, vol. 48, 7-35.

Rauch, J.E. (2001): 'Business and Social Networks in International Trade', *Journal of Economic Literature*, vol. 39, no. 4: 1177-203.

Rauch, J.E. and V. Trindade (2002): 'Ethnic Chinese Networks in International Trade', *Review of Economics and Statistics*, vol. 84(1), 116-30.

Ravallion, M. (2001): 'Growth, Inequality and Poverty: Looking beyond Averages', *World Development*, vol. 29, 173–97

Rebelo, S. (1991): 'Long Run Policy Analysis and Long Run Growth', *Journal of Political Economy*, vol. 99(3)(June), 500-21.

Reynolds, L.G. (1985): *Economic Growth in the Third World, 1850-1980*, New Haven, Conn.: Yale University Press.

Rivera-Batiz, L., and P. Romer (1991): 'International Trade and Endogenous Growth', *The Quarterly Journal of Economics*, vol. 106 (May), 531-55.

Rodrik, D. (2003): 'Institutions, Integration, and Geography: In Search of the Deep Determinants of Economic Growth', in Rodrik (ed.), pp. 1-20.

Rodrik, D. (2003, ed.): *In Search of Prosperity: Analytic Narratives on Economic Growth*, Princeton, NJ: Princeton University Press.

Romer, P.M. (1986): 'Increasing Returns and Long-Run Growth', *Journal of Political Economy*, vol. 94(5)(Oct.), 1002-37.

Romer, P.M. (1990): 'Endogenous Technological Change', *Journal of Political Economy*, vol. 98(5)(Oct.), S71-S102.

Ronald, K., and S. Hope (1996): *African Political Economy: Contemporary Issues in Development*, New York: M.E. Sharpe.

Rose, A. (2004): 'Do We Really Know that the WTO Increases Trade?' *American Economic Review*, vol. 94, 98-114

Rostovanyi, Z. (1993): 'Clash of Civilizations and Cultures: Unity or Disunity of World Order', unpublished paper, March.

Roy, T. (1999): *Traditional Industry in the Economy of Colonial India* (Cambridge Studies in Indian History and Society, vol. 5), Cambridge: Cambridge University Press.

Rubin, J., D. Pruitt, and S. Kim (1994): *Social Conflict: Escalation, Stalemate and Suppression.* New York: McGraw-Hill.

Rumer, B. (1996, ed.): *Central Asia in Transition: Dilemmas of Political and Economic Development,* New York: M.E. Sharpe.

Ruttan, W. (1991): 'What Happened to Political Development?' *Economic Development and Cultural Change,* vol. 39(Jan.), 1-16.

Salman, M., A. Salman, and K. Uprety (1999): 'Hydro Politics in South Asia: A Comparative Analysis of the Mahakali and Ganges', *Natural Resources Journal,* vol. 39(2), 295-344.

Salvatore, D. (1995): *International Economics,* 5th edn, New York: Prentice-Hall International, Inc.

Salvatore, D., and R. Barazesh (1990): 'The Factor Content of US Foreign Trade and the Heckscher-Ohlin Theory', *International Trade Journal,* vol. 16(winter), 149-81.

Samuelson, P.A. (1948): 'International Trade and the Equalization of Factor Prices', *The Economic Journal,* vol. 58 (June), 165-84.

Samuelson, P.A. (1949): 'International Factor-Price Equalization Once Again', *The Economic Journal,* vol. 59 (June), 181-97. Reprinted in Bhagwati (1981, ed.), pp. 3-16.

Sapienza, P. and L. Zingales (2006): 'Does Culture Affect Economic Outcomes?' *NBER Working Papers* No. 11999, National Bureau of Economic Research, Cambridge, MA, USA.

Sapir, E. (1949): *Selected Writings in Language, Culture, and Personality* (edited by David G. Mandelbaum), Berkeley, CA: University of California Press.

Sapper, K. (1968): 'The Verapaz in the Sixteenth and Seventeenth Centuries: A Contribution to the Historical Geography and Ethnography of Northeastern Guatemala', *Occasional Papers of the Institute of Archaeology,* UCLA, Los Angeles, No. 13.

Savenije, H.G., and P. van der Zaag (2000): 'Conceptual Framework for the Management of Shared River Basins with Special Reference to the SADC and EU', *Water Policy,* vol. 2, 9-45.

Saville, J. (2002): 'Language and Equity: A Development Perspective', in Kockel (ed.), pp. 196-220.

Sayer, A. (1997): 'The Dialect of Culture and Economy', in Lee and Wills (eds), pp. 16-26.

Schattschneider, E.E. (1960): *The Semisovereign People: A Realist's View of Democracy in America,* New York: Holt, Rinehart and Winston.

Schnitzer, M.C. (1997): *Comparative Economic Systems,* 7th edn, Cincinnati, Ohio: South-Western College Publishing Co.

Schulz, T.W. (1961): 'Investment in Human Capital', *American Economic Review,* vol. 51 (March), 213-26.

Scott, W.R. (2001): *Institutions and Organizations* (2nd ed). Thousand Oaks, CA: Sage.

Sen, A. (2000): 'Culture and Development', Global Development Conference, Tokyo, January.

Shanbaugh, J., J. Oglethope and R. Ham (2003): 'The Trampled Grass: Mitigating the Impacts of Armed Conflict on the Environment', Washington DC: World Wildlife Fund (WWF).

Shanker, R. (1996): 'Culture and Development', *Development Express,* no. 8, Hull, Québec: International Development Information Center.

Shorrocks, A. (1980), 'The Class of Additionally Decomposable Inequality Measures', *Econometrica,* vol. 48, 613–25.

Shorrocks, A. and J.E. Foster (1987), 'Transfer Sensitive Inequality Measure', *Review of Economic Studies*, vol. 54, 485–97

Shultz, R., R. Godson, and T. Greenwood (1993, eds): *Security Studies for the 1990's*, Washington DC: Brassey's.

Sillis, D.L. (1972, ed.): *International Encyclopedia of the Social Sciences*, vol. 3, New York: The Macmillan Company & The Free Press.

Singer, M.R. (1998): *Perception and Identity in Intercultural Communication*, Yarmouth, ME: Intercultural Press.

Smith, C. (1990, ed.): *Practical Methods of Regional Science and Empirical Applications: Selected Papers of Walter Isard*, vol. 2, New Work: New York University Press.

Smith, M.S. (2003): 'Buffer Zones', In G. Burgess and H. Burgess (Eds.): *Beyond Intractability* (pp. 130–50), Conflict Research Consortium, University of Colorado, Boulder. Available at: www.beyondintractability.org/m/buffer_zones.jsp.

Solanes, M. (1992): 'Legal and Institutional Aspects of River Basin Development', *Water International*, vol. 17(3), 116–22.

Solow, R.M. (1956): 'A Contribution to the Theory of Economic Growth', *The Quarterly Journal of Economics*, vol. 71, 65-94.

Spair, E. (1916; 1949): 'Time Perspective in Aboriginal American Culture: A Study in Method', in Mandelbaum (ed.), pp. 389-462.

Spar, D. L. (2001): 'National policies and domestic politics', In T. Brewer, & A. Rugman (Eds.), *Oxford Handbook of International Business*. Oxford: Oxford University Press.

Spengler, O. (1928): *Decline of the West*, New York: A. A. Knopf.

State Council (1981): 'Regulations of the P. R. China Concerning the Resolutions of the Disputes on Borders of the Administrative Divisions', Beijing: State Council.

State Council (1988): 'Regulations of the P. R. China Concerning the Resolutions of the Disputes on Borders of the Administrative Divisions', revised version, Beijing: State Council.

Stephan, J. (1999): *Economic Transition in Hungary and East Germany: Gradualism and Shock Therapy in Catch-Up Development* (Studies in Economic Transition), New York: St Martin's Press.

Stern, R.M., and K.E. Maskus (1981): 'Determinants of the Structure of US Foreign Trade', *Journal of International Economics*, vol. 24, 207-24.

Stewart, J.Q. (1948): 'Demographic Gravitation: Evidence and Applications', *Sociometry*, vol. 2, 31-58.

Summers, R., and A. Heston (1988): 'A New Set of International Comparison of Real Product and Price Levels: Estimates for 130 Countries', *Review of Income and Wealth*, vol. 34, 1-25.

Sumner, W.G. (1906): *Folkways: A Study of the Sociological Importance of Usage, Manners, Customs, Mores, and Morals*, New York: Dover. Reprinted in 1959.

Swan, T.W. (1956): 'Economic Growth and Capital Accumulation', *Economic Record*, vol. 32(Nov.), 334-61.

Taagepera, R., and M.S. Shugart (1989): *Seats and Votes: The Effects and Determinants of Electoral Systems*, New Haven, Conn.: Yale University Press.

Tehranian, K., and M. Tehranian (1992, eds): *Restructuring for World Peace: On the Threshold of the Twenty-First Century*, Cresskill, NJ: Hampton Press.

The New Columbia Encyclopedia, 4th edn, 1975, New York: Columbia University Press.

The New Palgrave Dictionary of Economics, 1987, vol. 4, London: Macmillan.

The Oxford English Dictionary, Oxford: Clarendon Press, 1989, 2nd Edition.

Tinbergen, J. (1962): 'An Analysis of World Trade Flows, the Linder Hypothesis, and Exchange Risk', in Tinbergen (ed.), pp. 20-42.

Tinbergen, J. (1962, ed.): *Shaping the World Economy*, New York: The Twentieth Century Fund.

Ting-Toomey, S. (1988): 'Intercultural Conflict Styles: A Face-Negotiation Theory', in Kim and Gudykunst (eds), pp. 213-35.

Tocqueville, A. (1873): *Democracy in America*, 5th edn, Boston: John Allyn.

Tønnesson, S. (1999): 'Can Conflicts Be Solved by Shelving Disputes?' *Security Dialogue*, vol. 30(2), 179–82.

Toynbee, A. (1961): *A Study of History*, London: Oxford University Press.

Trubisky, P., T. Toomey, and L. Sung (1991): 'The Influence of Individualism-Collectivistism and Self-Monitoring on Conflict Styles', *International Journal of Intercultural Relations*, vol. 15, 65-84.

Tsakloglou, K. (1993): 'Aspects of Inequality in Greece', *Journal of Development Economics*, vol. 40, 53-74.

Tsui, K. (1993): 'Decomposing of China's Regional Inequalities', *Journal of Comparative Economics*, vol. 17, 600-27.

Tylor, E.B. (1871) (1958): *Primitive Culture: Researches into the Development of Mythology, Philosophy, Religion, Art and Custom*, (vol. 1: 'Origins of Culture'), Gloucester, MA: Smith.

UNESCO (1999): *UNESCO Statistical Yearbook 1999*, Paris: UNSECO, available at www.unesco.org.

United Nations (1986): *Annual Statistical Yearbook*, New York: UN.

United Nations (1996): *The United Nations and Rwanda, 1993–1996*, New York: The United Nations Blue Book Series (Volume X).

United Nations (2001): *Annual Statistical Yearbook*, New York: UN.

United Nations Development Program (UNDP) (1999): *Human Development Report 1999*, available at: www.undp.org/hdro/report.html.

USDA (2002): 'Hispanic American Influence on the U.S. Food Industry', USDA, October, available at: www.nal.usda.gov/outreach/HFood.html

Venieris, Y. and D. Gupta (1986): 'Income Distribution and Sociopolitical Instability as Determinants of Savings: A Cross-Sectional Model', *Journal of Political Economy*, vol. 94, 873-83.

Vlahos, M. (1991): 'Culture and Foreign Policy', *Foreign Policy*, vol. 82, 59-78.

Vona, S. (1990): 'Intra-Industry Trade: A Statistical Prefect or a Real Phenomenon?' *Banca Naz. Lavoro Quarterly Review*, December, 487-97.

Wagner, R.E. (1983): *Public Finance*, Boston: Little Brown.

Weber, M. (1904; 1930): *The Protestant Ethic and the Spirit of Capitalism*, London: Allen & Unwin.

Wheeler, L., H.T. Reis, and M.H. Bond (1989): 'Collectivism-Individualism in Everyday Social Life: The Middle Kingdom and the Melting Pot', *Journal of Personality and Social Psychology*, vol. 57, 79-86.

Wiegersma, N. and J. Medley (2000): *US Economic Development Policies Towards the Pacific Rim: Successes and Failures of US Aid*, London: Palgrave-Macmillan.

Williamson, J.G. (1965): 'Regional Inequality and the Process of National Development: A Description of Patterns', *Economic Development and Cultural Change*, vol. 13(4), 165-204.

Wilson, E.A. (1980): *Sociobiology*, Cambridge, MA: Belknap.

Wilson, R. (1997): *Economics, Ethics and Religion: Jewish, Christian and Muslim Economic Thought*, New York: New York University Press.

Wissler, C. (1917): *The American Indian: An Introduction to the Anthropology of the New World*, 3rd edn, Gloucester, MA: Smith.

Wolf, A.T. (1998): 'Conflicts and Cooperation along International Waterways', *Water Policy*, vol. 1, 251-65.

Wong, C. (1992): 'Fiscal Reform and Local Industrialization', *Modern China*, vol. 18 (Apr.), 23-42.

Woo, T.W., S. Parker, and J. Sachs (1996, eds): *Economies in Transition: Comparing Asia and Eastern Europe*, Cambridge, MA: The MIT Press.

World Atlas, Rand McNally & Company, 1994.

World Bank (1983): *World Development Report 1982-1983*, Washington DC: the World Bank.

World Bank (1986): *World Bank Atlas*, Washington DC: the World Bank.

World Bank (1996): *Social Indicators of Development*, Baltimore: Johns Hopkins University Press.

World Bank (1999): *World Development Indicators CD-ROM*, Washington DC: the World Bank.

World Bank (2001): *World Development Indicators*, Washington DC: the World Bank.

World Bank (2008), *Doing Business: An Independent Evaluation*, Washington, DC: World Bank Independent Evaluation Group.

World Commission on Culture and Development (WCCD) (1995): *Our Creative Diversity*, Paris: the UNESCO.

World Resource Institute (1999): *World Resources 1998-99*, Washington DC: WRI.

World Values Surveys (1999-2002), Michigan State University, Ann Arbor, USA.

Yergin, D. (1992): *The Prize: the Epic Quest for Oil, Money and Power*, A Touchstone Book. New York: Simon & Schuster.

Zhang, H. (1990): 'Importance of Adjusting the Transprovincial Borders in China', (in Chinese), *Journal of East China Normal University*, No. 1, 1-10.

Zhao, G. (2002): 'The Determinants of Transnational Water Pollution in the LMB', M.Sc. Thesis, CUMT, Beijing, China.

Zhou, F. (1994), 'Measuring the Interregional Inequalities in Terms of Single Index and Multiple Indices', in Liu, S., Q. Li, and T. Hsueh (Eds.), 1994, pp. 193–200.

Zipf, G.K. (1946): 'The $P^1P^2/D$ Hypothesis: On the Intercity Movement of Persons', *American Sociological Review*, vol. 11(6), 677-86.

# INDEX

## D

# F

**G**

## J

## N

## O

## S

## Y

## Z